Reading Series Fic

children's liter-
d an enormous
y children and
:en's literature.
ces and argues
id championed.

g is once again
h an interest in
st out of their

Homerton Col-
s on children's
for Routledge,
Guide to Chil-

First published 2000
by RoutledgeFalmer
11 New Fetter Lane, London EC4P 4EE

Simultaneously published in the USA and Canada
by RoutledgeFalmer
29 West 35th Street, New York, NY 10001

RoutledgeFalmer is an imprint of the Taylor & Francis Group

© 2000 Victor Watson

Typeset in Sabon by
The Running Head Limited, www.therunninghead.com
Printed and bound in Great Britain by Clays Ltd, St Ives PLC

British Library Cataloguing in Publication Data
A catalogue record for this book is available from the British Library

Library of Congress Cataloging in Publication Data
Watson, Victor
  Reading series fiction: from Arthur Ransome to Gene Kemp / Victor Watson.
  Includes bibliographical references and index.
    1. Children's stories, English – History and criticism. 2. Children's literature in
  series – History and criticism. 3. Ransome, Arthur, 1884–1967 – Criticism and
  interpretation. 4. English fiction – 20th century – History and criticism. 5. Kemp,
  Gene – Criticism and interpretation. 6. Children – Books and reading. I. Title.
  PR830.C513 W38 2000
  823.009′9282—dc21   99–042235

ISBN 0 415 22701 1 (hb)   0 415 22702 X (pb)

My thanks are due to a boy in Year 6 at Stapleford Primary School, Cambridgeshire, who, while talking to me about series fiction several years ago, explained that starting a new novel was like going into a room full of strangers, but starting a book in a familiar series was like going into a room full of friends. I have no record of his name, but he provided me with the starting-point for this book and the title of my Introduction.

Contents

Illustrations

Acknowledgements

The author and publisher would like to thank the following for permission to reproduce material in this book: Christina Hardyment for permission to reproduce illustrations and to quote extensively from the *Swallows and Amazons* series by Arthur Ransome; Gene Kemp for permission to quote extensively from the *Cricklepit Combined School* series; Orion Publishing Group Ltd for permission to quote extensively from *The Borrowers* series by Mary Norton; Chatto and Windus for permission to quote extensively from *The Dark Is Rising* series; Faber and Faber Ltd for permission to quote extensively from the *Marlow* series by Antonia Forest and the *Green Knowe* series by Lucy Boston.

Parts of Chapters 1 and 3 are adapted from an article originally published in *Signal 66*, September 1991. The author would like to express his gratitude to the editor, Nancy Chambers, for allowing him to rework these ideas.

All excerpts from Enid Blyton's books are copyright © 2000 by Enid Blyton Limited, London.

While the author has made every effort to contact copyright holders of previously published material reproduced in this volume, he would be grateful to hear from any he has been unable to contact.

Introduction
A room full of friends

Nothing to fear but interruption

There is often a chanciness in choosing to read a single novel. Readers may be tempted by a seductive cover, influenced by the recommendation of a friend, or so simply at a loss that almost anything will do. But series-reading is not like that: it is always conscious and always deliberate. You cannot read a series of twelve novels by chance.

Deciding to read the next book in a series implies a commitment which is quite different from the cautious reconnoitring curiosity which readers often feel about an unfamiliar book. Reading a series involves a special relationship between reader and writer which the reader has made a conscious decision to sustain. It is an advanced kind of play; the rules are slightly different, and the pleasures are acknowledged and savoured. Although there are readers who read eclectically or erratically, there are many more who insist on reading (and owning) the entire series, and will read – or reread – the sequence only in the correct chronological order. This is not just an obsessive eccentricity; it is for many young readers central to their discovery of the most important reading-secret of all – that fiction can provide a complex variety of profoundly private pleasures, and that these pleasures are repeatable and entirely within the reader's control. Like the young Jane Eyre concealed on the window-seat, such readers have 'nothing to fear but interruption'.

Yet there has been little recognition of the importance of series. In fact, they are rather looked down upon. If you look up *The Borrowers* in *The Oxford Companion to Children's Literature*, you will find the first of the series is given a detailed and illuminating consideration – but all that is said about the rest is that 'Mary Norton wrote four sequels.'[1] This perfunctory treatment implies that to follow a successful novel with a sequel is a shameful loss of writerly integrity, a falling-off into repetitive and formulaic pot-boiling. But that is not how a series is experienced by its readers: if they found the sequels less interesting than the first story, they would stop reading them.

It is that interest – and the centrality of series in the lives of many young readers – that *Reading Series Fiction* proposes to examine. But the criticism of children's books has always been problematic, and has become acutely so in the wake of recent developments in critical theory.

Literary criticism and critical literacy

I was recently struck by a comment made by Charles Sarland concerning the characters in *Point Horror* fiction:

> They play out stereotypical dilemmas of what it means to be a teenager surrounded by the most unlikely family and social situations, live through events guaranteed to mess up permanently the most stable and well-adjusted personality, and all they do is shrug, smile and go off on a shopping-spree. *I cannot find any reasons whatever to be interested in them.* Yet for the youngsters they are vivid realisations of the definitional dilemmas of a state they are yet to embark on. [my italics][2]

Sarland has indicated precisely a difficulty faced by many adult readers who are interested in children's literature, especially if they are also concerned with teaching: on the line between excellence and popular appeal there are points of embarrassment. People who care about children's *literature* probably believe that there are degrees of excellence within it and that a good deal of it may be of interest to a discriminating adult reader – quite apart from a professional interest in children's reading. People who believe in nurturing *readers*, however, will want to champion children's right to become independent in their own way and encourage their growing willingness and ability to choose what kind of readers they will be. The points of embarrassment become especially uncomfortable when we see young readers setting out on the road to independence by seeming to become addicted to popular series fiction, resolutely ignoring – or even ignorant of – the higher-quality fiction which we know to be available. This is acutely problematic for teachers whose professional responsibility is to extend reading and develop critical literacy.

This is a real and serious dilemma for anyone concerned with young readers and children's literature: how are we to champion the readers' right to read whatever they please without losing sight of the literary excellence which we rather uncertainly believe in? It is not a controversy between two opposing camps; it seems to me that many who are concerned with children's books are impaled upon the point of conflict.

The range of views is wide. On popular fiction, there are those who argue that bad writing is simply bad writing and that we should do everything in our power not to infect our children's minds and lives with its dangerous influence. There are others who believe that trash is mostly harmless, or that a healthy literary diet needs some roughage in it, or that you cannot appreciate good writing if you have no experience of bad. A rather different kind of defence believes that popular fiction provides an important transitional reading which may lead later to a developing interest in more nourishing literature. Another argument is the one about empowerment: that young readers *are* discriminating and know exactly what they are doing when they choose to read popular fiction; that if they choose to read escapist novels it is probably because they wish to escape; that the act of reading is itself a locus of complex personal and ideological pressures; and that in any case the reading strategies involved in reading a *Point Romance* are not unlike those involved in reading *Pride and Prejudice*. And, finally, there is the view that 'rubbish' is as culturally determined as 'literature' is, that a good deal of so-called 'popular fiction' is actually very well written, and that yesterday's rubbish may be tomorrow's classic.

It is probably worth reminding ourselves at this point that people who cling to traditional distinctions of excellence in children's books do not necessarily wish to impose compulsory reading-lists on schools, or believe in the existence of a fixed canon of fine literature, or in a Leavisite 'great tradition' of fiction for young readers. On the other hand, we also need to remind ourselves that a belief in the independence and the ultimate judgement of young readers is not just a current fashion or a self-imposed professional angst; it is part of a serious professional commitment to child-centred learning.

The most compelling argument in support of readers and readings has behind it the experience and authority of Margaret Meek, who has been telling the teaching profession for many years that literacies change with a rapidity which is best understood by the young readers who are learning them in their day-by-day experience of new kinds of text; and that the only way for us to become informed is to ask the children about it and attend to what they say. In that spirit, Charles Sarland concluded the article from which I quoted above by saying:

'If we want to know what they think, we have to talk to them, and if we do, they will have something to tell us.'[3] For a decade or more, this spirit of child-centred enquiry has informed the debates about reading. At its best such patient child-centred research has transformed our understanding of what young readers are capable of, what they want from us by way of support, and what they themselves know about their own learning.

However, while we are seeking to understand the 'reading lives' of young readers, our own adult deliberations about literature must not go by default. Adults interested in children's literature need to consider the *literature* as well as the *children*; we need to talk to each other about what we mean by 'quality fiction', or whatever we choose to call it. I was struck by a point made by Jan Mark in a recent article. She wrote: 'The prime innovator of our own times, William Mayne, frightens the grown-ups; they do not want to engage with his uncompromising style, his intellect, his wit, and for that reason withhold him from children. It is much easier to promote the works of Roald Dahl who makes rude noises and uses daring words like "knickers".'[4] Jan Mark is right; for – while there is a whole body of discourse on Dahl and, for example, Enid Blyton, whose work, if they are honest, few adults would willingly reread – little has been done to develop ways of valuing and acknowledging the complex and elusive appeal of Mayne; or, for that matter, of many other recent and living children's writers, including Jan Mark herself.

I am not going to try to define 'literary excellence'. We all know that it is a shifting and shifty cultural slogan. But somewhere in the midst of this confusion of cultural and personal variables there must be something we can intelligently reflect on and discuss with one another. Perhaps we should begin modestly. We could, perhaps, take Charles Sarland's words quoted earlier and develop what is implicit in them. 'I cannot find', he says of the characters in *Point Horror* fiction, 'any reason whatever to be interested in them.' *Interest* is not a bad starting-point, close cousin to *enjoyment*. The reason so few of us would find any pleasure in a rereading of the *Famous Five* series is precisely that we would find so little to interest us – though that is not to say that we should sneer at them, or at the young readers whose readerly desires impel them so passionately through the entire sequence.

If we are not to be accused by a later generation of a serious *trahison des clercs*, I believe we must exchange discourses of discrimination which articulate the varieties and degrees of interest in specific texts, and especially those written by authors whose work is difficult, innovative and complex. If adult commentators cannot explain to each other the elusive (and at times irritating) nature of William Mayne's fiction, or the complex challenges and delights of the extremely popular fiction of Diana Wynne Jones, we can hardly expect to be able to encourage young readers to approach it sympathetically. We must begin to explain to each other what we admire and why we admire it. And we should not seek to dodge this simply because our attempts to account for excellence in this way might be interpreted as aligning ourselves with the educational and political Right.

The kind of critical attention I have in mind *is* currently being given to picturebooks. Many analyses of picturebooks have recently been published, written from different perspectives ranging from art history and image-analysis to case-studies of young readers. At their best they have been illuminating, even inspiring. They have succeeded by virtue of their commitment to precisely an *analysis of interest*, providing a detailed text-based scrutiny of resonance, pictorial quotation, irony, intertextuality, evocativeness, using an appropriate technical vocabulary of line, colour, frame, perspective, and so on. And they do not leave the reader/beholder out of the account; indeed, part of the appeal of picturebooks to commentators is that, because they can be genuinely shared with children, the subsequent accounts can be simultaneously both book-centred and child-centred. I have done this myself and I know the powerful appeal of this opportunity to explore what is happening in a text with the help of a young reader while simultaneously attending to the young reader's understanding of the text.

But it is more difficult to do this with fiction for older children – or with poetry and drama, for that matter. Perhaps that is why there is little critical work which can help uncover and illuminate for all of us the varieties of interest to be found in the novels of, say, Jill Paton Walsh, Gillian Cross, Dianna Wynne Jones, Margaret Mahy, Robert Swindells, or Cynthia Voigt. In private, adults interested in children's books have no misgivings: in conversations with colleagues, and at conferences and other gatherings, they talk freely to each other using the shorthand of 'good books', 'good writers' and 'enjoyable reads' – as if they were entirely innocent of critical theory! Some of these discussions should be turned into reflective critical commentary – and made public. There is an even greater difficulty involved in considering the complex kinds of interest and pleasure involved in the reading of series, partly because this reading is often obsessively and lovingly private, and because hardly anyone has taken the trouble to discuss it.

Silence serves no one's purpose. It does not serve the interests of the literature or its readers. It certainly does not help teachers. Nor, incidentally, does it help new writers, whose condition is indeed a parlous one if the only adult reader interested in them is their publishing editor. An arena of critical debate is particularly important at a time when book-reviewing of new works for children is in such serious decline, and when the development of reading at Key Stages 2 and 3 is seen to be of such importance. Now that we have come to appreciate the importance of the contexts within which books are produced and read – and the extraordinarily complex economic, domestic, pedagogic, ideological and personal factors influencing those contexts – we ought to be able to address texts with some modest confidence in our usefulness. I do not see how we can develop *critical literacy* without *literary criticism*.

'A room full of friends' – the appeal of series fiction

It is likely that the most important continuous reading children do on their own is the reading of series. Their role in the development of reading is incalculable. And it may help us to appreciate the importance of this kind of reading if we bear in mind that in the period since Arthur Ransome began writing there have been more than 400 British and American series written for children, including sequels, trilogies and quartets – and that figure does not include publishers' format-series. I ought perhaps at this point to make it clear that, although the word 'series' has recently come to refer to books with an identical format, I am using it mostly in its older sense, of a sequence of related stories about the same groups of characters, usually by the same author. Our children's literature is particularly rich in these: E. Nesbit's *Psammead* and *Bastable* novels, the *Narnia* books, Antonia Forest's *Marlow* stories, the *Borrowers*, the *Green Knowe* stories, Cynthia Voigt's *Dicey* novels, and many others. One of the greatest of these was Arthur Ransome's *Swallows and Amazons*. He is still in print today both in hardback and in paperback; without him, possibly Malcolm Saville would never have begun the *Lone Pine* series, or Enid Blyton the *Famous Five* and the *Secret Seven*, Marjorie Lloyd the *Fell Farm* series, and so on.

A Year 6 child once explained to me why he preferred a series to single novels: when you begin a new novel, he explained, it is like going into a room full of strangers, but reading the latest book in a series which you already know is *like going into a room full of friends*. It is an obvious point but an important one: there is for most readers a wariness in beginning a new book, particularly with regard to the characters. The new reader has to work out not only who is who, and who is whose brother or sister or friend, but also the hierarchy of age and authority within the fictional group. A degree of watchfulness is required while reading those first few pages which may be difficult for a newly independent reader to sustain. This state of uncertainty is relieved only when the reader has chosen a character to identify with, whose activities they expect to be able to observe with interest, enjoyment, sympathy and hope. Adults, too, when they read novels in series know that instead of the uncertainty of watchfulness there is the pleasure of recognition – the familiar mannerisms, the bossiness of one character, the impatience of another, the jokes and the ways of speaking are all savoured and welcomed; and, above all, there is the familiar and inimitable voice of the narrator.

Finding characters in one novel whom we have already encountered in another seems a trivial narrative phenomenon, but its comforting appeal to our readerly desires is considerable – and remains so as we become adult readers. We do not grow out of series novels; we grow into them. The first novelist to realise their appeal was Trollope, with the *Barchester* and the *Palliser* novels. Today, Mary Wesley's popular novels are not strictly speaking a series, but her readers enjoy the fact that the main characters of one novel are likely to reappear as minor figures in others. Long before series novels were part of the literary landscape, Shakespeare understood perfectly the appeal of familiar characters reappearing in several plays; he knew how to win the roar of approval and delight which greeted Falstaff, Mistress Quickly and the rest of the gang in the two parts of *Henry IV* and *The Merry Wives of Windsor* – and the killing-off of Falstaff in *Henry V* shows that he also knew how to challenge such audience expectations.

Reading a series provides some of the pleasures of watching a television soap, in particular the continued satisfaction of observing the same characters over a long period of fictional and real time. But the narratives in a series also provide what soaps can rarely offer: the satisfaction of endings. A series is not a serial; it has resolutions as it proceeds. The promise of further related but separate stories is quite unlike the unending restlessness of a soap in which, as one narrative strand is tied up, fresh strands begin to unwind. In a group of related fictions each of which is complete, there is for the developing reader a stability – at its lowest a sequence of breathing-spaces, at its highest a series of profoundly satisfying narrative or thematic closures.

Time is either explicitly or implicitly a preoccupation in many children's books, but in a series of novels it assumes a different significance. A series of novels can express far more subtly than a single novel the ambivalence of age and time which is central to the experience of childhood. The ambivalence arises from a child's strange and contradictory perception of life as changeless and cyclical, and at the same time as shot through with change; the apparent stability of a predictable sequence of school terms, Christmases and birthdays is forever set against the unstoppable stages of teeth falling out, growing bigger, and experiencing personal and social rites of passage. The characters in a series reflect this: they both do and don't grow older – or they grow older very slowly.

Time may be a difficulty for writers: Antonia Forest once admitted in an author's note to *The Thuggery Affair* that her characters had aged only eighteen months in a historical period of seventeen years – and that was only the sixth novel in a series of ten. It may also be a difficulty for readers, many of whom believe that it is a sad let-down when an author allows the characters of a series to grow older. It is an aspect of genre: characters who remain the same age for ever inhabit an essentially magical and romantic world, however authentic the surface realism might be. But it is also a dilemma of readership, for an author has to decide whether to attempt to appeal to the same generation of readers as they grow older, or to new readers of the same age-group. The question of age and the passing of time is important because nostalgia almost certainly plays a big part in series-reading – a desire for the same story to be repeated along with a knowledge that it cannot ever be exactly the same, an impossible longing for a simultaneous sameness and difference.

For a child, reading a series may quickly become a matter of collecting all the titles, the first step in what used to be called 'building a library'. Publishers' format-series can also promote this activity, as many now-grown-up collectors of the *Ladybird* books will testify. Children's annuals have for 150 years served a similar purpose. More importantly, collecting books also gives a sense of belonging to a community of readers with whom you can exchange ideas – or even books. This sense of belonging to what Gabrielle Cliff Hodges has felicitously called a 'fellowship of readers'[5] will be enhanced if the series is itself concerned with characters who form their own club, with rule-books, oaths of allegiance, and secret codes and hideaways. The sense of a fellowship within the stories is inseparably enmeshed with the sense of fellowship outside in the social life where other readers share it.

My intention in this book is to argue that series fiction has played an enormous and largely unacknowledged part in children's reading throughout most of the twentieth century; and that the critical world has been content to accept a number of seriously misleading and simplistic critical assumptions about its nature and value. The approach I have adopted is an inward-looking and text-based one; I do not see any other way of explaining the kinds of interest I derive from reading than to look closely at texts.

I hope to demonstrate that series fiction is not generically or inevitably inferior. Everyone who has a personal or professional interest in children's literature knows how difficult it is to have its seriousness acknowledged by the wider literary establishment; and it is even more difficult with series fiction, which is often wrongly associated with third-rate and formulaic pot-boilers.

Part I of this book is devoted to the *Swallows and Amazons* series, and Parts II, III and IV focus on the work of Mary Norton, Lucy Boston, Susan Cooper, Enid Blyton, Malcolm Saville, Antonia Forest and Gene Kemp. I make no apology for devoting three chapters to Arthur Ransome: his work provides both a standard of excellence and a standard of difficulty, and I hope to demonstrate by analysing his writing the complexity and humanity – the *trust in children* – implicit in his apparently simple and beguiling accounts. In writing these chapters I have found myself repeatedly seeking to explain and illuminate what I have come to regard as the central and distinguishing characteristic of children's writing – a 'poetic' able to suggest subtle, complex and private values in simple, transparent and carefully crafted language and form.

Simplicity is not always banal; but it is always vulnerable to neglect, or even mockery. It needs, therefore, to be championed and understood. Accordingly, the Conclusion will directly address what I have called the 'invisible excellence' of the best children's books.

Part I

Innocence aboard:
Swallows and Amazons

1 A fellowship of innocence

I have never found 'realism' to be a very helpful term; it muddies the waters of critical discussion and it always comes as a surprise to me when I hear Ransome described as a realistic writer – or criticised for not being realistic enough. I regard him as essentially a *magical* writer. He is realistic only in the sense that he is a great describer, a painter of word-pictures, with an extraordinary commitment to the faithful representation of the workaday realities of boating or camping. I want in these first chapters to show how this surface authenticity works to sustain an altogether magical representation of childhood and landscape. Ransome's creative enterprise is not to represent landscape and childhood as they are but as they may be imaginatively transformed within what is ultimately a Wordsworthian vision. And I hope to show that, while *The Prelude* celebrated the privileged perceptions of a solitary male boy, Ransome was altogether more generous in allowing into his stories many different approved ways of responding to the experiences of childhood.

And he does this so unobtrusively that no young reader is ever likely to be troubled by a sense of bewildering complexities.

Swallows and Amazons and *Swallowdale* are perfect books of childhood. They come closer than any book I know to expressing in terms of metaphor and plot the nature of innocence.

The theme of *Swallows and Amazons* (1930) is newness. It is a book of first-times – the first time the Swallows are allowed to camp out, the first time Roger swims without one foot on the bottom, the first time they sail at night. Every island, every river, every inlet and bay, is a discovery. Eden lies within this story. The children are like Adam and Eve naming the beasts and the flowers, and at such moments of discovery Ransome's prose has a light and unpretentious lucidity. Here is Titty respectfully observing a dipper:

A round, stumpy little bird, with a short tail like a wren's, a brown back and a broad white waistcoat, was standing on a stone that showed above the water not a dozen feet away. It bobbed, as if it were making a bow, or a quick, careless kind of curtsey.

'What manners,' said Titty to herself. She lay perfectly still, while the little brown and white bird bobbed on its stone.

Suddenly the dipper jumped feet first into the water. It did not dive like a cormorant, but dropped in, like someone who does not know how to dive jumping in at the deep end of a swimming-bath. A few moments later it flew up again out of the water, and perched on its stone, and bobbed again as if it were saying thank you for applause.[1]

The details of the landscape and the realities of sailing are described with such convincing authenticity that it comes as something of a surprise to note that the behaviour of the children is actually quite improbable. There is no quarrelling, nobody sulks, nobody is ever malicious – for such realism would work against the book's gentle imagery of innocence. The children are their own safe family within the wider community of the world. The Swallows are a small hierarchy of four, bound together by a loyalty and a morality whose structure derives from naval discipline. Captain John and Mate Susan are rather solemn youngsters, lacking humour; but they are firm and kind in their dealings with their young brother and sister, attentive both to practical matters of health and safety, and to matters of personal achievement like Roger's swimming. The concern of all four children is to increase their skill and knowledge, a task undertaken without the intrusion of their parents. The almost complete exclusion of adults from the children's adventures has often been remarked upon; this absence throws into relief the special significance of their mother when she visits Titty on the island and they talk about when she was a girl in Australia – mother and daughter in a continuity of childhoods.

The narrative has a special interest in Titty. She is the imaginative one, the reader, who enriches her make-believe with literary possibilities. Her knowledge of *Robinson Crusoe* informs their adventures. She does not have her brother's technical knowledge of boating, but she knows about pirates and parrots, treasure and typhoons. It is she who names the Peak of Darien, and when the children are pretending a shipwreck, it is Titty who remarks quietly, 'Someone has killed an albatross.'[2] She is the story's questioner; she wants to understand and experience. While the other three have adventures together, it is Titty who experiences and relishes solitude.

The story is told with great skill. The opening – with Roger, aged seven, tacking up the grassy hillside to his mother – is outstanding. Then comes their father's famous telegram ('BETTER DROWNED THAN DUFFERS IF NOT DUFFERS WON'T DROWN'[3]), and thereafter the narrative moves at a steady pace. The Amazons add a touch of abrasiveness and several instances of humour. There is real danger, too, when the Swallows sail in the dark.

But there are no enemies in this story, and no wickedness – only a burglary which is kept at a safe distance from the children. When all these matters are resolved, Ransome still has one more surprise in store – the account of the storm during the children's last night on the island. The novel ends on a lyrical and elegiac note of closure as the two boats leave the island, the fleet breaks up, and the four children sing sea-shanties as their mother walks down the field to meet them at the water's edge. This concludes with perfect artistic propriety what is in fact a very gentle book – a book relating the two themes of innocence and discovery.

Next came *Swallowdale* (1931) and I doubt if there is any other substantial novel in our literature in which there is no wickedness and so little folly. All the adults in this story – the charcoal-burners, the boat-builder, the young man who is courting Mary Swainson – are true, honest, skilled and kind. Even Captain Flint, who was a clown in *Swallows and Amazons*, is shown now to possess firmness, decisiveness and tact.

The poetics of the novel are concerned with exploration. The surface narrative allows the children to discover Swallowdale and its fishing possibilities, the paths and deceptive dangers of High Moor, the River Amazon and Mount Kanchenjunga. There is no end to the possibilities of travel and exploration, and Ransome subtly attaches this theme to the idea of the children's absent father.

> 'If we went on and on, beyond the Isle of Man, what would we come to?' asked Roger.
> 'Ireland, I think,' said John, 'and then probably America . . .'
> 'And if we still went on?'
> 'Then there'd be the Pacific and China.'
> 'And then?'
> John thought for a minute. 'There'd be all Asia and then all Europe and then there'd be the North Sea and then we'd be

coming up the other side of those hills.' He looked back towards the hills beyond Rio and the hills beyond them, and the hills beyond them again, stretching away, fold upon fold, into the east.

'Then we'd have gone all round the world.'

'Of course.'

'We will some day. Daddy's done it.'[4]

There is more in that than geography. While the territorial space of the four Swallows expands considerably (as the endpaper maps show), the children's understanding of time develops too. There are cross-references to a past and future in which the children are enabled to place themselves in a pattern of beginnings and endings. When Captain Flint visits the Swallows' cave there is more than a hint of seriousness in the language.

'It's smaller than I thought it was,' he said when he was inside and was able once more to stand up. He turned to the right inside the doorway and there, carved with a knife on the rock, he found the name 'Ben Gunn' in big sprawling letters.

'We'll put Captain Duck's name there too,' said Titty.

'Ben Gunn'll be glad to meet him,' said Captain Flint.

'Did you carve it?' asked John.

'More than thirty years ago,' said Captain Flint.[5]

And at the top of Kanchenjunga the children find a small brass box containing a note reading

> 'August the 2nd. 1901.
> We climbed the Matterhorn.
> Molly Turner.
> J. Turner.
> Bob Blackett.'

to which they add:

> Aug, 11. 1931.
> We climbed Kanchenjunga.[6]

Over and over again, Ransome weaves into the plot brief unremarkable incidents which relate the children to the big human issues.

This incident is not simply a happy coincidence; it is a recognition of continuity and having a place in the processes of human time. At this point a darker note is briefly sounded.

'Who is Bob Blackett?' asked Susan.
'He was father,' said Nancy.[7]

That is all she says, but it recalls another sombre incident when the great-aunt is said to have made Nancy's and Peggy's mother cry with her criticisms of the children, and Captain Flint was heard comforting her with the words: 'Bob would have liked them as they are.'[8]
   The narrative seems at times to be debating with itself on child-rearing. The great-aunt has her comic uses, but her real role is menacing. She is a threat to the familial ideal that the novel upholds; she is insensitive to the poetry of generations united in time and landscape, and she wrecks the summer's boating possibilities as effectively as the loss of the *Swallow* does. She is the only person in the novel to make someone else cry. This unpardonable offence is set against the loving-care of Young Billy when Roger is lost and crippled in the mist on the Moor. Later, the old man's eccentric gentleness becomes part of the process of revealing to the small puzzled boy the mysterious energies of memory.

> There would likely be some wrestling, and when Roger asked what that was, Young Billy said it was high time he was taken to see some. And then he told how long ago he was taken, when no bigger than Roger, to see his old dad wrestle for a belt with a bit of a silver buckle on it, and then of how the time came when he was wrestling in that place himself. And with that his back straightened and he swung his old arms and rubbed his old hands and clapped them together and rambled away with talk that Roger could not understand at all, about half-Nelsons and cross-buttocks and fair throws and lost handgrips. But Roger did not say that he did not understand. He just listened and the words went over his head like great poetry, only leaving him the feeling that the old man who was talking was very much stirred up by something or other that had happened a very long time ago.[9]

For each of the children exploration means something different. For Roger it means new first experiences like camping out on a hillside, hobbling with a crutch and sleeping in the charcoal-burners' wigwam.

For John, it is a developing pattern of loyalties, for he is by nature a defender; he champions his boat, his brother and sisters, his favourite camping-place, and when he has climbed Kanchenjunga he sees all other hills as 'hummocky' in comparison. Susan's exploration is experienced in terms of camp-building and home-making. She has a narrower range of adventure, and gets cross about the cooking. She is often sharp-tempered, and the narrative seems uneasy about this; Chapter 26 ends with an eloquent tribute to her domestic reliability, but it reads more like conciliation, propitiatory rather than generous.[10]

The connection between the 'realistic' surface narrative and the novel's underlying concerns is Titty. The early *Swallows and Amazons* novels are preoccupied with play as serious activity, and this novel in particular develops the theme of pretending. Titty transforms every moment through the power of make-believe, insisting on the constant imaginary presence of Peter Duck, and correcting the others when they forget him. But pretending is a kind of magic and may not always be free of risk – as she discovers when she makes a wax image of the great-aunt intending to cause her a little discomfort, but drops the image in the fire by mistake. When she realises the implications of this, her horror is almost overwhelming. Of course, the great-aunt comes to no harm and Titty learns a lesson about the power of magic to distress the magician more than the victim. The lesson learned is not one of make-believe versus reality, but of error reassured by love, for when the others come back John is instantly concerned (for Titty, not for the great-aunt) and the chapter ends with a quiet reassuring cadence.

> But late that night Susan heard Titty stir uneasily in her tent. Susan wriggled a hand out from under her tent and into Titty's which was close beside it. Titty found the hand and held it tight.
> 'I didn't mean to kill her,' she whispered.
> 'Of course you didn't and you haven't,' said Susan.
> 'We'll know in the morning.'
> 'We know now,' said Susan. 'Go to sleep.'[11]

The children's boat inspires them almost to poetry. The account of *Swallow*'s sinking and subsequent salvage employs a mixture of the practical and the lyrical which is a distinguishing feature of Ransome's writing at its best.

> They took hold of *Swallow*'s anchor rope and pulled, gently at first, and then harder. Something stirred far down and sent a

quiver through the rope into their fingers. They pulled again and it was almost as if they could hear *Swallow* move on the bottom of the lake.[12]

That 'almost as if' expresses precisely the imaginative connection in Ransome between realism and magic. The little boat is speaking to them, alive and persistent under the water.

Again they pulled. The rope came in and they could feel *Swallow* lifting over the stones. With her ballast out she weighed very little more than water.
 'I can see her,' said John, almost under his breath, as if he were telling of a miracle.[13]

That last clause is significant; it exemplifies the way in which Ransome represents ordinary practicalities as transformed into something almost miraculous or magical. Reality is transcended but never lost sight of. For the rest of the narrative *Swallow* is out of the action, laid up in a boat-builder's yard. But she reappears in the end to become an image of healing, a simple metaphor for the values implicit in the story, and at the same time a focus for a complex patterning of words of *new* and *old*, of *youth* and *renewal*.

They could not have told, if they had not known, where that dreadful hole had been. She was a new ship, better than new, for she had renewed her youth and kept her memories and was still at heart the same old *Swallow* – more, far more, to them than any other vessel could be, anywhere, in all the world.[14]

The novel ends with a triumphant race against the Amazons, and then the joyous return to their old camping-place on Wildcat Island, where Susan has the last significant word:

'Pouf!' said Susan, raking the sticks together in the fire-place. 'Isn't it a blessing to get home?'[15]

which, from Susan's point of view is narrow and domestic, but which also invokes a wider, Rousseauistic, ideal associated in the 1930s with the joys of camping.

Peter Duck (1932) is supposed to be a story made up by the children in winter. However, I suspect that most of its young readers have probably accepted it simply as the account of the Swallows' and Amazons' third summer adventure. It is, I believe, one of the best children's stories of the century, concluding and completing the themes of the two preceding works.[16]

Peter Duck is concerned with the conflict between good and evil, and with the way goodness defines itself in terms of opposition. I believe Ransome sustained his interest in the series by almost secretly shifting his imaginative interest. The first time he did this was in this third narrative, which is not primarily interested in the individual children but in the ship, and the children as crew. The entire adventure is presided over by Peter Duck, who in the previous story was a fantasy figure invented by Titty, but who in this story is a solid and convincing Everyman of the Sea, a personification of centuries of traditional sea-faring values. Ransome's creation of Peter Duck is an imaginative master-stroke. He is an Ancient Mariner with a fund of sea-going know-how; in his unfussy way he cares for the children, and is wisely sceptical of the value of treasure. Furthermore, he is a kind of guarantor of the joys of sailing, a presider over the poetry of the sea.

There is a great deal of such poetry in *Peter Duck* – moments of fine writing, unselfconscious, subdued and balanced, like the description of the lightships and buoys of the Channel as 'the signposts of the sea',[17] or the account of the *Wild Cat* moving slowly through thick fog and making 'hardly as much noise as the wind blowing over soft grass'.[18] Such careful and unpretentious phrasing is frequent: the boat is described as 'picking her way almost in her sleep in and out among the mountain ranges of the sea';[19] or 'resting . . . easy as a sleeping gull upon the heaving waters'.[20] Ransome's language makes no fuss about its moments of imaginative perception: when Bill climbs out at night to the end of the bowsprit, we are told simply that he sits 'astride of the spar, swaying on and on ahead of the ship, above the dark water in the moonlit night'.[21] In the final chapter the novel's interest in poetry becomes explicit as Peter Duck demonstrates to Titty that the sailors who made the *Spanish Ladies* shanty must have been tacking up Channel against a north-easter – a rare case of practical criticism illuminated by a seaman's know-how.

This lyricism of the sea is not ornamental. The *Wild Cat* crew is an idealised community – six children learning, sharing and practising new skills, and bound by a tacit and deeply felt loyalty to the ship. The *Wild Cat* is an embodiment of values; she combines the security of home with the uncertainties of voyaging; she defines in her movements social and moral, as well as aesthetic, values; she is huge, yet responsive, and she elicits love. Something of this is conveyed in the account of their first time at sea:

> Titty looked back at the lengthening wake astern. This was like sailing *Swallow* only somehow better. A touch on the wheel and this whole ship obeyed with the whole lot of them aboard, a regular house of a ship, with towering sails higher than lots of houses. There was a lump in Titty's throat, and John's lips were pressed tight together.[22]

Apart from an amateurish burglary, evil and menace were absent from the first two books. But in *Peter Duck* Ransome brings the children to face real danger. Black Jake – hot-tempered, dark-faced, with gold ear-rings – is only a villain from Titty's reading of pirate stories, but when he and his gang of stereotypes capture the *Wild Cat*, there are no clichés – just a solid and distressing realism. Peter Duck is knocked out and tied up; Bill is beaten up, and they stuff a lump of soap into his mouth, and lock him up in a cage. The account is economical, lucid and grim. There is something outrageously shocking about that lump of soap. It does not matter that Black Jake is a stereotype; he represents a force which would destroy everything gentle and peaceable that the *Wild Cat* stands for. Innocence here is toughened and defined through intimate contact with violence. It requires courage, and the seriousness of this need comes across strongly in the understated firmness with which the two oldest children endure their darkest moments in defence of it.

The children see their danger in terms of *loss*. 'Earthquake and landslide had not been enough to make this kind of difference. It was the coming of the *Viper* that had changed the island for them.'[23] All along Peter Duck had warned them not to underestimate Black Jake; now Nancy and John must face him alone. As they light the lantern which will be a beacon for Captain Flint in the dark, but also a clear target for the pirates, there is a sombre note in the prose.

> [The lantern] lit up the yellow oar with which Nancy fended off. It lit up their faces, oddly white, as they looked at each other across it, and then, as John turned towards the shore and held the lantern at arm's length, it seemed to Nancy to turn him into monstrous flickering shadow between her and the light.
>   'He ought to see that all right,' said John.
>   'They'll see it, too,' said Nancy.[24]

That is all they say. There is no parading of courage, just an acknowledgement of the reality. When they hear footsteps stumbling through
the dark, John simply stands up, 'holding the lantern before him as
high as he could'.[25] It is an act of extraordinary bravery. Stevenson,
Kipling and perhaps Conrad lie behind this writing.

Peter Duck, the teller of tales and possessor of mysterious knowledge of the sea, is not entirely predictable. He occasionally teases,
and Titty does not know how seriously to take him when she plans
her first swim in tropical waters. '"It don't seem fair to give a shark
his breakfast before you've had your own," said Peter Duck.'[26] He
seems unconcerned, but a few moments later Captain Flint has to be
hurriedly hauled out of the water 'just as a long grey shadow flashed
white in the water, and the shark turned over and a horrible mouth
snapped only an inch or two below his foot'.[27]

The old salt's memories are unreliable, for the enormous crabs
which had so horrified him when, as a boy, he had been abandoned
on the island seem disappointingly small to Roger. It is, characteris-
tically, Titty who imagines the old man as a frightened shipwrecked
child.

> '. . . Miracle, it seems to me. If I'd come ashore anywhere else I'd
> have missed sixty years of sailing. Sixty good years I'd have
> missed. Think of that now.'
>
>   Titty stared at him. She tried to think of him sixty years ago,
> small and wet and wretched, tied to a spar, and washed ashore
> from a wreck, not like Robinson Crusoe, with lots of useful
> things to help him, but with nothing at all but a pocket-knife.[28]

Titty and the narrator remind us that Peter Duck is not super-human;
and when, during John's and Nancy's final moment of danger, he
feels sure they have been murdered on the dark beach, he is described
as 'a little, bent old man, bowed down perhaps by the weight of his
fears'.[29] That 'perhaps' is revealing; it is the text's own tribute to
Peter Duck's mystery. Behind his creation lie *Robinson Crusoe*, *The
Ancient Mariner*, *Treasure Island* and Ransome's own boating masterpiece, *The Cruise of the Racundra*. He embodies the toughness and
continuity of humanity and the vulnerability of humanity's innocent
pleasures.

Despite its fantastic nature (its earthquakes, storms, tornadoes and
water-spouts), *Peter Duck* in a poetic and thematic sense triumphantly
and with sustained seriousness completes *Swallows and Amazons*
and *Swallowdale*. The three books are like a trilogy, defining a social

ideal of companionship based on respect, decorum, and love of sea-scape and landscape. Ransome was aware of the special connectedness of the three novels, for he makes it explicit at precisely the point of John's and Nancy's greatest courage, when their rowing falls briefly out of time.

> 'Sorry,' said John.
> 'My fault,' said Nancy.
> They would have said just that if they had got out of time while rowing together on the lake at home. They said it now, though they were rowing in at dusk to an island of landslide and earthquake and half-mad pirates roaming about with stolen guns. Still, some things were the same as usual. Wherever you were you said 'Sorry' if you bumped 'stroke' in the back with the bow oar, and you said it was your fault if you had happened to change the time unexpectedly because you were thinking of something else.[30]

Ransome usually leaves these things unsaid – wisely, because such emphases easily become sanctimonious. In *Peter Duck* there are numerous references back to the children's adventures on the lake in England, for they are the same people with the same values. And, incidentally, they have brought *Swallow* with them on their Caribbean voyage – indeed, the little boat, their partner in a dozen lakeland adventures, gets a pirate's bullet in her timbers.

According to Hugh Brogan, Ransome insisted that *Winter Holiday* (1933) was to be the last book about the Walkers and the Blacketts. And in fact, the text confirms the fact that Ransome's imaginative sympathy has been transferred to Dick and Dorothea Callum. He has removed Nancy from most of the action by giving her mumps, and the four Swallows are rather diminished stereotypes of their former selves – vigorous, cheerful but more than a little sanctimonious. In one revealing episode they are tempted to slip away to spend a secret night on the iced-in houseboat without telling Titty and Roger. They try to deceive the youngsters (unthinkable in the previous stories), and when Titty and Roger catch them at it, there is a rare example of vindictiveness. 'Can't we stop . . .?' says Titty. 'No you can't,' says Susan. 'It's because of you that we can't either.'[31]

Something has changed here. This *is* realism. But it undermines the idyll of unitedness which the first three books had poetically established. A hint in any of the first three stories that Susan and John regarded Titty and Roger as nuisances would have been inconceivable. *Winter Holiday* is a kind of closure. Ransome has finished with his six much-loved children. But he transforms this closure into a new opening by introducing two new characters, Dorothea and Dick, to whom he hands over the themes of innocence and discovery. The story of the two town-children is then developed into a quest for meaning in a bewildering world of coded messages.

The best writing in this complex novel is concerned with Dorothea and Dick. The episode at the beginning when they hear across the water the voices of the six Swallows and Amazons in their boat is powerfully evocative of the strangeness of the countryside and the longing of the two newcomers to be part of it. Thereafter the novel describes a process of initiation into languages and codes – Morse, Semaphore, naval flag-signalling, and various other ways of conveying secret information. Diagrams and illustrations reinforce the point that *meaning*, and access to it, lie at the heart of the story. The main activity is signalling, and the novel's predominant metaphors have to do with codes. The imagery of the winter landscape is itself a code to be cracked; it is composed of signs to be interpreted – the track of a bird in the snow, a change of light or cloud-movement, or the enigma of a fish frozen in the ice. In a deeper sense, Dorothea and Dick have to learn the unspoken code which holds together the companionship of the Walkers and the Blacketts – and, in a still deeper sense, the shared local codes of how to experience a Lake District freeze-up.

Dorothea and Dick construct meanings according to their natures. We see this early, in their different responses to the night sky.

'. . . How far away does it say the Pleiades are?'

Dorothea went back to the fire and found the place in the book.

'The light from the group known as the Pleiades (referred to by Tennyson in *Locksley Hall*) . . .'

'Oh, hang Tennyson!'

'The light from the group known as the Pleiades reaches our planet in rather more than three hundred years after it leaves them.'

'Light goes at one hundred and eighty-six thousand miles a second,' said the voice of the astronomer out in the darkness.

But Dorothea was also doing some calculations.

'Shakespeare died 1616.'

'What?'

'Well, if the light takes more than three hundred years to get here, it may have started when Shakespeare was alive, in the reign of Queen Elizabeth, perhaps. Sir Walter Raleigh may have seen it start . . .'

'But of course he didn't,' said the astronomer indignantly. 'The light of the stars he saw had started three hundred years before that . . .'

'Battle of Bannockburn, 1314. Bows and arrows.' Dorothea was off again.

But Dick was no longer listening. One hundred and eighty-six thousand miles a second. Sixty times as far as that in a minute. Sixty times sixty times as far as that in an hour. Twenty-four hours in a day. Three hundred and sixty-five days in a year. Not counting leap years. And then three hundred years of it. Those little stars that seemed to speckle a not too dreadfully distant blue ceiling were farther away than he could make himself think, try as he might.[32]

This exchange has nothing to do with make-believe; it is astronomy and history grasped through two different kinds of imaginative reflection.

Because the two initiates are in many ways more sensitive, more thoughtful but less confident than their teachers, the account of their learning the codes of the Swallows and Amazons simultaneously questions the adequacy of the codes to be learnt and exposes some of the strains in the unity of the six host-children. Dick and Dorothea are more subtly articulate than their teachers. It is characteristic of this novel that this difference between them is revealed in terms of language.

John, Peggy, Titty and Roger made up the despatch between them. Here it is: –

'NORTH POLAR EXPEDITION
'Crossed Greenland. Reached Spitzbergen by ice.
'Captain Flint's houseboat is frozen in.
Signed – North Polar Expedition
'PS. – The D's have got a sledge. That makes 2.
Peggy.
'PS. – Mr. Dixon made it because Dick (and us too)
rescued a Polar bear which was starving.'
Roger.
'It is getting better with hot milk.'

Dorothea thought that this despatch missed a lot of things that might very well have been said. In her own story about the Arctic she would have one altogether different and more exciting. But she said nothing. After all, the despatch did say what had happened.[33]

She says nothing because she is a girl of great gentleness and tact. 'Nobody ever was angry with Dorothea', we are told.[34] This is demonstrated when Captain Flint unexpectedly returns to his houseboat and finds the Ds – whom he has never heard of – occupying his home. Anger is out of the question because the innocent seriousness and integrity of the two children are immediately apparent to the adult and command his response. Captain Flint is won over by Dick's interest in astronomy, which is systematic and scholarly, and has nothing to do with make-believe. The boy has knowledge which the Swallows and Amazons learn to respect – like how to deal with frostbite. And what impresses the Lake children most of all is the Ds' ability to skate; in this activity roles are reversed and the two town-children become the teachers.

Generally, though, the Ds are the learners. Throughout their lessons they remain doggedly loyal to each other, and their silent and almost telepathic concern for one another is in stark contrast to their noisy and voluble companions. After their first lesson in rowing, 'they looked at each other across [Peggy], smiled faintly, but said not a word'.[35] There are many such moments. Hugh Brogan has suggested that Dorothea and Dick are two aspects of Ransome's own character – the story-teller and the scientist. He may be right; it is certainly true that the narrative has transferred its allegiance and there is now an extraordinary authorial commitment to the quiet and heroic unassertiveness of the two new characters, who are more subtly articulate than can be provided for by the codes they are being taught.

The unity of *Winter Holiday* is sustained by the landscape, its beauty and its perils. The Ds are initiated into this; their danger derives from snow, frost and blizzard in a mountainous landscape realistically described. But there is more in the narrative than verisimilitude. A specific example is Dick's moment of initiation: it takes place during the sheep-rescuing incident, and he faces his danger heroically. At the heart of a novel about codes, communication and meaning, how appropriate that Dick's discovery is the private inwardness, the *incommunicable* solitariness of personal courage.

Nobody was there to see him, to say a heartening word. This was something to be settled between him and himself.

He slipped the loop over his head and sat still for a moment, holding it. Then he untied it. A doubled rope would make more difficult what he had to do. He gave himself a short lecture on Centres of Gravity. After all, he told himself yet again, while he sat there and did not look down he was as safe without the rope as with it. And suddenly his mind was made up, and the thing seemed almost easy.[36]

In a surprising imaginative shift, in this fourth book of the series, the Swallows and Amazons themselves are not so much explorers in the lakeside landscape; they are for Dick and Dorothea part of its appeal, its strangeness – and in the end part of its dangerous unreliability too, for it is because of a signalling mistake made by the Swallows and Amazons that the Ds set off across the frozen lake and are caught in a blizzard which might have killed them. This is a considerable irony after all that code-learning.

In 1937, Ransome – writing of two child authors – said, 'We elders look back to a world that once was young. For them, the dew is still on the grass.'[37] It is a revealing remark, especially as in *Winter Holiday* 'elders' was the word he frequently used of Nancy, Peggy, Susan and John. The 'elder' Swallows and Amazons were imaginatively shifted into the background to become kindly but rather puzzling features of the winter landscape. Ransome probably believed he had finished with them and at the same time had secured a future with Dorothea and Dick.

Beneath the surface of these four outstanding books for children – the narrative sureness, the balanced lyricism, the sense of pace – there seems to have been a shifting and questing authorial search for varieties of innocence which no other children's writer except E. Nesbit had ever attempted. This was a challenging creative undertaking for it runs counter to our cultural expectations; it associates innocence with confidence, and assumes the possibility that increasing knowledge, a developing awareness of danger, and inclusion in an adult world, will confirm innocence, not annihilate it. This preoccupation, despite the manifest differences between them, links Ransome with E. Nesbit, Lewis Carroll and ultimately William Wordsworth and William Blake. Blake's vision of the realities of innocence in a contemporary industrial society was altogether more austere; he understood far more acutely its ambiguities, its fragility, and its connection with sexuality.

Ransome – in *Peter Duck* – brought the six Swallows and Amazons into direct contact with brutality and greed; he brought Innocence face to face with Experience. Then – in creating Dick and Dorothea – he went back again in search of Innocence.

It was not a realistic representation of the Lake District that Ransome was interested in – it was Arcadia.

When the series resumed in 1934 with *Coot Club*, the Swallows and Amazons were abandoned, reflecting Ransome's loss of imaginative interest in them. But it didn't matter – what sustained his creativity now was his excited personal discovery of the Norfolk Broads.

Coot Club is a comic adventure story embedded in a guide-book. Ransome's artistic commitment is to the Broads – its waters, birds, boats and people. The text requires the reader to encompass the geography of the region, and to realise and appreciate its particular visual beauty as it was perceived in the 1930s by a man who recognised that the new motor-cruisers would threaten the pace of older and more leisurely forms of boating. The language of the novel is concerned above all with *seeing*, and accordingly there is a great deal of Ransome's characteristic and carefully stated observation.

> The sun had gone down. The tide was on the point of turning, and up-river a calm green-and-golden glow filled the sky and was reflected on the scarcely moving water. A heron came flying downstream with long slow flaps of his great wings. Only twenty yards away he lifted easily over the tall reeds and settled with a noisy disturbance of twigs on the top of a tree in a little wood at the edge of the marshes. The heron had a little difficulty in balancing himself on the thin, swaying branch, and Tom, watching him, dark against the glowing sky, very nearly forgot that he, too, had an uncertain perch.[38]

There are many such accounts in *Coot Club*, economical vignettes of water and sky, sometimes rather conventional, but always clear and unpretentious word-pictures. They are often inspired by bird-watching.

> The two birds were flying one above another and no longer so far apart. Suddenly the first hawk dropped or threw from it the small bird it was carrying. The other turned almost on its back in the air and caught the quarry as it fell.[39]

Such descriptions combine careful observation and restrained enthusiastic affection.[40] It is apparent again when the children, sailing at South Walsham – 'that beautiful little broad'[41] – find a crested grebe on her nest.

> They sailed silently by, and she let them come to within a few yards before she quickly covered her eggs with some rotted weeds and slipped off into the water. She was back again on the nest before they had gone far, and, after they had had dinner, when they brought Dorothea to see her, she let them sail close by without stirring from her nest, sitting with neck and crest erect, following them with her eyes and moving nothing but her head.[42]

Often such lyricism exists unobtrusively as nothing more than a modest illuminating detail, as when the wash of a cruiser is described as 'sending long bustling waves chasing one another over the mudflats';[43] or the description of Beccles viewed from under its bridges, 'houses almost standing in the water, rowing boats tied to the walls, and a flock of white ducks swimming from one back door to the next'.[44]

The prose frequently conveys in the rhythm of its syntax the author's sense of excitement:

> And so, rejoicing in their freedom, the outlaw and his friends sailed on their way, through a country as flat as Holland, past huge old windmills, their sails creaking round, pumping the water from the low-lying meadows on which the cows were grazing actually below the level of the river. Far away over the meadows other sails were moving . . .[45]

The reference to Holland is apt here, for the passage seems to combine the restrained aesthetics of Dutch landscape painting with a very Dutch interest in the realities of drainage-engineering. The writing wants its readers to realise, or internalise, in a dramatic and personal way, the extraordinary geographical shock of seeing the imagery of the sea amid the imagery of the land, and of cows 'grazing *actually* below the level of the river'. That 'actually' is significant – we are being reminded to make an imaginative effort.[46]

This novel makes the reader 'see' the Broads, and the word-painting is aided by the two endpapers and various other maps[47] in the text. The villages and waterways are given their real names, not fictional ones, indicating a transfer of authorial interest from the transforming imaginations of the children to the realities of an actual landscape. The processes of visualising are aided by Ransome's own illustrations, many of which successfully capture the horizontals and verticals of masts and reeds in a flat landscape of waters and wide skies. Many chapters end with a small tailpiece, resembling a tiny wood-engraving – a heron in some reeds, a windmill on a bank, a pair of spoonbills, a Norfolk wherry with its sail reflected in calm water.

This narrative is particularly excited by movement and records it with eager faithfulness. Everything in this landscape is on the move – flowing waters, tidal transformations of water-scape to mud-flat,

HADDISCOE·BRIDGE

1 and 2 From *Coot Club*

changes of wind and cloud, fogs that come rolling unpredictably in from the sea, and – above all – the movements of birds. The boating people of the Broads are nomadic. All the plots and sub-plots are about voyaging. While Mrs Barrable – 'a wrinkled old lady in a little brown dinghy' who 'jolly well knows how to row'[48] – is boating down to Beccles, the twins are making their own unorthodox journey by hitching lifts on boats. Simultaneously the Death and Glories are either cycling all over the area in search of information or rowing frantically about in their makeshift craft. This authorial interest in movement may account for the narrative's and the illustrations' concern with bridges. Often these bridges move too; they swing aside or open up. When they don't, they test the skill of the crew and simultaneously indicate progress along a river.

The best writing in the novel is the account of the *Teasel*'s long voyage down from Horning to Yarmouth, through the Yarmouth bridges, and along the Waveney almost to Oulton.

> The sun had set, the wind was dropping, but the *Teasel* was still gliding on, so smoothly, so easily, that it seemed impossible to stop. On and on they sailed. A sunset glow spread over the sky, and the reeds stood out black against it. On and on. They could hardly see where the reflections ended and the banks began. Nothing else was moving. Windmills, dark against the darkening sky, seemed twice their proper size. At last, peering forward, they could see that the river was dividing in two.
>
> 'Oulton Dyke,' said Tom, hardly above a whisper.[49]

The language here evokes with fine precision an end-of-the-day, end-of-the-voyage feeling of weariness and triumph. It is a climactic closure, suggestive of journeying and joy consummated and recorded.

At the same time, on another Broad, the twins are experiencing a different kind of bedtime aboard Mr Whittle's Thames barge.

> The dark closed down over the marshes and the river. A light was hoisted up the forestay, for even in inland waters the *Welcome* of Rochester did not forget that she was a sea-going vessel. Down below, under a lantern hanging from a beam, her crew and her passengers ate fresh herrings and bread and butter. And there was talk of London river and Rochester Bridge, and of Rotterdam and other foreign ports. And Mr Hawkins brought out his mouth organ and gave them a tune when invited to do so by Mrs Whittle.

At last Mr Whittle was spoken to by his wife for yawning. Mr Hawkins covered his own mouth with a huge and tarry hand, said 'Good night,' and went off up the ladder and away in the darkness to his berth forward.[50]

Conrad and Stevenson have given way to Dickens, enabling Ransome to express his respect for the eccentric water-people of the Broads – their generosity and the validity of their lives. It is well done, but there is a price to be paid. His preoccupation with the people and landscape of the Broads has led him to pay less attention to the individuality of his child-protagonists. They are little more than ciphers. Dick and Dorothea are reduced copies of the sensitive and intelligent brother and sister who appeared in *Winter Holiday*; the twins have little to interest us beyond the fact that they are identical and are nicknamed Port and Starboard. But Tom Dudgeon is more substantial; with his local knowledge of the Broads and his acquaintance with almost every boatman he encounters, he is to the Broads what Peter Duck was to the world's great oceans (a kind of Peter Coot?).

I find *Coot Club* a slightly unsatisfactory novel. There is too much activity and not enough action; too many 'characters' and not enough character. Yet it is an extraordinary work in many ways – it must have been something of a shock to country children of the thirties who took it for granted that the natural thing to do with birds' nests was to rob them. *Coot Club* will probably always appeal to ornithologists, boating people, and nostalgic lovers of the Broads. But it stands apart from the main thrust of the *Swallows and Amazons* because the children in it are of minimal interest – they are there simply to crew the narrative on its celebratory voyage and to stand back and allow the reader to feel something of the author's pleasure in the unique visual appeal of Norfolk. Any boatload of children would have served this purpose, provided they responded with appropriate pleasure to the people and places of the Broads. Perhaps that is the real reason for the absence of Nancy and John and the rest – Ransome might have been unable to make them acquiesce in such an enterprise; in all their sailing adventures they were never content to be tourists.

2 The storm before the calm

Pigeon Post (1936) must have seemed to many readers a welcome return to the earlier, more robust, mode of the series – a return to the Lake District, the Swallows and Amazons, and the unpredictability ensured by the presence of Nancy. But it is significantly more than an imaginative home-coming. Beneath the surface confidence of the writing, *Pigeon Post* is in many ways a strange and daring story. This novel, and its successor *We Didn't Mean to Go to Sea*, are concerned primarily with real danger – and this concern is somehow related to a new authorial interest in Susan.

How young readers must have loved the beginning of *Pigeon Post*, with the gathering of the clan for the long summer holiday, the commitment to prospecting for gold, and the determination to establish a camp up in the hills. But this carefully staged opening, with its atmosphere of scoutmasterly insouciance, is deceptive. Although there are periods of busy tranquillity, they are rare interludes in a narrative which is uncharacteristically tense. The book's predominant imagery has to do with heat. The landscape is parched, streams have dried up, and local people are irritable and frightened of fell-fires. Astonishingly, for the children's central activity Ransome has chosen mining, charcoal-burning and smelting! The narrative plays with fire and takes its characters to the volatile perimeters of danger. It seems intent upon testing the holiday-adventure's fundamental assumption – that reliable and well-brought-up children will come to no harm if left to themselves. Four of them are almost buried alive in a derelict mine-working where they have no business to be; all of them are almost burned alive in a fell-fire of terrifying ferocity; and in a drought-baked landscape Ransome allows his children to try to heat a furnace to 2060 degrees.

The structure of the narrative reinforces this sense of tension. It is composed of a series of achieved gratifications, each frustratingly delayed and dependent on the children overcoming some apparently insuperable difficulty. Ransome does not allow the children to make their camp until the seventeenth chapter! Suspense in this novel has little to do with wanting to know what happens; it has to do with *making the reader wait*. The narrative edges slowly forward to its successive moments of triumph by way of delays, deferments and frustrations. The prospecting for gold is slow and tedious for the children, and the narrative comes close to tedium too. Ransome is risk-taking, pressing close to the edge of the acceptable boundaries of comfortable children's fiction.

In this flammable and volatile story, nothing is what it seems. Sight is repeatedly dazzled by the brilliance of the sun, and the narrative itself is equally unreliable, confusingly offering alternative perspectives. Here, it seems to say, are eight loyal and sensible children gamely going about their innocent business. Yet those same children almost get themselves killed, and their activities might easily have set fire to several square miles of countryside and destroyed two or three farms. These children are dangerous – especially Roger. In the earlier books he tagged on, an enthusiastic little boy with an egocentric and uncertain grasp of what was happening. But in *Pigeon Post* he has a mind and will-power of his own. He is cheeky, he plays tricks, and he makes silly noises. He is subversive, disobedient and dangerous. It is Roger who leads Dorothea, Dick and Titty into a tunnel where they are almost crushed to death. On another occasion he slips off and stays away so long that the others are sure something has gone badly wrong.

> And just then the pale red glimmer of a dying torch showed between the trees and Roger walked into camp.
> Pity and fear for him were gone in a moment.
> 'Miserable little idiot,' said John.
> 'Where have you been?' said Susan.
> 'Hullo,' said Roger, seeing what was in the frying-pan that Peggy was holding . . .
> 'Shiver my timbers,' said Nancy. 'If you were a ship's boy in *my* ship . . . *or* an able-seaman.'
> He came slowly towards them, keeping one hand behind his back.
> 'What have you done to your hand?' said Susan.
> 'Nothing,' said Roger.
> 'Why are you hiding it?'
> 'Got something in it,' said Roger.

> He faced the whole indignant company and held out a large
> lump of white quartz.
> 'Gold,' he said simply. 'Look at it and see.'[1]

This is a new kind of writing. Readers of the *Swallows and Amazons*
stories have not been accustomed to anger like this.

The emotional price for Roger's recklessness is paid by Susan. In
this novel we know little about her. The impassioned Nancy, like the
others, assumes she is keen to get on with the cooking, but Susan is
given no chance to comment. In this novel she is a silent brooding
presence, angry, worried and preoccupied. The others think of her as
nearly 'native', but for the reader she is a narratorial seismograph
registering the gravity of the risks the rest of them take. For example,
when the four youngest children escape from the disused mine they
see the older children searching in the distance and send them a
semaphore message: ALL WELL.

> 'What are they doing?' said Roger. 'Susan's turned round and
> she's walking away.'
> 'She's jolly mad,' said Titty.
> 'And John's beckoning,' said Dorothea. 'And Peggy's gone
> after Susan to bring her back.'[2]

Susan is given no speech, just a gesture and a movement of anger and
worry. And a little later –

> They came back to the camp to find Susan stirring the cocoa
> rather grimly, and Roger, oddly silent, watching her. She had
> heard, at last, the whole dreadful story of how the tunnel had
> fallen in on the heels of the explorers.[3]

In the earlier stories, Susan was identified as a competent and caring
surrogate mother. Here, however, she is powerless to check the behaviour of the others, partly because they are growing more independent and more wilful, but also I think because Ransome is writing
a different kind of story – a story which allows him to suggest without explaining Susan's unknowable and intimidating passions.

Nancy has stopped being a character altogether. Perhaps she never
was one. She is a kind of child-demon, a spirit of the determined and
benevolent craziness of children in the holidays, an inspirer of irra-
tional enterprises. Peggy and Dorothea hardly exist. John and Susan
seem to have moved to helpless adulthood and by-passed adolescence

altogether. *Pigeon Post* is primarily a novel about the three youngest
– Roger, Titty and Dick. Dick's ingenuity and knowledge, and his
practical approach to science, keep the gold-prospecting alive and are
set against Roger's disruptive recklessness.

However, even Dick's scientific sobriety is baffled by the mysterious episode when Titty discovers she is a dowser and finds a hidden
spring. When the others have failed and Roger has made a joke of it,
Titty reluctantly has a go.

> 'Half a minute,' said Captain Nancy eagerly. 'Didn't it give a
> sort of jerk just now?'
> Titty looked round miserably. 'It can't have,' she said.
> 'There it is again,' said Nancy. 'Look here. Come back a yard
> or two and go over that bit again.'
> Everybody was alert now, and watching.
> 'What happened?' said Roger. 'I didn't see.'
> 'Slowly . . .' said Nancy.
> Titty's eyes were swimming. She saw the ground of the yard at
> her feet through a mist. Something queer was happening that she
> could neither help nor hinder. The stick was more than a bit of
> wood in her hands. It was coming alive. If only she could drop it,
> and be free from it.[4]

Ransome is writing with a sure touch here. There is no rollicking
triumph (imagine the Famous Five in a similar situation) – just confusion and fear, and Titty's almost unbearable sense of being controlled by something unintelligible. She *fights* the hazel-twig. It suddenly
twists out of her hand and 'Titty, the dowser, startled more than she
could bear, and shaking with sobs, had bolted up into the woods.'[5]

Why this distress? In most of the previous novels, Titty has kept
the group in touch with deeper mysteries – mysteries of poetry, story
and the imagination. Titty has to do with magic. It was Titty who
once made a wax image of the hated great-aunt and accidentally
dropped it into the fire. Here, again, she is in touch with a mysterious
force, but whether it is a power she possesses, or a power which
possesses her, is problematical. For the others it is a simple practical
matter: they need her to use her power to find water for a camp
higher up the mountain. But the writing aligns itself with Titty's
confusion – never explained, but convincingly presented as a child's
fear at discovering a startling gift which sets her apart from the rest.

The question for Titty is whether she can bring herself to try
dowsing properly at the longed-for camp-site. After a chapter of

guilty hesitation (relieved by a comic interlude in which Nancy has a try), Titty makes up her mind to do it and sets off at dusk, alone, like a pagan child-priestess, up the track through the forest. At once a kind of benevolent magic comes into play.

> She listened. From far away down the valley she heard the mooing of a cow. A sheep-dog was barking. Hens were fussing loudly in the Tyson's farmyard. She could just see a bit of the grey slate roof far below her. It looked as if she could almost drop a stone on it.[6]

There is more than a hint here of Beatrix Potter's imaginative landscape, but transformed to reassure Titty that all is well – the familiar world is close by and, although she is alone, she is not set apart from it. Then the countryside offers a precise magic sign.

> It was growing darker very quickly. The glow in the sky over Swallowdale and the fells on the other side of the valley was climbing higher, and the dusk was coming up after it over the eastern hills. Just for a moment it felt a little queer to be alone there in the darkening wood. And then there was a sudden disturbance of leaves and presently the long 'Tuwhoooooooooooo' of an owl. Real owl, thought Titty, not an owl-call, and she remembered a night when she had been alone on Wild Cat island, and an owl had called like that and everything had turned out right just when it seemed to be going wrong.[7]

This is followed by an odd little incident, an encounter with a hedgehog trotting down the path and sniffing, which knew 'that something strange was about, but he looked for things of his own height, and never saw Titty, towering above him'.[8] The hedgehog is searching for water too. Yet what wonderful writing that is – 'he looked for things of his own height' – evocative, magical, yet exact.

Titty begins a strange little dialogue with herself, breathing hard as she takes hold of the hazel-twig. She feels it move in her hand, then it tickles and twitches, and pulls harder and harder. She is not so frightened this time – in fact, 'she was almost eagerly feeling the pulling on the twig'. Its twisting grows more violent and finally in a dramatic climax it seems 'to leap in her hands'[9] and almost springs out of her fingers.

> 'It's here,' said Titty. 'I've found it.' She had no longer any doubts. Dick was wrong. This was nothing of her imagining. No imagining could make the hazel-twig twist her hands until they

hurt. She was no longer afraid. This was a secret between her and the twig.[10]

Are we to interpret this sexually? Is Titty coming to terms with her emerging sexuality (such a popular theme today)? I doubt it. The narrative is undoubtedly concerned with an unintelligible power but it is specific to Titty, not generally female. Ransome does not explain it, or mock it, or question it. Dick is mystified by the unreason of it, the others joyously make use of it, and Titty herself feels an odd wish to cry when eventually they dig out an enormous hole and discover a small faithful spring just where the twig had indicated. The episode seems to me to be religious, not sexual – to be concerned with the readiness of the countryside to yield up its secrets as if they were gifts. But only when invoked by a 'magical child'.

In any case the ambiguous mystery surrounding Titty's strange power is entirely consistent with the kind of novel this is. Its imagery is the imagery of confusion and danger deriving either from the brilliant dazzling heat of the surface landscape or from the oppressive blackness of tunnels. *Pigeon Post* is an explosive narrative. The tinder-dry landscape is likely to catch fire at any moment. And the children are explosive too – subject to uncontrollable and unintelligible passions which erupt without warning and leave them for a time confused and troubled. Roger's dangerous mischief, Titty's unaccountable power, Susan's anger which is so terrible that the narrative shies away from describing it, indicate a fierce child-turbulence *just* contained within the safe limits of a holiday-adventure story. The ending of the novel – like the beginning – confirms the more reassuring perspective: the children are safe and acknowledged at last as heroes. But it has not been as simple as that comfortable rounding-off suggests. Even the pigeons are not to be trusted. In the narrative their role is to reassure Nancy's mother down in the valley by carrying messages that the children are safe; in the title their role is to reassure adult book-buyers that this is just another of the *Swallows and Amazons* books. But, significantly, one of the three pigeons almost falls victim to a hawk, and another never arrives on time anyway. They confirm that this is an unsafe narrative disguising itself as a safe one.

There was nothing disguised about the title of the next novel in the series, which was *We Didn't Mean to Go to Sea* (1937). It is a truthful sign that this story involves a danger survived and a broken undertaking. The novel has none of the equivocal tentativeness of its predecessor: it is openly an unsafe adventure story.

In the central section of the novel, the four Swallows find themselves through no fault of their own adrift in the North Sea. They
face unaided the perils of sailing in thick fog, impenetrable darkness,
and hurricane-force winds. The four children are tested in the boating skills, discipline and loyalties they have developed in Swallowdale.
For John in particular, the adventure is a *rite de passage* at the end of
which he is recognised – literally and symbolically – by his father. We
find in this central account of the children's night at sea some of
Ransome's best writing, an authentic and compelling account of John's
panics, his irritability, his mistakes, his generosity and above all his
boyish heroism. There is a different quality in the writing, a new note
of urgency in the prose.

> A sea broke over her bows, and sheets of water flew up over the
> cabin roof, into the mainsail, and splashed down over the strug-
> gling figures in the cockpit.
>
>   They came too near the wind and the jib flogged as if it would
> tear to pieces or pull the mast out of the ship. Another sea burst
> over the bows and came sluicing aft over the cabin roof. They
> were knee deep in water. John wrestled with the tiller. The thun-
> der of the jib stopped, and the *Goblin* again darted forward, met
> a sea as if it had been a rock, dived, and rose heavily, only to
> meet the onrush of another breaking crest.[11]

There is discipline here, a commitment to the accuracy of seaman-
ship, with no overstatement or sentimentalism. It is not surprising
that Nancy and Peggy are not involved in this adventure; the very
syntax excludes them. The dangers press upon the children with
unrelenting ferocity, and each is faced, endured and survived – not
with professional finesse but with a grimly realistic understanding of
the price of failure.

In so many ways this is John's story – an account of his initiation
through fear and resolve into the confident possession of an achieved
triumph in the face of overwhelming dangers. But it is also Susan's
story. The brooding and troubled girl who fretted and grumbled on
the sidelines of *Pigeon Post* now occupies the central imaginative
arena, where it becomes clear that her role is largely to register,
define and *resist* her brother's triumph.

> Susan's voice, now that she was back at housekeeping, giving
> people meals, sounded calm and cheerful. What would it be
> when he told her what he had in mind?[12]

These two sentences expose something of what this narrative does to Susan. To begin with, it makes assumptions about her role as house-keeper, and, taken out of context, this outrageous diminishing of Susan might serve as a rallying-point for a feminist denunciation. Yet there is a note of doubt in that word 'sounded'; and 'calm' is a singularly appropriate adjective in a narrative of storms, for in this novel Susan herself is the most stormy element that John has to contend with. To say that 'Susan's voice sounded calm' is to acknowledge unpredictable outbursts – and this is confirmed by the question which follows, for throughout that fearful night, every time John comes to a 'good' masculine decision he has to contend with Susan stormily resisting it.

Through much of the series the narratives have been uneasy about Susan. We know where we are with Roger, and with Titty too, in spite of her imaginative inventiveness; and we have great trust in the reliability of John, who is, after all, a recognisable boyish 'type' brought appealingly to life by Ransome's unpretentious writing. But the prose does not allow us to feel so comfortable about Susan. In *Swallowdale* there was a revealing moment at the beginning of the novel when the children were sailing for the first time to their island in the lake.

> [John] was looking straight forward, feeling the wind on his cheek, enjoying the pull of sheet and tiller and the 'lap, lap' of the water under *Swallow*'s forefoot. Sometimes he glanced up at the little pennant at the masthead, a blue swallow on a white ground (cut out and stitched by Able-Seaman Titty), to be sure that he was making the most of the wind. It takes practice to know from the feel of the wind on your cheekbone exactly what your sail is doing, and this was the first sail of these holidays. Sometimes he glanced astern at the bubbling ribbon of *Swallow*'s wake. At the moment, it did not seem to matter whether Captain Flint was flying a flag from the masthead of his houseboat or not. To be on the lake again and sailing was enough for John.

This is a moment of peace for John, the language suggesting the relaxed yet attentive pleasure of the skilled man of action. Susan, too, enjoys the moment, but her pleasure is of a different kind.

> She had had a tiring time the day before, looking after her mother and Bridget and nurse and the others and all the small luggage during the long railway journey from the south. She always took

charge on railway journeys and was always very tired next day. But nothing had been forgotten, and the number of things that would have been forgotten if Susan had not remembered them was very great. And then, this morning, there had been lists of stores to make out and check, besides the stowage of cargo in *Swallow*. So Susan was resting and happy, glad that for the moment everything was done that she could do, glad no longer to hear the din of railway stations, and glad, too, not to have to listen to strange voices in that din to make sure that they ought not to be changing trains.[13]

Despite the generous tribute to her sense of responsibility, it is ominously clear that, while John's happiness is in terms of achievement and action, Susan's is experienced mostly as a respite from worry.

In *Pigeon Post* Susan acted as an anxiety-indicator: if she was worried, the reader understood that the situation was grave. But in *We Didn't Mean to Go to Sea* her anger and fear are obstructive. From the point of view of navigation, to turn back into thick coastal fog would be an act of suicidal irresponsibility, and yet Susan's instinct throughout that ghastly night is to return to Harwich simply because they had promised not to go to sea. Susan is no longer left to fuss on the domestic sidelines; she is a central and dangerous antagonist.

At first Ransome presents her behaviour as a straightforward inner conflict of doubt and fear.

> Roger pulled at Titty's elbow.
> 'Susan's going to cry,' he whispered.
> 'Look the other way,' said Titty.
> But there was no need for that. Susan was not going to give in without a struggle. Talking to John was one thing. Talking to Titty and Roger was altogether different. Susan gave her head a shake, and as soon as she was safely back in the cockpit asked Titty why she had stopped banging the frying-pan. Titty gave the frying-pan a beating and felt better.[14]

This is cosy and agreeably reassuring. (They are using the frying-pan as an additional foghorn.) But then the narrative begins to punish Susan. It punishes her with sea-sickness, fear and humiliation. John and Roger are not sick at all, Titty only briefly; but every detail of Susan's distress is given to the reader with compassionate yet relentless vividness.

'Susan' said John again.

She turned, and he saw that tears were streaming down her face.

'It's all wrong,' she cried. 'We must go back. We oughn't to do it. I didn't want to, and I can't bear it.'

'We can't go back,' said John. 'It isn't safe to try.'

'We must,' said Susan.

Roger, who had just been going to give another three hoots of the foghorn, stared at her. This was a Susan he had never seen.

And then Titty suddenly clutched the coaming of the cockpit and leant over it.

'She's being sick,' said Roger.

John stretched out a hand to hold her shoulder.

'Leave me alone,' said Titty. 'I'm not. I can't be. It's only one of my heads. I'll be all right if I lie down just for a bit.'

She scrambled to the companion-way, got down one step, slipped on the next, and fell in a heap on the cabin floor.

'Titty, are you all right?' cried John. 'Look here, Roger. You go and help her. I can't let go of the tiller.'

This was too much.

'I'm going,' said Susan furiously. She took a long breath and struggled down into the cabin, leaving John and Roger looking at each other with horrified eyes.[15]

With that closing phrase the reader is nudged into sharing John's, Roger's and the narrator's collusive masculine moment of astonishment at this incomprehensible eruption of feminine emotion. Susan's moral misgiving about a broken promise is covertly transposed into physiological sea-sickness and presented as a weakness.

'Oh. . . . Oh . . . Oh. . . .' she groaned, and was sick over the side. She was sick again and again. When it was over she remembered that she was in the way so that John could not see the compass. She dragged herself across the cockpit and sat in the opposite corner, holding the coaming, ready to be sick once more.

'Susan,' said John at last. 'Poor old chap.'

There was no answer.

'Susan,' said John again. 'We've simply got to sound the foghorn.'

Susan leaned her head against the cabin and sobbed.

John's lip trembled. He bit it. There was a wetness behind his eyes. For one moment he thought of giving in and going back.

He looked astern into the grey fog. No. He must go on. The only hope of safety was outside. He wedged himself firmly with a foot against the opposite seat. He had the tiller with both hands.[16]

John's 'Poor old chap' says more about his school than about his perception of his sister's femininity. More significant is the way Susan's humiliation is transposed into John's moment of leadership: he is compassionate but firm, and above all he is *right*, with both hands symbolically on the tiller.

It is not surprising that reviewers of the day recognised a new note of realism and excitement in Ransome's writing. But to praise this book for its authentic representation of danger at sea is to employ an inadequate critical language. There is something here that goes beyond realism and transcends mere vividness. For, in the dynamic that is driving this narrative, it is not enough that John should be right; Susan has to be made to concede. Reluctantly John agrees to turn round the boat into the teeth of the hurricane; it is, of course, a hopeless attempt and comes close to disaster, so that Susan begs him to stop.

> 'Stop it, John! Stop it! I can't. . . . I can't. . . . Ough! . . . Oughgulloch! . . . Ough! . . . Oh! . . . Oh! . . . .' And Susan, shaken almost to pieces with this new violent motion of the battling ship, lay half across the cockpit, with her head over the coaming, and was sick. A wave broke across the cabin roof and a lump of green water hit her on the side of the head.
>
> 'John! John!' she cried. 'I can't bear it. Stop it! . . . Stop it just for a minute!'[17]

There is still one more ordeal for them to face: if they are to survive hurricane winds they must reduce sail. This is probably the most uncompromisingly and compellingly dangerous moment in the whole *Swallows and Amazons* series, and the account is composed with a constant reference to John and Susan as two polarities of fear. John – inching his way forward across the cabin roof of the bucking boat: 'Lonely? It was as if he was outside life altogether and wouldn't be alive again till he got back.'[18] And Susan – '. . . something that was hardly Susan's face, blotched and white, with wisps of bedraggled hair across her eyes, a face wet with rain and tears'.[19] At the climax of this episode John is almost washed overboard – and in her relief that he is safe Susan notices that she no longer feels sick. The chapter is ironically called *A Cure for Sea-Sickness* – but what precisely has cured it? Her concern for John? Her 'manliness' at the helm? Or her final admission that his judgement should be deferred to?

From that point the dangers faced by the four children diminish in intensity, and there is a new mood of joyous unity.

> Titty, climbing out, looked from John to Susan and from Susan to John. She was just going to ask a question, but did not ask it. She felt that the ship was suddenly full of happiness. John was grinning to himself. Susan was smiling through tears that did not seem to matter.[20]

It is a wonderful moment, but this recovery of mood ('the ship was suddenly full of happiness') has been earned at a price paid largely by Susan.

I do not mean to suggest that this great children's adventure story is flawed by the writer's unconscious sexism. After the worst of the danger is over, there is a moment when John is alone at the tiller, and we can test the text for sexism by experimenting with it.

> If anybody could have seen his face in the faint glimmer from the compass window, he would have seen that there was a grin on it. John was alone in the dark with his ship, and everybody else was asleep. He, for that night, was the master of the *Goblin*, even the lurches of the cockpit beneath him as the *Goblin* rushed through the dark filled him with a serious kind of joy. He and the *Goblin* together. On and on. On and on. Years and years hence, when he was grown up, he would have a ship of his own and sail her out into wider seas than this. But he would always and always remember this night when for the first time ship and crew were in his charge, his alone.[21]

The watchfulness, the secret grin in the night, the affection, the pride, and above all the solitariness, all serve to place John's secret moment of manliness in a long tradition of boy-heroes involved in great world events or moments of private peril. There is something predominantly masculine about this moment of achieved leadership and, if we substitute Susan's name throughout, the result would be inconsistent with everything we know of her character. But it is not *exclusively* masculine, for, if we try making Titty instead of Susan the subject, we find the substitution quite feasible. The self-sufficient Titty – a little older – might well have achieved such a moment (especially that 'serious kind of joy') and have imagined herself grow-ing up into a modern Clare Francis.

My purpose in improvising with the text in this way is to suggest that this piece of masculine discourse does not exclude from Ransome's concept of leadership the feminine in general, but Susan in particular. Her passion, her rages, her insistence on the letter of the law, define her as a force to be mastered; yet at the same time she is the breath of this story's great energy. There seems to be in *We Didn't Mean to Go to Sea* a strong authorial need to 'deal with' whatever Susan represents. What she represented in Ransome's life can only be guessed at; but we can know what she is in the story. Ransome's account of her is not, I believe, a masculine criticism of the feminine, but a discourse which concedes bafflement while acknowledging respect. Susan is Storm.

We Didn't Mean to Go to Sea is a bold book. Its dangers are real, there is nothing playful about it. It draws its vitality from powerful needs – like a boy's need for the respect of his father – and it has to do with the three-way dynamics of Men, Women and Danger. Much of this is familiar to feminist critical theory – the explicitly male story told against the implied, or silenced, female one. In Ransome's imagi-native world, there is a kind of femininity which is as dangerous and unpredictable as the elements of sea and hurricane – or, more specifi-cally, in Susan's domesticated and law-abiding heart there resides a spirit of stormy rebellion.

There are qualities of strength and endurance too; it is worth noting that when their quarrel is over Susan steers the boat through half the night while her exhausted brother sleeps.

What was Ransome to do next? The seventh story of the series had brought two of his principal characters to the frontier of adulthood, though it had in the long closing section restored them, so to speak, to childhood again. How was an author of Ransome's distinction to continue writing about his beloved characters without keeping them trapped in an artificially prolonged childhood and without repetitious plots? He had written himself into a developmental cul-de-sac.

With these difficulties unresolved, he began the first of two more East Anglian novels. They are less urgent and less tense, as if the East Anglian landscape induced in Ransome a different imaginative mood.

Whether this mood constitutes a diminishing of the range and drama of the series is a matter of personal taste; I confess that I am relieved that Ransome eventually took the bold imaginative risk of *Missee Lee*. First, however, there was *Secret Water* (1939), a sedate

3 From *Secret Water*

and untroubled account of an idealised group of children behaving with exemplary good-nature and restraint. There have never been children like these. There are no quarrels; there is no jealousy; if there is anger occasionally, it arises from misunderstandings, never from malice. John and Susan are in charge, but there is nothing to suggest that these two survivors have been changed by their great adventure on the North Sea. The imaginative indicators in the text point to Titty.

Secret Water seems to have been written in a benevolent mood; it is above all an affectionate narrative, especially in its vignettes of little Bridget.

> Bridget, already in her pyjamas, crouched at the door of the big tent looking out at her first camp-fire and at the figures of her elders moving in the dusk.[22]

The ostensible task of the children given them by their father is to map the locality – but the activity which really determines the tone of *Secret Water* is caring for Bridget on her first adventure as ship's baby.

> A faint whiff of burnt reeds drifted in through the open mouth of the tent. A curlew called. Again there was a sudden chatteration of gulls. Yes. They were alone, on an island. And she was old enough to be with them at last. She put out a hand to feel for Susan.
>
> 'That you, Bridget?' said Susan. 'Are you all right?'
>
> 'Very all right,' said Bridget. 'I was only making sure you were there.'[23]

Everyone is gentle with Bridget, even Nancy, Peggy and the ferocious new children who share this adventure with the Swallows and Amazons. Her presence transforms the other children into an idealised family of cheerful protective carers. The text itself is gentle with her. Mostly, it is Titty who spends so much of her time looking after Bridget and the kitten. She fulfils this responsibility with a careless disregard for the proprieties of cleanliness and clothing, and with an altogether unfussy and sensitive recognition of the real needs of her little sister. Titty is more imaginative and reflective than any of the other characters. She is, as it were, Ransome's idealised representative within his own narrative, capable of total self-absorption and complete unselfishness; she never fusses; she never grumbles; and she admits a wider range of thought and feeling.

THE ROAD ACROSS THE RED SEA · AT HIGH AND LOW TIDE

4 From *Secret Water*

These qualities are most apparent in the episode in which Titty, Roger and Bridget are trapped on the Wade – a muddy causeway submerged at low tide. This rather low-key novel is worth reading for this chapter alone; it is vivid and dramatic in Ransome's best unhurried way, and the urgency of the situation is given a new perceptiveness by Titty's understanding that they must face this unexpected crisis without allowing Bridget to know that there is any danger at all.

> 'Are we going to get wet?' asked Bridget suddenly.
>
> 'You can't get wetter than you are,' said Titty. 'You've been in once when I fell down. Look here. Don't let the ship's kitten get frightened. You tell him they'll be coming for us in a minute.'
>
> 'All right,' said Bridget and went to the post on which Sinbad's basket was hanging, to give the kitten words of comfort.
>
> Titty and Roger went to the water's edge.
>
> 'Hadn't we better swim now?' said Roger.
>
> Titty looked towards the island. 'No,' she said. 'Not till we can't help it.'[24]

For the patient reader there are many muted pleasures in this gentle novel – the den that the Mastodon has made in the sound section of an ancient decayed barge; Bridget's indignation when she is *not* to be a human sacrifice; and many descriptions briefly evoking the quiet and mysterious character of a tidal landscape of marshes, islands and mud-flats. Only Titty comes near to responding to the magic of nature with any of the imaginative intensity that is an essential element in such narratives. We find it here, when they are crossing the Wade at low tide:

> 'What is it? What is it, Titty? Hawk? I can't see anything.'
> Titty did not answer. She did not hear him. She was standing between the four tall posts, the tops of which had been awash when they had sailed through. She was looking straight above her and seeing not hawks or larks or infinite blue sky, but a few feet of swirling water over her head and the red painted bottom and centreboard of a little boat.
> Bridget wriggled a hand into the basket to stroke Sinbad. Roger pulled at Titty's elbow. 'I can't see anything,' he said again.
> 'Neither can I,' said Titty, 'not really.'[25]

Poor Titty has to disown her perception. As for the others, their approach to the countryside is either playful or practical – and always literal.

Secret Water is relaxed and unexacting, its accounts of the children external – a narrowing of the series' previous imaginative breadth, especially after the emotional rigour of *We Didn't Mean to Go to Sea*. *The Big Six* (1940) has a similarly reduced imaginative horizon. Its theme is injustice, but the moral world of the narrative is limited. Furthermore, the story is not told with Ransome's usual skill. There is a great deal of repeating of information which the reader is already in possession of, and the bad characters are presented as so obviously 'bad' characters – and the only bad characters in the district! – that it is difficult to understand why these intelligent protagonists take so long to work out what is quickly obvious to even the least skilled reader. It is impossible to agree with Hugh Brogan that 'the screw of suspense is tightened relentlessly until the very last chapter'.[26] As Peter Hollindale says:

> *The Big Six* . . . must count as one of the most incompetent detectives ever told. The Coot Club are unjustly accused of vandalism, when someone goes around loosing boats from their moorings. From the first chapter it is perfectly obvious who the real culprit is, and it takes over three hundred pages to expose him. But this is not the book's real subject. At its heart is the universal experience of being unfairly accused of a crime, of fail-

ing to persuade friendly adults of your innocence, of being thought to transgress standards that you passionately hold.[27]

Fortunately the novel improves when Dorothea and Dick arrive and begin to direct a systematic gathering and interpreting of evidence, but this change of narrative gear does not occur until almost halfway through a text of 400 pages. Dick brings a scientific and practical approach to the discovery and recording of evidence, and Dorothea brings an imaginative insight which to the three local country boys is comically incomprehensible. At first her involvement is playful, and she re-creates what is happening in the language of one of her own stories.

> 'From end to end of the country the net was set,' said Dorothea. 'Day and night patrols were out, risking their lives against a ruthless enemy. Here a chance word, there a suspicious glance was noted. The telephone bell rang continually . . .'[28]

This won't do, says Tom; his father's surgery telephone cannot be used for this.

> 'All right,' said Dorothea. 'It doesn't matter. The order had gone out that the detectives were never to telephone. The wires were tapped. The villain might be listening. So the messengers, their lives in their hands, rode through the darkling night.'[29]

It is strange that Ransome's narrative should be enlivened by Dorothea's unconscious parody. Her contribution becomes more serious when she begins to predict the movements of her unknown antagonist.

> 'He's in just as much of a hurry as we are. He's wondering why you haven't been summoned already, and he's thinking that if something doesn't happen soon he'll have to start all over again.'
> They stared at her.
> 'Do you know him?' said Joe wonderingly.
> 'I'm thinking his thoughts,' said Dorothea.[30]

Then Dick has the idea of trapping the villain into leaving his fingerprints on the newly-painted chimney of the Coot Club's boat. It works.

Dorothea, looking at the chimney and its print, felt much as she felt when reading over a good bit in one of her own stories. She had been sure the villain would come, and now it was almost as if he were obeying her orders. 'I knew he'd do it,' she said. 'And hasn't Dick's idea worked beautifully . . . the wet paint, I mean.'[31]

From that moment she is the leader. She marshals the evidence, puts their case to a solicitor, and receives a tribute which is probably lost on many young readers.

'. . . Dad's pretty upset about it too. He called you Portia by mistake, instead of Dorothea.'
Dorothea blushed. She understood, but she did not explain.[32]

There is a great deal of rich comedy in *The Big Six*, especially in connection with the three local boys – their strategy for removing Pete's waggly tooth, their attempt to smoke eels in their chimney, and Pete's conviction that the crimes are being committed by the local policeman. In fact, the novel is a kind of 'comedy of childhood manners', but there are other pleasures too – in particular the account of the four boys spending a night with Harry the local eel-catcher, one of Ransome's eccentric survivors of a lost East Anglia. This benevolent old-timer refuses to endorse Tom's views on the conservation of wildfowl and tells them shameless tales of bittern-shooting. Another success, which probably ought to be a classic anthology-piece for fishermen, is the episode in which the three boys triumphantly land a 30-pound pike. Its aftermath is a small master-stroke:

The old fisherman with the white beard turned from looking at the pike to look at the Death and Glories.
'Are you the boys who caught that fish?' he asked.
'We didn't exactly . . .' began Joe.
'Poor lads,' said the old man. 'Poor lads . . . So young and with nothing left to live for.'[33]

Secret Water and *The Big Six* – and the earlier East Anglian story, *Coot Club* – are the least successful of the series. There is no sustained imaginative urgency in their language and the plots have to be frothed up to fill the creative spaces. But the next novel of the series marked a return to Ransome's old controlled and impassioned excitement.

Despite its stereotypes of race, *Missee Lee* seems to me to be one of the greatest children's books of the century – a thriller-romance set in a distant exotic place, vividly and economically described, among strange and ferocious people.

3   Nancy Blackett – champion of goodness

In the last two novels of the series, Nancy Blackett is represented as the most important of the older children – no longer a kind of zany clown and instigator of wild enterprises, but an energetic and imaginative supporter of the needs and interests of the younger members of the group. But more of that later. First, she had to meet a real pirate.

Missee Lee shows Ransome writing at his most confident. It is a fairy-tale disguised as a sea-yarn, a climactic and concentrated expression of all the imaginings and pretendings of the previous narratives. It begins in a noisy Japanese harbour and without a sentence of explanation describes the children setting out at night for the coast of China.[1]

It is an opening chapter in an ancient tradition – beginning with a departure, a journey, and a prohibition. 'Don't go and fall foul of Missee Lee', the harbour-master[2] has said to them. ('Don't stray from the path', said Red Riding Hood's mother.) *Missee Lee* is a story about the 'old firm'. There are no Ds, no Coots, no extras – just the four Swallows, Nancy and Peggy, Captain Flint, together with Titty's parrot and Roger's monkey. *Swallow* and *Amazon* are with them too – the old magical fellowship of world-travellers setting sail from their hundredth port of call. They constitute a poetic community, a perfect company of travellers united by loyalty. Because there are no other children with them, there is no explaining to be done; as with fairy-tales, naming is sufficient. When they are captured by Chinese pirates, they must do what other fairy-tale characters do; like children trapped in an ogre's cave or a witch's cottage, they must employ courage and cunning to propitiate or outwit their captors. To assist them they have another fairy-tale characteristic, an animal companion – Titty's parrot, which wins over the bird-loving tyrant Taicoon Chang. And they have a magical gift, which – surprisingly – turns out to be Roger's grasp of Latin.

Missee Lee is a 'told' story. It lends itself to the speaking voice. It is composed as if the narrator was more than usually aware of actual children reading it. It deals repeatedly with horrors and repeatedly reassures. In none of the previous nine novels is one so conscious of Ransome's gentle concern for his readers. There is more humour in *Missee Lee* than in any of the others, more narratorial mischief – comedy with an edge of danger, cruelty with the release of laughter.

In a tradition of quest-making fictional characters that goes back through Sinbad as far as Aeneas and Odysseus, something goes wrong. *Wild Cat* is becalmed. Briefly, without fuss, with the understated economy of the great story-teller, Ransome gives his young readers a powerful sense of the frustration and the heat.

> . . . 'One o'clock.'
> John said nothing but struck the ship's bell, one . . . two . . .
> Titty looked up as the clear tone of the bell rang in the still air.
> 'It sounds quite happy,' she said.
> Captain Flint laughed. 'Got more sense than we have,' he said. 'What's the use of us all getting edgy because we aren't reeling off the knots? This isn't the first calm we've had to put up with.'
> 'It's the hottest,' said Nancy. 'Barbecued billygoats are nothing to it. Look out, Peggy, you can't sit there. The pitch is bubbling up out of the decks.'[3]

Titty's wistful observation has an ominous effect on readers who have already observed that the chapter is called 'The Loss of the *Wild Cat*'. We are made to wait through the slow hot afternoon. There are no descriptive intensities – just Ransome's judicious and homely phrasing:

> . . . looking round the horizon for the first sign of a ripple.[4]

> . . . still the little green schooner lay motionless like a toy ship on a looking-glass.[5]

> . . . a few square feet of shade.[6]

What happens next is the monkey's doing. He repeatedly gets them all into trouble and danger. He is, I suspect, an extension of Roger's unpredictable mischief-making; on this occasion he throws a lighted cigar into the fuel-tank. In eight lines of lucid compressed writing, Ransome conveys the danger.

A sheet of flame shot upward. A screaming monkey was gone, over the deckhouse roof, and up to the top of the mainmast. Peggy, without a word, got the fire-extinguisher from behind the galley door and gave it to Captain Flint, who had already thrown the three full cans of petrol overboard and was trying, with John and Nancy, to put the flames out with the bucketfuls of sand that were kept under the bulwarks. Susan was rubbing out a smouldering bit of Titty's skirt.[7]

There is here a narrator's recognition of the reader's need to understand – quickly and convincingly – the urgency of the situation. Only two pages later, the whole ship's company is adrift in *Swallow* and *Amazon*. The narrative does not pause to tell us how any of the characters are feeling; there is none of the private 'inwardness' of *We Didn't Mean to Go to Sea*. Here, distress is described in terms of activity; panic is contained – and the rest of the chapter describes the burning of the *Wild Cat*, told as a seaman might tell it who had, perhaps, read *The Ancient Mariner*.

Down came the foremast and the *Wild Cat*, crackling and roaring, lay a flaming, mastless wreck, reflected on the mirror of that oily sea.[8]

A few paragraphs later:

And suddenly, as he spoke, the burning stern of the *Wild Cat* lifted from the sea. Her bowsprit quenched its flames as it plunged. There was a long drawn hiss as the sea swept through her and the last flame went out as the little schooner disappeared for ever.[9]

Ransome leaves space for his readers to experience this catastrophe in several different ways. We can take it as Nancy does ('Shiver my timbers. This is going to be a lark.'[10]); or like Susan as she puts tannic jelly on Roger's burn; or, like Titty, we can register poetic and emotional meanings.

Ransome's characterisation in *Missee Lee* challenges assumptions about the centrality of character-growth in children's fiction. Throughout this episode – throughout the novel, in fact – the presentation of character is secondary to the telling of story. The children are still the children they always were, but less explicitly, less stridently. Susan is still a caring motherly elder sister, but with more tact and less insistent fuss. John is still the responsible navigator in command, but there is less pompousness in him, less worrying; he simply calculates and decides. Is Ransome reflecting upon the maturation likely to take place in a boy who has been through the adventures John has experienced? I don't think so; there were no signs of an achieved maturity in *Secret Water*. It seems more likely that Ransome has discovered a narrative mode – or rediscovered an old one deriving from the *Arabian Nights*. It is a mode in which, with a subtle narratorial tact, the characters make and present action by welcoming and defining it while remaining implicitly true to themselves. Here a moment of great beauty is made available to the reader by the transforming power of Titty's welcoming imagination.

> The man was sitting in the stern of a long brown punt. He was not hurrying. Working a paddle only now and then, he was moving crabwise across the channel between their island and the great cliff on which the morning light showed up that shining track. His hat, yellow and round, going up to a point in the middle, seemed as big as an umbrella. Along the gunwale of his punt was a row of ten or a dozen black lumps. Suddenly one of them stirred and spread and shook black wings.
> ... 'Cormorants,' breathed Titty.[11]

The point I want to insist on is that this is not just competent descriptive writing; it is description transfigured and made available to the young reader by Titty's response. It looks so easy and effortless that we hardly notice it. I can think of a dozen children's writers of the period who could have written a description like that; but they either would not have had Titty's response at all, or they would have gone into explicit and explanatory raptures. Ransome combines intensity with economy.

This understated tact is often apparent in dialogue.

> 'Pieces of eight!' shouted the parrot.
> ... 'Funny, Polly shouting in the dark,' said Titty.
> ... 'It isn't dark,' said Roger. 'Look over there.'
> ... 'Dawn coming,' said John.
> ... 'John,' said Susan suddenly. 'I smell cinnamon.'[12]

This is a masterpiece of concentrated narrative: five short utterances (if you count the parrot) to tell the reader that the stormy night is over, the dawn is coming, and there is hope after all. And Susan's words (said *suddenly*, bracing us with renewed expectation) suggest with an almost poetic intensity the magic and mystery of China. To set four English children adrift in a small boat on the China Sea, and to have one of them say, simply, 'I smell cinnamon', indicates a story-teller working at his most controlled and confident. It is writing such as this which has led me to believe that in the hands of some writers children's stories have more in common with poetry than with realistic prose-fiction. Who else but Ransome could have so unpretentiously united the bracing realism of the sea-thriller with the poetry of discovery? Perhaps stout Cortez standing on Darien is one of Ransome's imaginative antecedents here; certainly Robert Louis Stevenson is. Or perhaps this combination of poetry and plainness derives, as Fred Inglis has suggested,[13] from Conrad:

> Dawn in the tropics comes up as fast as dusk comes down. While they were eating rations of dates and chocolates it flared up out of the east. They stared at the shore and at each other, strangers all after that night of storm.[14]

For the next few chapters Titty is the heroine, the lucky fairy-tale child, the special person who has instant access to kings and princes. In this case, it is the Taicoon Chang, pirate-ruler of the island and lover of birds; the lucky heroine has her animal-helper, her parrot, who saves them all from instant death by commanding the Taicoon's interest. Titty shows tact, courage and maturity in this dangerous episode.

> The Taicoon was delighted. He talked away in a sort of pidgin English of which Titty understood one word in ten, and Titty talked to him in English of which the Taicoon understood about one word in twenty. But this did not matter. There were the birds. In Titty, the Taicoon felt he had found another bird-fancier, and while Roger and Gibber were having a good time with the bananas, the Taicoon and Titty were moving from cage to cage feeding the larks and not exactly talking but somehow managing to show good will.[15]

Communication has often been at the heart of Ransome's best writing. Here, the meaning of signs and gestures is unmistakable: the Chinese children in the Taicoon's fortress keep 'grinning from ear to ear and hitting the backs of their necks with the edge of a hand'.[16] The message is sinister, the manner cheerful. Then, as the others are being led away, Titty asks what is going to happen to them.

'Supper,' [said the Taicoon.] 'Perhaps to-mollow no supper. No heads . . .'

Not very cheering, thought Titty, but the Taicoon did not seem to think it mattered.[17]

Captain Flint is in a bamboo cage, the children are prisoners, and their execution is likely to take place next morning. Blithely Ransome conducts his readers through this piratical grimness, finding comedy at every turn. The account of the children's enforced Chinese meal – which could be their last – is comedy of manners at its funniest.

> The Taicoon, who had just used his chopsticks to put something in his mouth, had picked a titbit off his plate and, smiling politely at Titty, was poking at her face. Titty looked at it and at him. There was nothing else to be done. She opened her mouth. The Taicoon popped the titbit in. Titty chewed it up, wishing she could spit it out instead, and then, seeing the Taicoon's face, smiled at him, smacked her lips and said 'Thank you.'
>
> It was as if a signal had been given. Looking right and left along the table, Titty saw that all the captains were doing the same for their next-door neighbours.
>
> 'Here, I say,' said Roger, but, when he saw what was happening even to Susan, opened his mouth and smacked his lips like the rest of them.[18]

So, while Titty with her kindly diplomacy restrains the Taicoon's wrath, the narrator with his comic story-telling eases his readers' anxiety.

A brief explanation makes it clear that these pirates are operating a cynical and lucrative protection-racket on the high seas. But Ransome makes no judgements; this is the way things are, the narrative seems to say, and if you can't pay up you get your head chopped off – without malice, but just as finally. We are never allowed to forget the danger the Swallows and Amazons are in; there are repeated reminders of the likely outcome as they are transported from Chang (who is only a ten-gong Taicoon) to Missee Lee herself (a 22-gong Taicoon).

Chapter 12 is a masterpiece of unpleasant uncertainty as the children wait in the great courtyard of Missee Lee's palace. Around them prisoners are paying their ransoms and bowing and smiling as they are released. Young readers are not told – but they know if they care to think about it – what is happening to those who cannot pay up. With gentle good-humour the narrator guides his reader through this grim business, maintaining the level of anxiety and simultaneously providing reassurance. This is a very timely moment for Captain Flint to discover that John has managed to keep hold of the ship's sextant – a kind of fairy-tale magic object which might ensure their escape. Throughout this episode, Ransome provides for his young readers 'comfortable places' in the narrative. They are allowed, like Titty, to notice 'John and Susan looking at each other as if they thought that something might have gone wrong'.[19] Or they might shift that worrying detail to the imaginative sidelines and prefer to brace themselves briskly with Nancy: 'Look here, John. She's a she-pirate. Let me do the talking.'[20] Or they might prefer to keep an eye on Captain Flint, who infuriates his captors by doing a gorilla-act, and who winks at the children at this moment of crisis. In such almost imperceptible ways Ransome makes provision for different readers with different imaginative modes. That wink is also for the reader – one of the oldest story-telling signals indicating that all will be well – probably.

Missee Lee herself is the strangest adult character in the series – a piratical tyrant educated at Cambridge, exchanging her gun-belt for a Latin primer, conducting with ruthless skill the politics of gangsterism and retaining a secret room done up as a university study.

> She unbuckled her cartridge belt and her pistol holster and hung them on a clothes hook behind the door as if she had been out for a walk and was hanging up a mackintosh.
>   'Now,' said Missee Lee. 'Dulce domum. Please make yourselves at home.'[21]

Her rescue of the six children is less benevolent than it seems – for slowly it dawns upon them that she intends to keep them as prisoners to Latin lessons.

> 'Latin first,' said Miss Lee. 'Pelhaps Gleek next year or the year after that . . .'
>   'But we can't . . .' Susan began in horror. She caught Miss Lee's eye and was silent.[22]

Missee Lee, required by the wishes of her dead father to take his place and devote her life to ruling the Three Islands, is Ransome's only attempt to portray an adult character in conflict. It would be wrong to describe her as a tragic figure, but there is poignancy in the position of this small lonely woman, scholar of Virgil and Ovid, and powerful autocrat in a peasant world of brutish and greedy men.

And humour too. What an irony that Nancy the pirate – with her galoots and barbecued billygoats – should discover at last her ideal she-pirate, only to find her a frustrated Latin teacher.

At the climax of the novel, during the escape down-river by night in a stolen Chinese junk, Missee Lee shows she is also a superb sea-woman. This episode shows Ransome's writing at its best. There is only one way to the open sea – a perilously narrow gorge of churning rapids and dangerous rocks. In this gorge, with massive cliffs towering above them on either side, the current takes the escaping Swallows and Amazons so powerfully that Captain Flint can neither see nor steer. Then there is a strange noise:

> A door slammed below the poop.
> 'What's that?' said Peggy with a gasp. 'There's someone in the cabin . . .'
> 'Gibber exploring,' said Roger. 'May I go and get him?'
> 'Lie still,' said Captain Flint almost angrily.
> 'Gibber!' called Roger.
> 'Shut up,' said Captain Flint.
> 'But he'll come if I call him . . .'
> 'Damn that monkey!' said Captain Flint.
> Titty felt about her, found Roger's wrist and held it firmly. She knew. They all knew. For the first time since they had known him, Captain Flint was afraid.[23]

All is surely lost, but the master story-teller has one more surprise.

> Roger jerked suddenly. Titty felt somebody stepping over her . . . soft, silent feet against her body . . .
> 'Who's standing?' shouted Captain Flint. 'Lie down, I say. Lie down!'
> 'Solly. Better let me have tiller, I think,' said the voice of Miss Lee.[24]

The Chinese she-pirate with the classical education does what Captain Flint could not do – she guides the junk along this perilous path and out to sea as dawn breaks.

Then there is a serious moment of truth for Nancy. Captain Flint, though grateful to be alive, assumes they are still Missee Lee's prisoners. But while he accepts defeat, Nancy is angry and defiant – and, for once, there is nothing comic about it.

Captain Flint spoke. 'If Miss Lee hadn't taken the tiller in time we'd never have got through at all. We're lucky to be alive and we're a lot better off as her prisoners than if we'd been caught by Bo'sun Wu or Mr. Chang.'

Nancy turned her back on him. Suddenly she flung round again. 'Rot,' she said. 'No guards now. We're not her prisoners. She's ours. Shut her up in the cabin.'[25]

But the real pirate confronts the pretend-pirate, the teacher assesses the pupil.

In the dim light of early morning a little smile showed on Miss Lee's face. 'Nansee,' she said. 'You are a blave but foolish child. I am coming with you. Going back to Camblidge.'[26]

Of course, Missee Lee decides after all to stay and do the duty placed on her by her beloved father; and the magic band of six children, and a Captain, resume their voyage around the world without her. Ransome ends the novel with a simple distancing sentence.

And you may, yourselves, have read in the newspapers how the people of St. Mawes, in Cornwall, woke one morning to find a little Chinese junk, with a monkey at the masthead, anchored off their harbour mouth.[27]

This direct address to the reader reminds us that, more than with any of the other stories in the series, *Missee Lee* is 'told by a voice', the voice of a known and trusted story-maker. Readers – especially if they are devoted lovers of the series – trust this story, and know that the six famous children will come to no harm despite the ferocity of those repeated references to beheading. *Missee Lee* shares this characteristic, perhaps, with oral folk-tales – cruelty and violence are unlikely to be harmful to young listeners when the story is told by a known member of the community. Ransome, by virtue of his established reputation, and the endurance of the nine previous books, was in the 1940s a known and trusted teller of tales. Writers of series have this advantage: that they can earn through continuity a secure role as a community story-teller. The *Swallows and Amazons* books were like children's annuals – there had been a new one every Christmas. It must have been clear to all readers that the six children *must* survive.[28]

In *Missee Lee* there is a story-teller's protective concern for his readers. Perhaps in the wartime context of 1941 Ransome was aware of his readers as troubled children in need of diversion and reassurance. So he tells them a story of his six magical children journeying to a place far beyond the cockpit of the war with Hitler – a Sinbad-story which Scheherazade might have told. Ransome knew that the east coast of England bristled with barbed-wire and fears of an invasion, and in that closing sentence of the novel there is an invitation to his child-readers to look the other way – to a far-west Cornish harbour suggestive of famous settings-out and heroic returnings.

There are ironies in that. For thousands of wartime readers could – as I did – happily switch from the *Swallows and Amazons* to *Biggles* and back again – and without any sense of inconsistency.

In the last two novels of the series Ransome turned his imaginative attention to Nancy. In almost imperceptible and totally credible ways, *The Picts and the Martyrs* and *Great Northern?* give substance to her character and transform her into a champion of innocence. Dorothea and Dick reappear in these last two novels as central protagonists whose role is specifically to experience and enjoy their summer adventures under the guardianship of Nancy.

In *The Picts and the Martyrs* (1943) Nancy and the Great Aunt preside over the narrative; they are the two realities which have to be reckoned with. For rather contrived reasons (though most young readers probably disregard such contrivances), it is necessary for the Great Aunt not to discover the existence of Dorothea and Dick. They must live a secret life in the woods (like Picts), while Nancy and Peggy must keep the Great Aunt happy by behaving for ten days like model schoolgirls (hence, Martyrs).

> 'Just coming, Aunt Maria.' That was Nancy's voice, but oddly gentle, not like her usual cheerful shout. . . .
> . . . The boat had come into sight below the lawn, gliding down the river. They had last seen it with a crew of wet dishevelled savages. Now it was being rowed by a girl in a white frock with a pink ribbon round her hair. Another girl, just like her, was sitting in the stern, idly trailing a hand in the water. The boat turned into the boathouse. A minute later, they saw the two girls walking hand in hand towards the house.[29]

There is a hint of satire here, a conscious overacting in the two girls walking hand in hand, and in Nancy's 'oddly gentle voice'. An outdated view of girlhood is being ridiculed.

This kind of mischief is clever and amusing. But, in fact, the autocratic old lady is not straightforwardly funny. She derives in part from the Lady Bracknells of literature, but also from Alice's Queen of Hearts. There is cruelty in her as well as comedy; in an earlier novel she had said unforgivably hurtful things to Nancy's and Peggy's mother. In the end, however, the old lady is redefined as a courageous eccentric, and we are told that the 'Great Aunt is remarkably like her Great Niece'.[30] Both of them are bossy, decisive, brave and determined; and they are born leaders. However, the joke almost obscures the fact that Nancy is capable of a heroic generosity which we see no sign of in the Aunt. The comedy almost distracts the reader from the seriousness of Nancy's commitment to Dorothea and Dick – and from the author's commitment to Nancy. *The Picts and the Martyrs* is a sustained demonstration of Nancy's goodness – and, by implication, a tribute to the kind of childhood which is allowed to define itself through play rather than confine itself within adult expectations. Nancy sustains her freedom through language – the brilliant, subversive release of comic insult.

> '. . . And then we've got to be all proper in party dresses ready to soothe the savage breast when the Great Aunt comes gorgoning in. We'll manage her all right so long as we can keep you secret. What her codfish eyes don't see her conger heart can't grieve over.'[31]

With such eloquent gusto Nancy heroically commits herself to an enterprise which will be extremely unpleasant for herself and Peggy. She assumes responsibility for Dorothea and Dick, combining adult caring with the cheerful inventiveness of childhood. It is no small self-sacrifice for action-loving girls like Nancy and Peggy to submit to ten days of imprisonment, as Dorothea generously acknowledges.

> . . . deposed from her place at the head of the table, not allowed to order meals, made to wear the clothes she hated, forbidden this, forbidden that, and, in spite of all, determined to keep the Great Aunt happy. And Peggy was the same. There they were, the two of them, their own holiday spoilt but determined to see that she and Dick had just the holiday Mrs. Blackett had planned for them.[32]

Meanwhile the Picts are living in hiding in the woods and the chapters which describe their camp-building and home-making are subdued

evocations of childhood contentment in which Ransome can redis-
cover the mode of the early novels in the series. There is anxiety at
first, for Dorothea is troubled by their solitariness 'in a hut with
holes in its roof and no glass in its window',[33] and by the strange
night-noises of the wood. But she is a stalwart girl and comforts
herself with the sensible thought that 'the ghostly wood all round
them was only full of natural history'.[34] Next morning she wakens
early:

> She put on her sandshoes, took soap, toothbrush, towel and
> kettle, opened the door and went out into the morning sunshine.
> There was that pheasant again. And now a new noise, the tap,
> tap of a hammer on a tree-trunk. For a moment Dorothea stood
> still, listening, half thinking that there might be someone work-
> ing in the wood. Then she remembered that she had heard that
> noise before, last summer, in the woods below High Topps, and
> Dick had told her what it was. A woodpecker. No. There was
> nobody about. She and Dick were the only people in the world.
> And Dick was asleep. She had the world to herself.
>   She filled the kettle at the pool in the beck, washed her face
> and hands and cleaned her teeth.[35]

These are idyllic images – Edenic almost. The stone hut with its huge
chimney establishes the two children in an old and secure world of
abiding certainties. It also evokes fairy-tale memories of more sinister
houses in the depths of dark forests; but, with perfect timing, the
appearance of Dick in his pyjamas unobtrusively restores the reader
to a familiar and homely mode. Dorothea and Dick are Hansel and
Gretel without the witch, without the fear, with nothing before them
but promise.

In these woodland episodes Dorothea defers to Dick in ways that
Ransome's age would not have questioned. It is not a matter of
which one of them is the leader; he *experiences*, she *interprets*.
Dorothea has her own experiences, of course, but her role in the
novel is to suggest meaning and value. There are two Ransome set-
pieces – trout-tickling and rabbit-skinning – and both these two con-
trasting experiences are given to the reader through the perceptions
of the gentle Dorothea. The rabbit-skinning is an ordeal, the cooking
takes hours, and a fearful storm rages. That is a bad night for the
children. But the two slightly uncertain youngsters make the best of it
– and the chapter ends with a timely confirmation of their success
when they have a visit from Nancy:

Squelching footsteps sounded outside. The next moment there was someone in the doorway, wet and piebald, in bathing things that glistened in the flickering light of the lantern and the fire.

'Shiver my timbers,' said Nancy. 'You're warm in here. Gosh! What a lovely smell.'[36]

Ransome's unpretentious touch is sure here. The tireless Nancy has come to check that the young novices are safe – and then she has to hurry back through the storm to look after Peggy, who is frightened of thunder.

In *The Picts and the Martyrs* Ransome has rediscovered his original commitment to newness. 'We've got to learn everything,' Dorothea says,[37] and this takes us back to the early stories in which Roger learned to swim and Titty sailed alone at night. But the difference here is that the learning happens only because Nancy supports, encourages and enables. When Dick is learning to sail *Scarab*, he is uncertain and tentative at first, but under Nancy's wise direction he begins to get the hang of it.

He was finding that he could watch the flag and the sail and yet keep a look out. No other rowing boat was going to be close in front of him before he saw it. Things were all right after all. *Scarab* was no harder to sail than *Titmouse*, and faster, lots faster.

'Listen to her,' said Dorothea. 'She's enjoying it.'[38]

There is a three-way dynamic here: Dick sails the boat scientifically, Dorothea brings it to life imaginatively, and Nancy presides, encouraging the two young novices, and then wisely leaving them to get on with it – precisely what the Great Aunt fails to do.

This is Nancy's novel. It would be simplistic to say that her character has developed; there seems to be no inner maturation, no increase in self-knowledge. Yet she has changed. In the earlier stories her energy always had system and purpose; she was never just scatty. Now, however, we are given fresh instances of an older and more substantial Nancy – a girl of extraordinary kindness and sustained cheerful toughness. What else could Ransome do with her in an age of reticence? Writing about Nancy 'coming to terms with her sexuality' was culturally out of the question. So there is bound to be something of the school prefect in his conception of her – as almost a young woman, accepting a free-spirited and protective responsibility for the younger children around her.

In the next story Nancy demonstrates the same qualities. *Great Northern?* (1947) is the last of the series and one of the most interesting – a narrative composed of puzzles, hints and unresolved issues. The question-mark of the title indicates the ornithological question Dick must answer: are there really Great Northern Divers nesting on a Scottish loch? But there are other, less explicit, questions too; the behaviour of the local people is mysterious and hostile, and their silent and apparently motiveless menace gives the novel an unnerving quality.

At the imaginative heart of this story is Dick's self-effacing and patient bird-watching and his entirely innocent eagerness to understand the world without using it for self-aggrandisement. There is a touching appeal in this timid and short-sighted boy's reverence for those 'big ocean-going birds, wild and shy'.[39] The chapter describing his day of patient watching and waiting with his camera deserves to be recognised as a classic account of timeless and impassioned ornithological devotion. But Ransome seems also to be concerned with moral ambivalences: Dick, the innocent bird-watcher, reflects that it was his own interest in the birds that brought to the island the rich bird-collector who intends to shoot them and stuff them for his collection.

Great Northern? is concerned with the moral and psychological uncertainties of *watching*. Its plot is a web of strategies of surveillance and its characters are repeatedly spying on each other and being spied upon. The talismanic objects are binoculars, telescopes, cameras, and Dick's spectacles, which he repeatedly wipes in the hope of achieving clarity. Perspectives are insisted upon. Even in the opening paragraph of the first chapter, the language of observation places the reader alongside an unknown boy, watching:

> On a hill above the cliff a boy in Highland dress turned from watching the deer in the valley to look out over the sea. He saw a sail far away. It was no more than a white speck in the distance and presently he turned his back on it and settled down again to watch the deer.[40]

From the moment they set foot on shore the Swallows and Amazons become actors in processes of hiding and spying – willing actors for the most part, except for Titty.

> So far as she could see there was no one else in the valley and the three explorers had the hillside to themselves. Yet, suddenly, she

had the feeling that they were being watched, and watched from close at hand.[41]

The uneasiness of not knowing if you are being observed provides a persistent and disquieting motif throughout the narrative

> They jumped up.
> 'People . . . quite near . . .' said Titty.
> 'I can't see anyone,' said Dorothea . . .
> 'You can't tell,' said Titty. 'Somebody may be seeing you.'[42]

Not since *Robinson Crusoe* has a narrative been so consistently composed of the language and incidents of *spying* and *seeing*. Crusoe associates seeing with mastery (especially with a spy-glass, from a safe distance); wrongly, in fact, for sight rarely guarantees certitude. It is similar in *Great Northern?*: seeing fails to ensure understanding. It simply menaces.

> 'No,' said Dorothea, and suddenly grabbed Nancy's arm. 'There's one of the Gaels watching us NOW.' Not fifty yards away, in the shadow of the shore under the cliff, all three of them saw the flicker of a match. Someone was lighting a pipe. The tiny spark quavered and died. They could see nothing where it had been but the dark mass of the cliff against the sky.
> 'What's he there for?' said Dot.[43]

As far as Roger is concerned, watching is power; but being watched is an intolerable intrusion. Most of Roger's part in this story has to do with his taking possession of a hill-top look-out from which he can spy out the land and sea. But his occupation is an uncomfortable one, for he knows it is someone else's look-out and he can never be at peace in it. Captain Flint's role in *Great Northern?* is minimal, but he too is caught up in this uncomfortable activity: he and the bird-collector spend an entire day bluffing each other with mutual surveillance.

However, watching can be benevolent, as it is when John and Nancy keep a critical eye on Dick the landlubber as he earnestly tries to row a straight course across the loch.

> 'She's a bit of a beast,' said Nancy. 'Never mind. He's getting her along.'

'But how,' said John.

The folding boat had left the reeds and was making a very zigzag course of it along the shore towards the island. The surface of the loch, smooth in the windless, early morning, was broken by row upon row of long ripples.

'Gosh!' said John. 'Even Roger'd do better than that.'

'Nobody could do much worse,' agreed Nancy, and the two old shellbacks, one-time captains of the *Swallow* and the *Amazon*, sat up with impatience as they watched the ship's naturalist glance over his shoulder, pull hard with an oar, glance over his shoulder again and pull hard with the other.[44]

Here, watching is linked with guardianship. Dick's enterprise – to provide proof of the great northerns' presence by photographing them – needs the support of the six Swallows and Amazons. They watch over him as he watches over the birds. They make everything possible for him with a complex plan mostly devised by Nancy. Dorothea's role is to 'explain' Dick to the others; again, she is his interpreter. But it is clear from the start that Nancy is the leader. Captain Flint is only a token-captain, overruled and disregarded at every turn. It is Nancy who is in charge, and her ingenuity and generous leadership are placed at the service of Dick. She understands little of what this bird-business is all about, but since it matters to him she generously devotes herself to his enterprise.

In this last novel Roger is a puzzle, for he is persistently represented as a rebel. He repeatedly escapes from what he sees as the irksome bossiness of the others. In several earlier stories, he was naughty and wilful, but now he is directly disobedient. In Roger, Ransome convincingly presents the psychology of sulking:

He had a pleasant feeling of badness, to which he was well accustomed. He knew very well what Susan and the others would be thinking of him. Anyhow, they could not be expected to understand.[45]

Roger does nothing very wicked – but he repeatedly exiles himself from the others and professes to despise what they do. Nothing goes well for him in this story; he vows vengeance on the Highland boy who spies on him and insults him – but Ransome does not allow him the gratification of that vengeance. No moral is pointed, but Roger defines himself in this story as an outsider, disagreeable and disgruntled.

The series ended there, though there might have been a thirteenth story: in 1988 Hugh Brogan edited a collection of little-known and unpublished works by Ransome, one of which consisted of some unfinished fragments and an outline of another story which Brogan called *Coots in the North*. It was to have taken the three East Anglian 'Death and Glories' to the Lake District for a shared adventure with Nancy and the others.

The series is open to accusations of sexism – and it is certainly true that Ransome makes the same assumptions about gender-roles as almost everyone else in the thirties and forties. But it is not as simple as that. When Nancy Blackett fired arrows into the Swallows' island camp in the first story of the series, it was as if she was serving notice on them that she would disrupt the comfortable certainties of the Walker family and provide an alternative liberating version of the possibilities of girlhood. 'Possibilities' is precisely the right word, for Nancy is a maker of new possibilities.

It seems to me that Ransome was unconsciously working into fiction a shifting and complex preoccupation with the feminine. This was particularly true in *We Didn't Mean to Go to Sea*. His writing appears to have been directed by three imperatives. The first is concerned to create a 'good' or 'authorised' version of the feminine (Titty and Dorothea); this version is quiet but articulate, unassertive, imaginative, responsive to mysteries – an enricher of life. The second imperative seeks to propitiate or subdue the 'hysterical' feminine, who is also the 'law-maker' (Susan). The third seeks to escape the feminine altogether in a world of 'masculine' play (mapping, exploring, fishing). My point here is that Nancy Blackett eludes these categories. And to some extent so does Titty, who remains for Ransome an almost secret and deeply needed ideal whose image fades and reappears with intermittent clarity in this long sequence of narratives.

The series has been condemned because it is concerned almost exclusively with the privileged children of well-off upper-middle-class families, or because in some uncertain way the stories are said to convey middle-class values. 'It won't do', as Fred Inglis says in his excellent chapter on Ransome in *The Promise of Happiness*. It is certainly true that until the late fifties there were no children's novels which reflected the lives of working-class or inner-city children – an extraordinary and quite indefensible cultural lop-sidedness. E.W. Hildick, William Mayne, Philippa Pearce and John Rowe Townsend should be applauded for changing this situation – as long as we remember that there is no necessary correlation between subject-matter and excellence. Any reader who still feels uncomfortable about the socially privileged status of the Walkers and the Blacketts should read Inglis' chapter, which argues that 'a gifted novelist, though starting inevitably from his or her class, criticises the narrow limits of its horizon by showing in the creation of a narrative what it would be like truly to live up to the terms of its best values'.[46]

John Rowe Townsend once pointed out that Ransome's young characters 'maintain a sexless companionship which does not quite accord with the facts of adolescence'.[47] But such criticisms are wide of the mark, for the twelve linked novels are closer to the quality of magical fairy-tales than their surface realism seems to indicate. I believe Ransome's child-characters constitute a fellowship of innocence, a company of magical children sailing in search of experience, yet never losing their innocence. They are not realistic children maturing into adolescence.

And in any case the objection that Ransome has nothing to say about adolescent sex ignores the historical context. Children's fiction in the 1930s had found no way of writing about sex. Ransome's banishment of this turbulent and problematical subject-matter was not personal but cultural – a consequence of that gigantic western conspiracy to silence sex, in which children's fiction unresistingly acquiesced. Hardy had said that 'English society opposes a well-nigh insuperable bar' to the 'honest portrayal' of 'the relations of the sexes'.[48] This had been true in 1890, and it was still true as far as children's books were concerned in the 1930s and 40s.[49]

The tradition Ransome drew sustenance from embraced classical mythology, folk-tales and fairy-tales, the *Arabian Nights*, sea-shanties and Romantic poetry, *Robinson Crusoe* and all the other Robinson-nades, along with Conrad, Kipling and Stevenson. The qualities which distinguish him – his gentle and word-perfect prose, his story-telling, his love of landscape and seascape, his preoccupation with the goodness of children, his recognition of the enduring possibilities for happiness – cannot be demonstrated without a close and detailed attentiveness.

Ransome's children are *magical* characters, and during the twelve books of the series they mature into characters of myth. Though they are recognisable English children messing about on recognisable English and Scottish waters, they have something in common with Jason, Odysseus, Lancelot and Robin Hood. Their business is to appear unexplained at the beginning of each narrative, and go adventuring into our imaginative lives, always recognisable yet never predictable, sometimes mistaken yet always reassuring. They belong to the mythology of childhood, not to realistic fiction. Their meaning connects on one side with the benevolent young leadership that was such an important ideal in the heyday of Scouting and Guiding, and on the other with the potent appeal of Flash Gordon, Batman, Tarzan, Biggles, and – at a younger level – Rupert Bear. Although these characters may have been presented in various debased forms, and although adults may perceive in their crusades moral obliquities (for example, the righteous use of violence), what unites them is their unfailing defence of innocence and justice.

Ransome's achievement was to combine the energy of this mythology with characters and situations which were at the same time plausible and convincing. His narratives are composed of possibilities for pretending and ideas for imagining; they are resource-books for dreamers. At its best, his language is the language of desire. Within a perfect equilibrium, it is in love with what it creates and creates what it longs for. Ransome mediates for young readers a wide cultural continuity, and he does this through the creation of something resembling a childhood mythology. His six magical children are benevolent champions of goodness. They sail in search of Experience, yet never lose their Innocence. His narratives are escapist – but his children are escaping *into*, not from. They learn new knowledge, yet are never disillusioned and never cynical. There is no arrival for them – only a perpetual voyaging in an extended holiday of expanding childhood.

Part II
Series galore

4 Camping and tramping fiction, 1920–1960

For reasons which are not altogether clear there was a great outpouring of fiction series after 1920. Like long extended fiction-caravans, they made their way across the literary landscape of the period. It was the great age of the series; young readers who read fiction at all in that period were likely to be series-readers.

Probably the first extended series to capture the widespread allegiance of young readers was Hugh Lofting's *Doctor Dolittle* stories; the first was published in the USA in 1920 and in Britain in 1922, with new titles added annually until 1929,[1] after which the remaining four titles were released intermittently until 1953. This was not a small-scale enterprise: by 1942, the first of the series alone, *The Story of Doctor Dolittle*, had been reprinted in the UK nineteen times. At about the same time, Dorita Fairlie Bruce began the *Dimsie* series, nine titles published between 1921 and 1942. In 1920[2] Elsie J. Oxenham's *Abbey School* series began, and in 1925 Elinor M. Brent-Dyer published *The School at the Chalet*, which was to be the first of a series with new releases issued at the phenomenal rate of almost one a year until 1970. And in 1930 Arthur Ransome published *Swallows and Amazons*, with new titles being added almost every year until 1947, by which time the first in the series was into its 24th impression. A series of a rather different kind had been running since 1911 – the *Twins* series by Lucy Fitch Perkins, each of which ran into several reprints.

These are impressive figures, indicating a massive readership. To become a reader in the thirties or forties – as I did – was to become a series-reader. If by any chance a young reader of my generation missed out on Ransome, Brent-Dyer and Lofting, it was impossible to be a reader and not discover Richmal Crompton's *Just William* books, begun in 1922 and still going strong with new titles in the 1950s and 60s. There was *Biggles* too; Captain W.E. Johns' series had begun in 1932, but its heyday was to be the period between about 1940 and 1950, beginning with *Biggles in the Baltic: A Tale of the Second Great War*, published – very topically – in 1940.

There were many more, all published in hardback – and the success of Enid Blyton in the 1940s and 50s must be seen in this context. Children's publishing was awash with series, for publishers understood that a series, once established, markets and advertises itself: a child who comes across any of a series is instantly introduced to all the rest.

To put together a complete list is impossible. Many are now forgotten, except sometimes by small groups of adult enthusiasts. Children's literature is popular literature, and it is inevitable that many works will not survive beyond their own generation; but historians need to know about them, and a start might be made by looking at some dates.[3]

1911	*The Dutch Twins*, first of Lucy Fitch Perkins' *Twins* series.
1919	*A Go-Ahead Schoolgirl*, first of 5 titles in the *Rocklands* series by Elsie J. Oxenham.
1920	*The Abbey Girls*, first of around 40 titles by Elsie J. Oxenham.
1921	*The Senior Prefect* by Dorita Fairlie Bruce, later renamed *Dimsie Goes to School*, first of a series of 9 stories.
1921	*The Two Form-Captains*, first in Elsie J. Oxenham's series of 5 works set in Switzerland.
1922	*Doctor Dolittle*, first published in the USA in 1920, 12 titles by Hugh Lofting.
1922	*Just William*, first of 42 titles by Richmal Crompton.
1922	*La Rochelle* series begun by Elinor Brent-Dyer, 7 titles.
1923	*The Girls of St Bride's*, first of a series of 9 by Dorita Fairlie Bruce.
1923	*The Junior Captain*, first of 4 books in the *Gregory's* series by Elsie J. Oxenham.
1925	*The Chalet School* by Elinor Brent-Dyer, first of 58 titles.
1928	*Just Jane*, 11 titles by Evadne Price.
1928	*Springdale*, series of 6 school stories by Dorita Fairlie Bruce.
1930	*Swallows and Amazons* by Arthur Ransome, 12 titles.
1932	*Biggles*, almost 100 titles by Captain W.E. Johns.
1935	*John and Mary*, first of a series of 12 stories by Grace James.

1936	*Lockett Family*, a series of 21 titles by M.E. Atkinson, beginning with *August Adventure*.
1937	*The Far-Distant Oxus*, first of three by Katharine Hull and Pamela Whitlock.
1939	*Bunkle* series, 11 titles by Margot Pardoe.
1939	*She Shall Have Music*, first of Kitty Barne's stories about the Farrar family.
1940	*The Naughtiest Girl in the School*, 3 titles by Enid Blyton.
1941	*St Clare's School* by Enid Blyton, with 6 titles.
1942	*Famous Five*, 21 titles by Enid Blyton.
1943	*Lone Pine* series, 20 titles by Malcolm Saville.
1943	*Mystery* series by Enid Blyton, 15 titles, beginning with *The Mystery of the Burnt Cottage*.
1944	*Island of Adventure*, 8 titles by Enid Blyton.
1946	*Malory Towers*, 6 titles by Enid Blyton.
1948	*Jilly Family* series, 6 titles by Malcolm Saville.
1949	*Secret Seven*, 15 titles by Enid Blyton.
1950	*Buckingham Family* series, 6 titles by Malcolm Saville.
1950	*Jennings Goes to School*, first of the series by Anthony Buckeridge.
c. 1950	*Ian and Sovra* stories by the excellent Scottish children's writer, Elinor Lyon.
1951	*All Summer Through*, first of a series of 4 by Malcolm Saville.
1954	*Susan and Bill*, first of 8 stories by Malcolm Saville.

It is hard to appreciate the sheer scale of this output. These series alone amount to more than 560 separate titles, all published in hardback and mostly reprinted many times. And there were many others: David Severn's *Waggoner* series; John Verney's series about the Callendar family; Garry Hogg's *Explorer* series, and *Nat and Jonty* series; Helen Dore Boyson's *Sue Barton* – a nursing series – and *Carol* – a theatre series; and Pamela Brown's popular *Blue Door* series about the theatre, which started with *The Swish of the Curtain* in 1941. To these have to be added the various ballet series, the best-known of which was Jean Estoril's *Drina* series, begun in 1957, and Lorna Hill's *Sadler's Wells* series, begun in 1950. There were other series too, by popular authors who are largely forgotten now, like Eric Leyland and Rita Coatts. There were also, of course, many American series, the best of which was probably Edward Eager's outstanding (and now almost forgotten) Nesbit-like series which began with *Half Magic* (1954). It is also worth bearing in mind that another major factor in the history of children's reading was the popularity of annuals, in which series-characters often made an appearance in short stories – not by any means the same as a series but appealing to similar habits of collecting and reading a numbered series of continuous volumes.

However, young readers did not become series-readers only when they were capable of managing a full-length novel. There was then, as there still is, a wide range of series of shorter books, picturebooks and chapter books which helped younger readers to acquire the habit. There were Alison Uttley's *Little Grey Rabbit* books (1929–75), *Sam Pig* (1939–60), *Tim Rabbit* (1937–64) and *Little Brown Mouse* (1950–71); the *Josephine* books by H.C. Cradock and illustrated by Honor Appleton (1915–53); Kathleen Tozer's *Mumfie* books (from 1935); Joyce Lankester Brisley's *Milly-Molly-Mandy* books (1928–67); the *Orlando* picturebooks by Kathleen Hale (1938–72); Constance Heward's *Ameliaranne* stories (1920–48); the *Mary Plain* stories by Gwynedd Rae (from 1930); Barbara Euphan Todd's *Worzel Gummidge* series, begun in 1936 and continued until 1963, when the series was continued by other writers; and Beatrix Potter, whose books are not strictly speaking a series but are often read and collected as if they were.

Rosemary Auchmuty's excellent *The World of Girls*[4] has made superfluous any further analysis of series fiction based on schools. As she has shown, school stories fall naturally into series because of the nature of the subject: a boarding school by its very nature exemplifies stability and change in a perfect balance – ideal material for a series, with the constant opportunity to introduce new pupils and new teaching staff. But Arthur Ransome's *Swallows and Amazons* was a move in a new direction – out of school and into the holidays – and it led eventually, alongside the many series of schoolgirl stories, to an astonishing growth in camping and tramping adventure stories. These books were enormously popular for many years and nothing more powerfully demonstrates cultural change than their subsequent almost total disappearance.

Ransome was a major influence on holiday adventure fiction. Almost as important was the work of M.E. Atkinson's *Lockett* series. When *August Adventure* was published in 1936 (the first of a series of 21), its first chapter explained with considerable originality (and length) how the novel came to be written. The fictional Bill, Jane and Oliver Lockett agree that they should write their own accounts of their 'big adventure'; the result is a terrible muddle of shifting narrative voices and perspectives, and their Aunt Jane agrees to 'jot down their united "outpourings", sorting them out later at [her] leisure'. Aunt Jane insists on emotional authenticity.

> Before we actually started I made a little sort of speech. I said, 'Look here, this book isn't going to be any good if it isn't *real*. All the things in it really happened, I know, but you people in it won't seem *alive* if I can't write down quite honestly just how you *felt* about everything.'[5]

In the 1930s this insistence on *feeling* attached itself particularly to the word 'adventure', which seems to have acquired for itself a particular emotional resonance, a thrill of promise and a special association with children in the school holidays. Atkinson may have been partly responsible herself, for the children's story is referred to as the 'Great Adventure' and the children in later novels are called 'adventure magnets'. The first chapter of the second novel in the series, *Mystery Manor* (1937), is called 'THINGS DO SO HAPPEN TO US', and the word 'adventure' is repeated like a mantra. This insistence was to become a feature of camping and tramping series, and one is reminded of Enid Blyton's series and all those repetitive complaints (usually from younger female characters) that 'surely we aren't going to have *another* adventure this holiday!' – providing young readers with a simple lesson in irony and an agreeable frisson of anticipation.

Most camping and tramping novels were devoted to the excitements of hiking, exploring, boating, map-reading and the practicalities of camping. There were some popular individual novels, and a number of major series, published mostly between 1930 and 1960, as well as numerous short stories published in children's annuals. They quickly developed their own generic predictability: the fictional children of these books had ready access to camping equipment, or a handy caravan (sometimes with an available horse conveniently grazing in a nearby meadow), free entry to friendly farmhouses, and the guaranteed loyalty of passing gypsies and circus-folk.

They were to a large extent an expression of an age in which Boy Scouts and Girl Guides – and numerous similar organisations – were flourishing. In addition to the official Guiding and Scouting periodicals, there was a wide range of fiction devoted to camping activities. Percy Westerman wrote a series of fourteen Scout novels beginning with *Sea Scouts of the Petrel* (1914). A writer called F. Haydn Dimmock, editor of *The Scout* from 1919 to 1954, wrote sixteen

Scout novels and countless other tales in the pages of his magazine. Dorothy Osborn Hann's *Peg* series began with *Peg Junior* (1931) and was followed by *Peg's Patrol* (1924), *Captain Peg* (1928) and finally *What Happened to Peg* (1932). Frances Nash wrote the *Audrey* series, beginning with *How Audrey Became a Guide* (1922).[6]

There were other camping and tramping writers who set themselves apart from such 'official' fiction associated with Guiding and Scouting: for example, in *Fell Farm Campers* (1960) a group of incompetent working-class Boy Scouts are given some friendly but patronising assistance by the *real* campers – and incidentally taught how to behave.[7] This was one of the *Fell Farm* series by Marjorie Lloyd, in which a family of children spend their school holidays on a farm in the Lake District.

The *Fell Farm* series exhibits both the worst and the best features of camping and tramping fiction: the action is leisurely, there is little interest in characterisation, there is a stereotypical farmer's wife fussily providing huge meals, and all this exists in a generally cheerful and trusting world. On the other hand, the camping and exploring adventures of the children are represented with a detailed and affectionate authenticity which appealed to thousands of young readers. Another popular series, beginning with *Out with Romany* (1937), by 'Romany of the BBC' [G. Bramwell Evens] and running through several titles and many reprints until 1949, was committed to the observation and understanding of British wildlife. In David Severn's *Warner Family* and *Waggoners* series, the narrative voice reinforces its passion for its subject with beautiful and dramatic wood-engravings and line-drawings by J. Kiddell-Monroe.

Like much camping and tramping fiction, Severn's narratives were essentially love stories in which the loved-one was the English countryside, and the authorial desire was to initiate young readers into a similar devotion. The influence of Rudyard Kipling – especially *Puck of Pook's Hill* – was a powerful factor in works like *South Country Secrets* by 'Euphan' [Barbara Euphan Todd] and her husband 'Klaxon', in which a group of children returning from South Africa explore not only the geography but also the history of southern England. Another, almost sacred, text was Richard Jefferies' *Bevis: The Story of a Boy* (1882).

Camping and tramping fiction assumed an ideology of patriotism: a specifically English continuity was implicitly celebrated, stretching from Bronze Age settlers to the defeat of Germany. Despite its popularity, much camping and tramping fiction lacked the imaginative

5 Endpaper illustration by Joan Kiddell-Monroe for *The Cruise of the Maiden Castle* by David Severn

and meditative quality of works like Alison Uttley's *The Country Child*, and it had little of the dramatic pace of Enid Blyton's famous series. Furthermore, as if they sensed their own narrowness, camping and tramping narratives were constantly having to turn into other kinds of story – pony stories, wildlife natural history books, and especially adventure stories.

It is a fact of the history of children's books that for about thirty years children's literature was for the most part a version of pastoral, a sustained and essentially *adult* elegy on a massive scale for dearly loved and vanishing rural ways of life, mediated through fiction intended for young readers. The fictional world represented was fundamentally conservative, the narrative posture reclusive, and the tone elegiac – but the combination of rapturous lyrical description with sharply defined illustrations was often genuinely affecting. That many of the illustrations were wood engravings was appropriate – a nineteenth-century mode of illustration employed to illuminate a backward-looking vision of the English countryside.[8] Pastoral is inevitably adult and nostalgic; and this may in part account for the fact that camping and tramping series are currently so popular with adult collectors keen, perhaps, to cherish fictional accounts of a country-side which they remember from their own childhood.

David Severn's *The Cruise of the Maiden Castle* is typical of the genre: its first eight chapters describe movingly and accurately the practicalities of taking a longboat on England's canals in the 1940s. There is a good deal of explanatory description of using the tiller, managing lock gates (especially the famous 'staircase'), with accounts of shopping, cooking and swimming. Then, in Chapter 7, the lei-surely plot is given some urgency when the four longboat children have to endure a thunderstorm, and two chapters later a fight with some local working-class boys. The chapter which describes the chil-dren's trip through a canal tunnel deserves to be seen as a classical set-piece.

> On and on they chugged; David keeping well in the centre and away from the wall. Then a dim pool of light drew nearer and they passed through a patch of almost ghostly radiance. Looking up, they saw the round opening of a ventilation shaft, and some-how, the sight of the link with the fresh, breezy hillside above, cheered them all. Joan found Alan *was* beside her, and before the blackness swallowed them again, they exchanged a fleeting smile.

This is reminiscent of Ransome, especially that shared smile.

> Three more shafts passed by, at long intervals, and they chugged on through an eternity of night. The storm seemed hours and hours behind them; the hot midday laze under the trees might have belonged to quite another holiday. And then, at last, a twinkle, a star, shone in the darkness beyond the gleam of their headlamp. Slowly, steadily, the point expanded; became recog-nizable as a half circle; and they began to make out the damp, rough brickwork ahead, as daylight penetrated the tunnel. Gradu-ally they all emerged from the blackness, bathed in the cold, blank glare of the sky beyond the arched mouth.[9]

(There is a similar account in Garry Hogg's *Explorers Afloat* (1940); perhaps 'the trip through the tunnel' was obligatory if you were writing about canal longboats.)

Descriptive writing of this order is a salutary reminder that quality is no guarantee that a work will survive.

In Chapter 11 the novel turns into an adventure story as the children discover a disused factory full of stolen goods. However, there are no self-indulgent heroics: Severn's child-protagonists are described as frankly terrified. There is some light comedy when they report their find to a local policeman who suspects they are pulling his leg and indulgently calls them 'young whippersnappers'. The case is reported in the national press and the children become reluctant national heroes.

It is easy to ridicule this, but the formula was extraordinarily popular with young readers for three decades. There is a strong sense in Severn's fiction of England as a beautiful and derelict land known fully only to the initiates who could penetrate her secrets.

> There was the towpath, just below them. They could see the brown earth, dry and baked, showing through the grass. But no-one walked there, and now that they had left the moorhen far behind, nothing moved on the canal. There was little to show that this was a thoroughfare; part of a great network of waterways stretching over England. It was all so modest and quiet; deserted – and a little derelict.[10]

A myth is being invoked here, the myth of an old historical England still *there*, still holding things together beneath the surface of modern times. In the following quotation the proprietorial air is unmistakable, not complacent exactly, but celebratory, almost sacramental – and profoundly and nostalgically appealing to readers today who, like me, grew up in exactly such a countryside.

> He faced forward and could see the wash spreading out to the right and left as the blunt bows prodded forward; turned, and looked back over the stern to the woggly line of bubbles left by the screw. This was his Kingdom! And from his vantage-point on the roof, he could inspect the fields beyond the towpath; the fringe of woods opposite, that crept down to the canal. Harvesters waved to him; the men standing on a trailer behind a tractor, jolting over a rough stubble between stooks of yellow corn. And proudly, Christopher waved back, and watched them as they started to load, the sun sparking from the prongs of their pitchforks; the sheaves tossed up into the sky.[11]

Camping and tramping fiction shared an assumption that the entire British countryside was a safe playground for middle-class youngsters. The background to that assumption was the great agricultural depression which began at the turn of the century and which left rural England almost empty. Since the First World War the young had left the countryside in their thousands, leaving a beautiful and rather run-down rural landscape. This was infinitely appealing to the middle classes, who could see it as a lovely playground full of history and mystery, and suitable for hiking, boating and all manner of adventures for children. The rural background to all those friendly and welcoming fictional farmers was, in reality, one of economic and social stagnation in which farmers had to supplement their incomes in any way they could. When farmers began to prosper and agriculture became intensive, an entire genre of children's fiction was effectively wiped out by Common Market farming subsidies. And at about the same time the Beeching cuts closed down the branch lines that had taken so many fictional children by steam to their favourite holiday destinations.

> As manufacture seemed to become more important to England than agriculture, the Government neglected farming because food could be bought cheaper abroad. Only the best farms paid. The poorer farms were allowed to go out of cultivation and thousands of acres were only kept for sport. Arable land was turned into pasture for cows or into sheep runs, because ploughing and harvesting takes more labour. So more and more labourers left the land. Many farm houses and cottages lapsed into ruins, or were taken as week end houses by the townspeople. The first world war gave the country a shock and for a few years farms were pressed to produce more, but after that war, prices fell, and things became worse than ever on the land.

That quotation is not from a political pamphlet, but from a book for children, *A History of the Countryside*, one of an outstanding format-series which began in the 1940s, the Puffin Picture Books.[12]

Camping and tramping fiction was eclipsed by rural development, by the skilful marketing of the 'new wave' of young writers in the 1960s, by changes in reading habits, and by the overwhelming popularity of Enid Blyton's series – most of which derived from the camping and tramping fiction they had helped to displace. However, it survived into the 1960s and 70s in at least one specialist form, the pony story. In what we sometimes refer to as the 'world of children's books', pony stories constitute an entire continent the size of Asia! Ruby Ferguson's *Jill* series began in 1949 and the Pullein-Thompson sisters wrote over 150 pony stories from 1946. Probably the most distinguished writer of pony stories was Monica Edwards, whose two related and overlapping series, the *Punchbowl Farm* and the *Romney Marsh* series, ran to more than twenty titles, written over twenty years from 1947. Alison Haymond – to whom I am indebted for her work on pony stories – has pointed out that Edwards' reputation suffered because 'she acquired the pejorative and inaccurate label of writer of pony stories'.

A similar point might be made about series-writers generally: Enid Blyton has given the genre a bad name. More of that in the next chapter.

5 The great Nanny-Narrator and the children of the War

Enid Blyton wrote more series than most novelists write novels. It is also true that she has written more works that have subsequently fallen out of print than any other children's writer. Nevertheless she remains the monarch of series-writers. According to David Rudd, in 1951 this astonishing writer published thirty-seven books, an average of one every ten days.

I do not propose to go yet again over every aspect of the great Blyton controversy. My own view is that, in spite of its imaginative limitations, its formulaic plots, its stereotyping and its racist, classist and sexist bias, her work must for the time being be taken seriously by anyone genuinely interested in contemporary children's reading; I say *for the time being* because it is only her series that are proving durable. Her days are numbered, and I predict that within fifty years she will probably be of interest only to academics. In the meantime, thanks to a number of critics – notably David Rudd and Charles Sarland – it is possible now to have a much greater understanding and a much fairer appraisal of the work of the world's best-selling children's author.

But other questions remain to be asked: why was she so successful, and what was the effect of her success on children's books in general?

I believe that the key to an understanding of Blyton's phenomenal popularity is an understanding of the specific period in which she was writing. That her series fiction should succeed in the middle of the War years is not surprising. Most young readers at that time were fatherless; they had no role, yet were aware of a national crisis. Not all children enjoyed the new freedoms Robert Westall was later to describe in his fiction; and not all children were evacuated. But it was impossible not to be affected by the War: there were troop movements everywhere, and all children witnessed the signs of War activity:

if they were not actually blitzed, they saw dog-fights in the air, fighters and bombers taking off from or returning to air bases, barbed wire along the sea-shore, searchlights in the night sky, POWs working in prison camps, long army convoys passing through country towns and villages, streetlights switched off for six long years. They carried gas-masks and had lessons in how to use them, and were hurried into air-raid shelters when the sirens sounded. The dangers were real – but the children had nothing to do but wait.

In the midst of all this there came the sudden appearance of child-centred adventure series.

In the abundance of series described in the last chapter, there were two major writers – Malcolm Saville and Enid Blyton. Both began their best-known series in the middle of the War, the *Famous Five* in 1942 and the *Lone Pine* in 1943. By 1949, *Five on a Treasure Island*, published by Hodder and Stoughton, was into its sixth reprint and *Mystery at Witchend*, published by Newnes, was doing a little better with its seventh. For the next few years the two series kept pace with one another. Yet today much of Blyton's work is still in print and read by large numbers of children, while Saville's work is more or less completely out of print and yet sold in large numbers to adult collectors. This difference I will address in the next chapter.

Enid Blyton's stories appealed at first to the children of the War, and later to new generations of readers, because they are *contracts of narrative desire*, breathless, exciting, smoothing away difficulties with the ease of make-believe. I was at first tempted to use the phrase *carnivals* of desire, but that word suggests something reckless and anarchic – quite inappropriate for Blyton's swift but orderly narrative processes.

Debates about quality are wide of the mark. If only because there were so many of them, and because so many thousands of adults admit they became readers because of her work, Blyton's series seem to express some essential longing and potential associated with childhood. With many adult readers today they seem to have won some of the authority of myth. But, if so, it is a different kind of myth, for classical myth is essentially adult, with little interest in children and concerned with darkness, mystery and ambivalence; it places men and women in dilemmas and forces them to endure the sometimes terrible consequences; it is about an implacable universe where tragedy may be a deserved retribution or a purely arbitrary misfortune, but is almost always irreversible.

The *Famous Five* stories are the opposite in almost every respect. Blyton's narrative is like a powerful spotlight; it seeks to illuminate, to explain, to demystify. It takes its readers on a roller-coaster story in which the darkness is always banished; everything puzzling, arbitrary, evocative is either dismissed or explained. Nothing is left to chance: the motivation, emotions and actions of her characters are always explained, sometimes twice, so that there is nothing here for the reader to brood upon. Myth broods. But Blyton's narratives – committed to reducing everything to a condition of lucid banality – rush forever forward with her narrative beam of light illuminating the shadows. The numerous tunnels, underground passages and caves in her narratives provide a fictional darkness which is always made visible. Torches have both a practical and a symbolic significance for her young characters. The torch is an important trope, a central metaphor serving to exemplify the nature of her narratives. For your torchlight to begin to fade is a catastrophe, and not to have spare batteries is a personal failure.

Enid Blyton's adventure series offer the notion that there is in children an idealised and generous desire to belong to a benevolent group which goes out into a landscape to help adults put right the wrongs of a predominantly pastoral world. Her child protagonists are like child Knights of the Round Table (but happily free of the moral ambiguities of adultery and the challenges of the Holy Grail). In *The Sea of Adventure*, after a dangerous encounter with gun-runners, the children are reunited with their adult companion, Bill.

> 'It's been pretty thrilling,' said Philip. 'We had some scares, I can tell you, Bill.'
>
> 'You're good kids,' said Bill. 'Good and plucky kids. I'm proud of you. But there's one thing I don't understand. Why didn't you make for safety, when you captured Horace's boat? Why did you mess about here?'
>
> 'Well . . .' said Jack, 'you see – we had the choice of making for safety – or trying to find you. And we chose to try and find you, Bill. Even Lucy-Ann voted for that.'
>
> There was a silence. Then Bill put his big arms all around the huddled-up four and gave them such a hug that Lucy-Ann gasped.
>
> 'I don't know what to say,' said Bill, in a queer sort of voice. *'You're only kids – but you're the finest company of friends anyone could have. You know the meaning of loyalty already, and even if you're scared you don't give up. I'm proud to have you for my friends.'*

'Oh, *Bill!*' said Lucy-Ann, tremendously thrilled to hear such a speech from her hero. 'You *are* nice. You're our very very best friend, and you always will be.'

'Always,' said Dinah.

The boys said nothing, but they glowed inwardly at Bill's praise. Friendship – loyalty – staunchness in face of danger – they and Bill both knew these things and recognised them for the fine things they were. They felt very close to Bill indeed. [my italics][1]

This passage exemplifies the difficulties adult critics have with Blyton. In many ways it begs to be parodied; the attitude-striking and gender assumptions are absurd, and the writing is slipshod. *But to the child reader there is nothing inherently ridiculous here.* An entire generation of wartime readers existed who were well aware of the implications of defeat; who saw the action on newsreels and read about it in newspapers; who listened to Churchill on the wireless; but who were utterly unable to contribute. Their fathers were mostly away, their mothers preoccupied, and out of such an ethos came a kind of 'myth-play' of child-power that outlasted the War years – innocent, determined, active and committed to traditional values of honour, truthfulness and loyalty to friends. While the USA in the thirties and forties was generating the super-hero in a period of dangerous cult political leaders, children's writers in Britain were generating the notion of the benevolent group.

This is not the making of a myth of childhood, at least not in the classical sense. In fact, it is hardly a representation of childhood at all; rather, it *sets childhood aside* for the duration of the reading. The complications and difficulties of actual childhood are simply discarded for the time being – and this brings her narrative approach closer to the character of make-believe. This is what children do when they pretend, either collaboratively or on their own: they set the realities of their lives aside and play. Or, to use one of Blyton's favourite expressions (which eventually became a title), they 'fall into adventure'. Children's make-believe is shot through with desire – desire to *experience* dangers, tests and rituals at an imaginative and vicarious level, and desire to *achieve* the promised happy and just outcome. Blyton's adventure stories are constructed on the basis of that desire; they promise the learner reader that desired vicarious experience, and they guarantee the desired outcome – and the promise is always kept, the consummation always achieved. 'Let's all play together!' says the great Nanny-Narrator. The desire of young readers to join in was never betrayed – and that readerly greed for more was the justification for the long extended series she wrote.

In 1944, Blyton published *The Island of Adventure*, the first of a series of eight adventure stories, which in many ways are superior to the better-known *Famous Five* series and exemplify her narrative strategies. Perhaps the best of the series is *The Mountain of Adventure* (1949). Its opening chapters represent a deeply appealing ideal of childhood. It begins with the excitement and promise of the family summer holiday:

> Four children were singing at the tops of their voices in a car that was going up a steep mountain-side road.
> A parrot was also joining in, very much out of tune, cocking up her crest in excitement. The man at the wheel turned round with a grin.[2]

This, to a young reader, is pure joy. Enid Blyton is laying down the terms of the contract. Accordingly, the four children are introduced to new readers: Philip the animal-lover, his sister the hot-tempered Dinah, and their friends Lucy-Ann and Jack, the latter a passionate bird-watcher and the former – the youngest of them – small and easily frightened. In the light of what is often said of Blyton's other young girl protagonist, Anne of the *Famous Five*, it is worth pointing out that it is stressed throughout that Lucy-Ann is frightened not because she is a coward but because she is the youngest, and the others are mostly very protective of her. In fact, the older children are generally protective towards younger ones, freely holding their hands and supporting them without embarrassment; and in *The Castle of Adventure*, when Tassie, a barefooted gypsy girl, has got her clothes wet and muddy, Jack coolly orders her to strip, wraps her in a rug and sits close to her to keep her warm![3]

There is also Kiki the parrot, used skilfully for comic effect. The place they are staying at is called something that sounds like 'Dothgoth-oo-elli-othel-in'.

> 'Gracious!' said Dinah. 'What a name! Not even Kiki could pronounce that, I'm sure. Tell her it, Bill. See what she says.'
> Bill obligingly told the name to the parrot, who listened solemnly and raised her crest politely.
> 'Now you just repeat that,' said Jack to Kiki. 'Go on!'

'This-is-the-house-that-Jack-built,' said the parrot, running all the words together. The children laughed.[4]

Kiki is running true to form, thinks the child reader; she is funny and mischievous, and she will probably get the children out of danger at some point in the plot. The more familiar you are with the other books in the series, the more you appreciate the terms of the contract. Then comes the arrival at the Welsh farmhouse where the children will be staying – another clause in the agreement.

It was a rambling old stone place, set on the mountain-side, with barns and out-buildings all around. In the evening sunset it looked welcoming and friendly.[5]

With such brief and sketchy details the narrative is keeping the implied promise to its readers and arousing their readerly greed for further fulfilments. And, as other commentators have observed, greed, hunger and food are central in Blyton's narrative world. So it is not surprising that after the arrival comes the feast:

A great ham sat ready to be carved. A big tongue garnished round with bright green parsley sat by its side. An enormous salad with hard-boiled eggs sprinkled generously all over it was in the middle of the table. Two cold roast chickens were on the table too, with little curly bits of cold bacon set round.

The children's eyes nearly fell out of their heads. What a feast! And the scones and cakes! The jams and the pure yellow honey![6]

Blyton can be relied on to go into stylistic overdrive when she is describing food as she never does when she is describing anything else. This is an edible still-life for a time of food rationing. The children eat the meal, 'looking out of the wide, low windows and the big open door' at the view.

Great mountains reared up their heads in the evening light. Deep shadows lay across the valley, but the mountains still caught the sunlight, and gleamed enchantingly.[7]

This is characteristic of Blyton's descriptions – a minimalist use of two or three visual details, and a few careless words ('gleamed enchantingly'). But its appeal to young readers, many of whom would never have seen a mountain, is unmistakable.

After the meal, the children go out into the twilight, where they discover some farmyard goats. Readers familiar with the series would immediately recognise that here was another detail of the contract – the strange power that Philip has over all animals, which is in this story to save the children from being torn apart by guard dogs:

> ... and with them was a kid. It was snow-white, dainty and altogether lovely. Philip stood looking at it, loving it at once.
> He made a curious little bleating noise and all the goats looked round and stopped eating. The kid pricked up its little white ears, and stood quivering on its slender legs. It was very young and new.
> Philip made the noise again. The kid left its mother and came leaping to him. It sprang right into his arms and nestled there, butting its soft white head against Philip's chin.[8]

Kinship with animals is close to a child's deepest fantasy: when the children have gone to bed, 'there came the scampering of little hooves' and the kid appears in Philip's bedroom.[9]

Chapter 3, entitled 'The first morning', begins:

> The next day the two girls awoke first. It was early, but somebody was already about in the yard. Lucy-Ann peeped out of the window.
> 'It's Effans,' she said. 'He must have been milking. Dinah, come here. Did you ever see such a glorious view in your life?'[10]

With such effortlessness, such slapdash carelessness even, Blyton seduces her readers into an authorial pact of promise and play. This is how all children's summer holidays should start! It is an idealised opening, a child-fantasy lovingly displayed with all the author's usual mixture of child-provision and slipshod language.

The Mountain of Adventure exemplifies the nature of her appeal: a magical and idealised opening, with an idyllic holiday-beginning beloved of a nation of children (many of whom never had summer holidays), with fictional children in an idealised landscape (presented as a beautiful wilderness, an empty continent) who stumble upon criminals in the mountain, and who are ultimately saved through their own heroism, the benevolent intervention of an adult 'guardian', and the mysterious/magical power that Philip has over the dogs. The series had always existed on the edge of fantasy; with Philip's magical power over animals it crosses the line. Magic underlies *all*

Blyton's adventure fiction, including the *Famous Five* stories. Timmy is a magical animal companion, not in the true fairy-tale manner because the magic is demystified. Nothing Timmy does is actually supernatural, but his instincts are always magically right, or a confirmation of George's.

It has been said that Enid Blyton, as she composed her stories, saw the action like a film. Her narrative is in the worst sense filmic – external, casual, viewed with little reflection and only a minimal interest in the inner life or the landscape. This is what makes her manageable for young readers; but it is also what sets her apart from the *Swallows and Amazons* and so outrages Ransome-lovers. The following extract from *The Sea of Adventure* (1948) illustrates how her filmic authorial mind works. Each character has a dominant trait, and each in a crisis can be summed up in a single statement.

> Lucy-Ann's knees went queer again. Her tummy felt peculiar too. Dinah was strung up and her breath came fast, although she was not rowing. The two boys were tense with excitement. Would they find the enemy's motor-boat there, with Bill already in it, ready to be 'dumped,' as the man had said that day? And would there be many men on guard?[11]

They are rowing in the dark towards danger, and what they become aware of is made available to the reader as if it were film, gradually through sound and sight, precisely as the protagonists themselves come nearer and become aware of it. Again, illumination in the darkness is structurally crucial.

> 'Whatever's that noise?' whispered Dinah at last, as their boat drew nearer to land. 'It does sound queer.'
>
> The boys paused in their rowing, and leaned on their oars to listen.
>
> 'Sounds like a band playing,' said Jack. 'Of course – it's a wireless!'
>
> 'Good!' said Philip. 'Then the enemy won't be so likely to hear us creeping in. Jack, look! – I think that's a little jetty there – you can just make it out by the light of that lantern. Can we possibly creep in without being seen or heard? And look! – is that a boat lying under the lantern?'
>
> 'I'll get the glasses,' said Philip, and felt about for them. He put them to his eyes. 'Yes – it *is* a boat – quite a big one. I should

think it's the one the enemy came to our island in. I bet Bill is on
it ...'

And a little later:

'Look! – can you see that little glow, Jack? I bet that's the end
of a cigarette the guard is smoking.'[12]

Filmic, yes; but the other dominant medium of the 1940s and 1950s
was radio. This is also constructed as a story that might be told on
the wireless – Children's Hour, perhaps – where listeners must be
carefully helped to imagine the scene.

If we compare that extract with Arthur Ransome's account of
the Swallows sailing in the dark, we can see that the two writers'
approaches are entirely different. Ransome is a truth-teller, concerned
to represent the difficulties and dangers the children have got themselves into. The occasional use of childlike language, and the reference back to their father's joke about 'duffers', is not allowed to
obscure the fact that the children here are in serious danger.

John said nothing. For one thing, he was counting to himself and
getting near a hundred. For another, the light of Susan's torch in
the bottom of the boat, where she was cutting hunks of cake and
breaking up chocolate, and the light of his own torch, when he
used it to look at the compass, made the darkness of the night
even darker than it really was. It was better than being stuck in
the river, much better, but Captain John knew very well that he
could not really tell how near they might be to the shore. He was
the captain of the *Swallow* and must not wreck his ship. Daddy
had trusted him not to be a duffer and, sailing in this blackness,
he did not feel so sure about not being a duffer as he did by day.
And there were no lights in Rio to help him. Everything was
black. He could only keep on tacking against the wind, and he
was wondering what he should do when *Swallow* came near the
islands off the Bay. And how would he know when she was
coming near them? It would not do to let his crew know that he
was worried. So he said nothing, except that he went on with his
counting. Perhaps he counted a little louder than before. He
reached a hundred, put *Swallow* about, and began again: 'One,
two, three,' as she went off on the other tack.

Backwards and forwards, *Swallow* scurried across the lake in
the dark. The islands could not be far away.

Suddenly John stopped counting.

'Listen,' he said. 'Trees. I can hear the wind in them. What's that?' He flashed his torch over the side. There was the white splash of water breaking on a rock.[13]

There is darkness, danger, torchlight, as there is in the Blyton passage. But the emphasis is on questions, uncertainty, and the way these are experienced *inwardly* by John. The unspoken question throughout is one of responsibility.

And that essentially is the difference between his writing and Enid Blyton's. Her narratives are *irresponsible*; they race forward in their eager and benevolent lust for completion without showing interest in any of the disciplining actualities of children's real lives. The only abrasivenesses in her stories are the ones she deliberately puts there to be smoothed away as her fictional children progress towards the desired conclusion – so that she can begin another story and do the same thing all over again.

But what was the great Nanny-Narrator really *interested* in?

It is a fair question, for an Enid Blyton narrative rarely slows down long enough to allow its reader to reflect. It does not invite its readers to consider the nature of their experience, the position of real children, or the nature of fiction. Nor does it invite them to take pleasure in words, or introduce them to other works of literature. Furthermore, Blyton showed no interest in narrative form, or in the particular dynamics of series fiction. It seems never to have occurred to her that she might attempt to develop the series format she was so committed to; quite the reverse, in fact, for she could be said to have removed everything from her series except the scaffolding of minimal description and essential dialogue.

She was not seriously interested in character, and she was interested in landscape only as a background setting; there is none of that strong sense of place that is to be found in Arthur Ransome, Malcolm Saville, Monica Edwards and many others. Landscape is dramatic for *action*, not *feeling*.

Occasionally in the last thirty years, when I have been discussing her work on children's literature courses, an enthusiast has drawn attention to some deliberate point of seriousness in Blyton's work, some ambiguous hint that there was a thoughtful mind at work. It often sounds plausible enough, but on closer inspection what is found is something so nebulous as to be almost accidental. It seems that, when Blyton's fiction does find itself in danger of addressing some issue worth reflecting upon, it hurries forward and the moment has passed before the reader can become aware of it.

This is the difficulty I have with her work: any supposed significance in it vanishes on the application of critical scrutiny, so that it is possible to discuss it only in terms of context – either the context in which it was produced or the context in which it is read. Her fiction has no interest in significance. It is never concerned with the implicit. Its commitment to the entirely literal banishes mystery, magic and the shifting psychologies of childhood.

Perhaps the more interesting question is not what the author was interested in, but what readers have found interesting in her work – and that is much easier to answer. Many adults remember with particular affection her early works, *The Enchanted Wood* (1939), and the two *Magic Faraway Tree* stories (1943, 1946).[14]

But what readers *really* recall with interest is George.

Five on a Treasure Island, published in 1942, was the first of what was to become the most famous series in the world. It begins with an explicit build-up of interest in George before the reader meets her. Within a single side the reader knows about Uncle Quentin, and that the children are 'rather frightened of him' because he is 'a very tall, frowning man, a clever scientist who spent all his time studying'.[15] Throughout the novel, there are strong signs of a breakdown between her and her father, with hints of unfairness and beatings. When the children arrive at Kirrin Cottage, Georgina has run off somewhere and is not to be found. They are warned that they 'may find George a bit difficult at first'[16] but the emphasis is squarely placed on her remote and bad-tempered father. '"She wants spanking," said Uncle Quentin. The children couldn't quite make out whether he was joking or not.'[17]

The reader's first encounter with George is also Anne's.

> 'I say! Are you Georgina?'
> The child in the opposite bed sat up and looked across at Anne. She had very short curly hair, almost as short as a boy's. Her face was burnt a dark-brown with the sun, and her very blue eyes looked as bright as forget-me-nots in her face. But her mouth was rather sulky, and she had a frown like her father's.
> 'No,' she said. 'I'm not Georgina.'
> 'Oh!' said Anne, in surprise. Then who are you?'
> 'I'm George,' said the girl. 'I shall only answer if you call me George. I hate being a girl. I won't be. I don't like doing the things that girls do. I can climb better than any boy, and swim

faster too. I can sail a boat as well as any fisher-boy on this coast. You're to call me George. Then I'll speak to you. But I shan't if you don't.'[18]

Here, and in the rest of the scene, we have passion, imperiousness, pride and rebelliousness – an unbeatable combination in a character who seems for once to have captured the author's interest. Blyton always appreciated the dramatic possibilities of naughtiness and non-conformity; here they are convincingly linked to issues of gender to provide a powerful narrative dynamic. The nature of the dramatic focus on George is quickly made explicit by the younger girl.

> Anne felt offended. 'You're not very polite,' she said. 'You won't find that my brothers take much notice of you if you act as if you knew everything. They're *real* boys, not pretend boys, like you.'[19]

That is a shrewd thrust, incidentally giving the narrative game away – for *Five on a Treasure Island* is essentially a male text, in which boys and brothers are the natural arbiters. George's struggle is not only against her gender and social expectations, but also against the text in which she is situated – a tension guaranteed to produce some narrative fireworks. The reader is given a hint of what is to come at the end of the chapter when George reveals that Kirrin Island belongs to her: 'At least, it *will* belong to me – some day! It will be my very own island – and my very own castle!'[20]

The other children are patient with George, especially Julian. And a firm bond seems to be established between them when they meet George's dog, Timmy. 'Oh, George – he's fine,' says Julian. 'Aren't you proud of him?' Then something strange happens: the authorial perspective suddenly shifts and the narrator's nanny-voice comes into play, exemplified by the external and grown-up observation of George as a 'little girl':

> The little girl smiled, and her face altered at once, and became sunny and pretty.[21]

George has little of the depth and complexity of many fictional characters; she is a two-dimensional case-study understood in the light of an entirely pragmatic psychology. We hear that her father has taken a dislike to Timmy and, backed by her mother, has banished the dog – and what makes this such a satisfying narrative to young readers is that the other children take her side on all issues, and *so does the narrative.* When it is explained to her that she has many things the children would like to share (an island, a dog, a wreck), the narrator provides a nannyish explanation:

> It wasn't [George's] nature to share anything. She had always been an only child, a lonely, rather misunderstood little girl, fierce and hot-tempered. She had never had any friends of her own.[22]

George's bad temper is clearly a consequence of loneliness, and her self-learning on that is made explicit through the rest of the narrative. But what happens is not an entirely predictable compromise in which the unruly feminine is obliged to accept the terms of the masculine world and the masculine text in which she exists. A bargain is struck – friendship in exchange for sharing and, with her father, affection in exchange for respect. But a new and rather startling assumption is also made explicit here in the form of some clear authorial acknowledgements that adults are likely to be unhelpful or worse. Nanny is on the children's side – though disguising her stance to appear like a perception of Julian's.

> Julian thought [George] didn't understand grown-ups very well. It wasn't a bit of good fighting grown-ups. They could do exactly as they liked. If they wanted to take away George's island and castle, they could. If they wanted to sell it, they could![23]

Where such a declaration came from in Enid Blyton's own psychology can only be guessed at. There is a child-centred perception here, and perhaps some bitterness – an authorial protest rare in children's fiction of the period, in which adults (unless they are crooks) are almost invariably represented as benevolent. It resurfaces again, later, when the ingots have been discovered and the delighted Quentin wants to know why George had not told him about them.

> The four children stared at him and didn't answer. They couldn't very well say, 'Well, firstly you wouldn't have believed us. Secondly, you are bad-tempered and unjust and we are frightened of you. Thirdly, we didn't trust you enough to do the right thing.'[24]

That is direct and persuasive writing, and very liberating for young readers in the 1940s and 50s. Subsequently, it would have been easy for Blyton to lose interest in George and allow this one powerful narrative idea to be diluted and extended into a series of endlessly repeated formulaic plots. But she did not do that – at least not at first. In the second in the series, *Five Go Adventuring Again* (1943), the problematic rebelliousness of her character is again central, with the added twist that George is proved right and the others – including her three friends and, of course, Uncle Quentin – wrong. Again, there are explicit statements about the powerlessness of children faced with adult authority, though such child-centred statements continue to be undercut by the frequent references to George as 'the little girl';[25] and whenever that happens, the Nanny-Narrator seems to be addressing her readers as if they too were nannies, chatting in the park about a difficult child. In the third in the series, *Five Run Away Together* (1944), the villainy-plot is the same as ever; but the character-plot is still driven by George, who hates the Sticks and intuitively knows they are villains. And, as before, she is right.

For child readers, George – with Timmy acting as her intuition, a kind of psychic scout – is a liberating character. But it is not just George; in this story, Julian's behaviour is extraordinarily confident and adult, pure wish-fulfilment for powerless young readers. 'If I've any nonsense from you I'll get you no other meals', says the odious Mrs Stick. 'And if I have any nonsense from you I shall go to the police', Julian says coolly in reply.[26] Totally implausible, but deeply appealing. And it goes on:

> 'How dare you!' yelled Mrs. Stick. 'First that girl slaps Edgar, and then you pull his nose! What's the matter with you all?'
>
> 'Nothing,' said Julian, pleasantly; 'but there's an awful lot wrong with Edgar, Mrs. Stick. We feel we just *must* put it right. It should be your job, of course, but you don't seem to have done it.'
>
> 'You're downright insolent,' said Mrs. Stick, outraged and furious.
>
> 'Yes, I dare say I am,' said Julian. 'It's just the effect Edgar has on me. Stinker has the same effect.'
>
> 'Stinker!' cried Mrs. Stick, getting angrier still. 'That's not my dog's name, and well you know it.'
>
> 'Well, it really ought to be,' said Julian, strolling off. 'Give him a bath, and maybe we'll call him Tinker instead.'[27]

There are some unpleasant assumptions about class here, but also a rather surprising reminder of P.G. Wodehouse (or is it Lord Peter Wimsey?) in the representation of Julian's coolly superior and confident repartee. But, in putting the adult disapproval of insolence into the mouth of the villain, Blyton has reversed the usual expectations and again skewed the narrative in favour of her child readers.

The sixth book in the series, *Five on Kirrin Island Again* (1947), reads like a closure. Not only does the narrative revisit the island which was at the centre of George's indignation in the first story, it also revisits the theme of ownership. It begins with George learning that her father has taken possession of Kirrin Island in order to complete some important scientific research. She is furious, and, when Anne defends him, she retorts:

> '*Your* father would talk to you about it first, and ask your permission, and see if you minded,' said George, sulkily. 'My father never does anything like that. He just does exactly as he likes without asking anybody anything.'[28]

Many young readers would recognise that sense of injustice. George's father has erected a suspiciously phallic-looking tower on the island – which is perhaps why Julian rather than George leads the way to the top of it. When, later, Quentin needs to borrow Timmy to stay on the Island with him as a watchdog (but without George), there is another confrontation and George is persuaded to be magnanimous. If Timmy understood that he was needed, says her mother, he would make the decision himself – which is precisely what he does:

> [George] looked at Timmy. He looked back at her, wagging his tail. Then he did an extraordinary thing – he got up, walked over to George's father, and lay down beside him, looking at George as if to say 'There you are! Now you know what *I* think is right!'[29]

This is simple symbolism for inexperienced readers – and further evidence that Timmy is more magical than naturalistic.

Five on Kirrin Island Again returns to the old fourfold theme of the first story: George, Quentin, Timmy and the Island. In the first story, George had convinced her father he had been wrong; now, in a dramatic climax, George singlehandedly rescues her father who is trapped in some caves, and also gets him to admit unreservedly that Timmy is a loyal and wonderful dog. This seems to settle the conflict conclusively in a father-and-daughter reconciliation, and everything seems to suggest that Enid Blyton was closing down this theme which had been the imaginative power-house driving the series of six books. There is an uncharacteristic finality about the closing paragraphs:

'We've had a lot of adventures together,' said Julian. 'More than most children. They *have* been exciting, haven't they?'

Yes – they have! But now we must say good-bye to the Five, and to Kirrin Island too. Good-bye, Julian, Dick, George, Anne – and Timmy. But only Timmy hears our good-bye, for he has such sharp ears.

'Woof! Good-bye!'[30]

Blyton had never before chanced upon such a richly psychological source for her narratives – and she never recovered it in the other fifteen titles she added to the series. They are adventure stories merely, and although George continues to be moody and bad-tempered and Timmy is frequently heroic, there is no imaginative return to Quentin, or George's sense of injustice.

However, although she had for the duration of six books given narrative expression to a powerful and impassioned insight about the power relations between children and adults, Blyton had never allowed the stories to be slowed by anything more than the most cursory allusion to the complex basis of George's unhappiness. And she had never done anything to point to – or point up – the occasional apparent symbolism. The consequence is that the critical adult reader is left with no way of telling whether she is one of the greatest unconscious children's writers of all time, a fully self-conscious provider for very young readers, or a lazy and slipshod author who was occasionally interesting by accident.

It might be argued that books for very inexperienced readers *must* be simple. But simplicity in children's books is profoundly complex, a sophisticated result of deep imaginative reflection. The simplicity in such great picturebooks as *Rosie's Walk*, *Where the Wild Things Are*, or – in my opinion the wisest of all 'simple' books for very young children – *Mr Gumpy's Outing*, is quite different from the breathless literalness of Blyton's series narratives. The trouble with her work is not its excessive reliance on exclamation marks (though she *does* use lots!), or its limited vocabulary (it is not, in fact, especially limited), or its predictable plots (readers have to learn prediction), or even its ideological assumptions (which were the predominant assumptions of her period anyway). What characterises her work is banality, especially in the representation of character and moral choice. Even with her most interesting character, George, complexity is seen only in terms of a crude sulkiness/good-nature conflict.

Banality is not an inevitable characteristic of narrative texts which are accessible to inexperienced readers. Think of *Charlotte's Web*, for example, or the fiction of Dahl, King-Smith or some of the great retellers of fairy stories. But Blyton was incapable of such impassioned, intelligent and witty writing. The busy Nanny-Narrator was in too much of a hurry, too preoccupied with the *process* of story-making; she had no time and, I suspect, little inclination ever to stop and reflect upon it.

6 Malcolm Saville
The price paid

Enid Blyton's effect on the development and understanding of children's books in this country is incalculable. How profoundly discouraging it must have been for other children's writers at that time! They must have wondered how any writer could keep pace with her phenomenal output. And there is another, more important, consideration: her work in the 1940s and 50s began to define for the general public what children's books were, and how they were to be perceived. The only consistent alternative view in Britain was that represented by the new Puffin paperback series under the inspired editorship of Eleanor Graham for its first 95 titles, and thereafter of Kaye Webb.

In 1961 Margery Fisher published *Intent upon Reading*, one of the most sensible and illuminating books ever written about children and the books they read. She refers only once to Blyton, remarking tartly that '[she] and others think that children are taxed too much if they are confronted by so much as a polysyllable'.[1] *Intent upon Reading* is in effect a critical study of the other writing for children that was going on alongside the great Blyton industry. But only a handful of the writers Margery Fisher admired have survived in print for youngsters today. Hers has become a history of a lost literature. Enid Blyton's success had an overwhelmingly oppressive effect on other children's writers of her day; furthermore, she is in danger of shaping our historical perspectives. What we have been inclined to see when we look back to the 1940s and 50s is the brilliance of her success – and not the achievements of other writers and publishers working in her shadow. Critical authority has allowed Blyton's reputation to overshadow the achievements of other writers and the view that she succeeded because she had no rivals has become an assumed orthodoxy.

One excellent author was Kitty Barne, a writer whose intelligent, pacy, witty and discriminating narratives have been described by one authority as 'a few unremarkable novels'. She is now almost forgotten and never read by children. Another is John Verney, who was also a distinguished illustrator and whose work receives no mention at all in the same reference work. David Severn's fiction, which I referred to in the previous chapter, is described as 'workmanlike but conventional'.[2] Another writer working throughout this period was Rumer Godden; this reference work has nothing at all to say about her novels of childhood, restricting itself to a few remarks about her doll stories. Elinor Lyon, whose series of novels about Ian and Sovra – set in the Scottish Highlands – have something of the character of William Mayne's early fiction, is not mentioned in any of the standard works.[3]

In 1947 Katharine Hull and Pamela Whitlock collaborated on a strange and innovative novel, *Crowns*, an experimental fantasy interesting in both style and structure, which might have led children's books in an interesting new direction; but it was so radically unlike anything Blyton was producing that it had little chance of success. Of course, there must have been many reasons for such neglect – but one of them, I believe, was that more contemplative narratives, dedicated to a careful and word-perfect faithfulness to the imaginative and affective inner lives of romantic fictional children, simply could not survive in a publishing climate dominated by the tyrannical success of Blyton's overwhelming and narrow-minded output.

But there was one writer who tried to match her and at the same time do better – Malcolm Saville, of whom it could be said that he started off as 'his own man' and was obliged to turn into a Blyton.

Saville wrote at least eight series for children – the *Jilly Family* books (from 1948), the *Buckingham Family* books (from 1950), the *Marston Baines* series (from 1963), the three *Lucy and Humf* stories (from 1959), the four *Nettleford* books (from 1951), the *Mike and Mary* series (from 1945), the *Susan and Bill* books (from 1954) and – his best-known – the twenty *Lone Pine* stories (from 1943). He also wrote a good deal of non-fiction, mostly about the countryside. His illustrators included Ernest Shepard and Joan Kiddell-Monroe.

There is a wholly admirable level-headedness about Saville's writing, a commitment to representing Britain (to be precise, England) as wartime children knew it. The first of the *Lone Pine* series begins with a scene which thousands of young wartime readers would recognise:

They changed trains at Shrewsbury.

'Promise me, twins,' said Mrs. Morton, when they had managed, with the help of a friendly but over-worked guard, to get their trunks out of the van, 'promise that you'll stay here with the luggage and look after Macbeth. Don't move till we come back. David is going to find a porter, and I'll see if I can get something to eat.'

'All right, Mummy,' said Richard. 'Trust us.'

'We swear,' said Mary solemnly as she sat herself firmly on a trunk and hoisted an agitated little black dog up beside her ...

David didn't feel particularly grown up as he went up the long platform. He knew he ought to be. He remembered what Daddy had said. 'Take care of Mummy for me, old chap, and look after those awful twins as well. I know you'll all love Witchend, and I want you to have a good time while I'm away ... But be sensible and remember that I trust you not to do silly things.'

He still felt a bit chokey when he thought of Daddy going off in his new uniform. 'Do all you can to help your mother,' he had said.[4]

In spite of the comic twins, this is unmistakably the serious and familiar world of evacuees, divided families, fathers going off to the forces and train journeys to unknown destinations. Although the War is never any more than a background, Saville was attempting something that Enid Blyton was never interested in – the visual and affective representation of the social, personal and geographical atmosphere of wartime England.

To attempt such a thing requires a highly developed ability to describe, and a determination to enable readers to 'see' an imagined landscape. Saville worked hard to achieve precision and clarity.

It was a cold, bright night, with millions of stars blazing out of a velvet sky. Although the moon was not yet up the reservoir glistened like a sheet of black glass, for a film of ice was already forming on its still surface. Above and beyond the water, the heathery slopes of moorland rolled up towards the summit of the Mynd, and all the world was quiet.[5]

The entire series is sustained by descriptive passages like this – unpretentious, conservative, sometimes a bit prosy, but always anchoring the narratives firmly in a real geographical countryside.

Saville's countryside has a dark aspect, often associated with its violent history and sometimes brought to the reader through dreams – Penny's disturbing dream of Roman soldiers attacking a small settlement in *Lone Pine Five*,[6] for example, or the compelling account of Peter's dream at the beginning of *The Secret of Grey Walls*, in which she and a strange companion travel through a dark and wintry landscape so that her mysterious partner can point out a particular house.

> Without a word to each other the two girls left the whispering trees behind them and went on down the cart-track together. And as they went it seemed to Peter that the light was changing, and before they had gone many yards the dream country was bathed in silver moonlight. Another few steps and the sky was flecked with scarlet, and when she turned to look over her shoulder Peter saw that all the moorland behind was on fire. Without either fear or surprise the two girls stood and watched the trees in the spinney flare up like giant torches and then, as the cruel winds swept the flames down towards them and the strange house, Peter woke.[7]

At this point I ought to confess that at the age of ten I fell in love with Petronella Sterling, otherwise known as Peter, heroine of the *Lone Pine* series. *The Seven White Gates* (1944) was the first full-length novel I read as a child, and when recently I looked again at the first illustration of Peter, stopping a runaway horse (which had been frightened by a passing tank) and saving the gypsy caravan from being smashed, I found I remembered it in such detail as to suggest that as a boy I had studied it with some attention.

I was fascinated by that story and by Peter in particular, and my interest is not surprising. There is in Saville's work a strong hint of sexuality that in the 1940s and 50s was not to be found in any other fiction. To a generation of boys attending for the most part single-sex schools (I cannot speak for girl readers), Saville's novels were highly gendered. They communicated a strong sense of 'girlhood' rather than girlishness, and at the same time managed somehow to suggest that girls were both *different* and *interesting*, and that companionship with them was exciting and full of possibilities. This was worlds away from William Brown's feelings about Violet Elizabeth Bott. The fact that Petronella is called Peter has nothing to do with gender issues and does not indicate a dissatisfaction on her part, but to a young male reader it added piquancy and made her femininity even more interesting.

6 Illustration by Bertram Prance, from *Seven White Gates*

But the *Lone Pine* series has had a humiliating history. When it was reissued in paperback from 1969 onwards, the novels were heavily revised and shortened. Whether this was to fit them to the practical limits of paperback fiction, or whether it was to speed up the pace of his plots, one of the effects of this editorial butchery was to weaken this pervasive and engaging sense of sexuality. The cuts were made on a large scale. In the hardback edition of the first in the series, *Mystery at Witchend*, Peter and David have a brief quarrel when they agree to go swimming in a mountain reservoir and David first allows himself to be distracted and briefly delayed by other interests. Then he remembers Peter:

> She was in a scarlet bathing costume with a bright blue rubber cap, and for a moment he wondered who it was. He called, but she didn't even look in his direction but ran straight into the water. He called again, 'Wait for me, Peter. I won't be a sec.,' but she made no answer, dived under[8] and swam rapidly away from him up to the dam where she pulled herself up and sat in the sun.
>
> David ran back along the little beach, but when he was within a few yards of her she dived in again and swam away. He was suddenly very angry and jumped down behind the dam wall, flung off his clothes and scrambled into his trunks. Instead of climbing up quickly and diving in he pulled himself up slowly and peeped over the top. Peter was now swimming lazily towards the deep end again and looking round to see where he had gone. He dropped down into hiding and, after a little, heard her pull herself up on to the wall. He waited a moment to see what she was going to do and then, as she made no further move, pulled himself slowly and quietly up. She was only about three yards away sitting with her back to him, with her feet in the water. As he watched she brushed a hand across her eyes.
>
> With a final effort he heaved himself up beside her and said, 'Hullo! Why didn't you answer me when I called?'
>
> She jumped in surprise and then would have slipped into the water if he hadn't grabbed her arm. She wriggled fiercely and turned on him in a fury. 'Let me go, you beast.'
>
> But the imperturbable David was also annoyed, so he held on. 'Don't be a silly ass, Peter,' he said. 'What is it all about?'
>
> She actually gulped and there were tears in her eyes as she said in a shaky voice, 'Fancy asking *me* what it's all about! There's nothing about! I can swim here if I want to, I suppose . . .'[9]

I have quoted this in full because it is a careful attempt to suggest the complexities of early adolescent friendship and flirtation, with some anger and provocation, and a power struggle masquerading as horse-play. But it is not essential to the plot and in the paperback edition *this is all that was allowed to remain*:

> Peter was angry with David for spending so much time messing about with sluices and wheels and things and had decided to go swimming on her own. When David saw her in the water he quickly jumped down behind the dam wall, pulled on his swimming trunks and dived into the water ...[10]

Later, three Home Guards in uniform wake up Peter so that they can question her about a stranger she has seen; she opens her bedroom window and looks out at them in her pyjamas.

> 'Good morning, Juliet,' said one. 'Speak to me from your window, I pray thee.'[11]

That was cut – perhaps because its reference to Shakespeare was assumed to be beyond the understanding of young readers, but also because of the implied acknowledgement that Peter is an attractive girl.

In *The Neglected Mountain*, the seventh in the series, Peter is described looking at an engaged couple who are friends of hers:

> As the light from the lamp lit up his brown, smiling face, she noticed how he looked down at the slim, lovely girl at his side and her heart began to thump and unexpected tears pricked her eyes.[12]

This small psycho-sexual detail was cut out. Yet a few pages later David 'suddenly realised that one day, and very soon now perhaps, other people would look at Peter and see that she was a very beautiful girl'[13] – and this for some reason was retained in the revised edition. But on its own it makes less sense because the exploration of 'beauty looked at and appreciated' has been excised from the novel. Accordingly, a later description of Tom noticing that Jenny 'was getting very pretty' was cut out, together with his very masculine appreciation of Peter: '[she was] upright, slim and yet so very feminine ... Her hair, bleached by the summer sun, was almost ash-blonde, and she gave him a lovely smile as she caught his eye.'[14] Saville's attempts to chart the emergence of sexual consciousness out of pre-sexual companionship were probably doomed to fail anyway because of the period in which he was writing; but such brutal editing ensured that he would fail.

On their own, none of these apparently arbitrary deletions amounts to much, but *Mystery at Witchend* was in total reduced by about one third of its original length, and cumulatively the cuts had the effect of seriously diminishing one of the distinguishing features of Saville's writing, his ability to suggest the shifting dynamics of young sexual friendship in an age of total sexual reticence.

In the story of my development as a reader, Peter was the first in a long line and was to lead eventually to Elizabeth Bennet, Tess Durbeyfield, Dorothea Brooke, Ursula Brangwen, Molly Bloom and a hundred others. I suppose other readers could claim that Blyton's George or Julian did the same for them. But there is a difference of self-conscious artistic purpose. Saville was serious about the nature of series fiction; he reflected upon it and was committed to representing his characters as *developing* young people. One consequence was that, while many of his novels remained in the camping and tramping genre, the later novels in the series were love stories as well as adventure stories. The boys and girls who have been such firm friends grow up, pair off and fall in love. The friendship which the earlier stories had charted now turns to romance, as seen here:

> [Jenny] no longer felt shy. She stood before him with her hands behind her back. She smiled into his eyes and then bent her head so that he could fix the clasp and this he found difficult because his fingers were shaking. When it was done he stepped back to look at her and was suddenly sure that he had never seen such happiness in anyone's face.
>
> 'Come here, Tom,' she whispered. 'I want to thank you.'
>
> She clutched the lapels of his old dressing gown, stood on tiptoe and kissed him as he had never been kissed before, then she turned on her heels and left. Tom was still standing dazed in the middle of the room when Mrs. Ingles came back.[15]

This, with its explicit acknowledgement of sex-as-reward, is dangerously close to sentimentality. But it is also a measure of how difficult it was at that time to write about sex at all. John Rowe Townsend once took Arthur Ransome to task because the Swallows and Amazons maintained 'a sexless comradeship which does not quite accord with the facts of adolescence'.[16] But even if Ransome had wanted to write about his characters' developing sexuality, he would not have been allowed to. Such a thing was both culturally and legally out of the question. Any reader who is unaware of how problematical this matter was – even in adult fiction – before the *Lady Chatterley* trial should read Catherine Storr's serious but flawed attempt to face the issue in *Marianne and Mark* (1960),[17] in which reticence and uncertainty combined to confuse matters of sex with matters of class in a way that Saville always avoided. Any hints of the ambivalences of sex, the danger and excitement of it, and, of course, the details of its physical processes, were entirely out of the question. Saville's suggestion that sexuality and friendship might be closely allied was a responsible one – and this was as far as any writer could go. If his externally observed descriptions of attractiveness seem now to be outdated and naive, it is all that was permitted in an age of sexual denial.

There were other kinds of revision in the paperback editions. A good deal of dialogue was cut out, along with occasional descriptions of landscape, and references to other stories in the series. But what most frequently fell casualty to the editorial pencil were the authorial explanations about understanding and integrity with which Saville maintained for his young readers an absolute clarity about how his fictional characters perceived and valued each other. Passages like these, for example:

> perhaps it was because Peter had such a love and understanding for the country and all wild things, and because she was so straightforward in her dealings with everybody, that she really liked Reuben and Miranda and the shy little girl whose life she had saved.[18]

> But Jenny knew everybody, and everybody liked her and had been sorry for her when her father had gone off to the war.[19]

> [David] had known [Peter] long enough now to realise that she set a very high standard for her friends – and also for herself. She was nearly always the same, too.[20]

The paperback editions of the *Lone Pine* series were a sadly emasculated version of Saville's work. Furthermore they had fewer of Bertram Prance's excellent action pictures, and sometimes none at all. A whole generation of readers was deprived of the pleasure of the character and feel of those hardback books – with the small pine tree blocked in gold (later, red) on the covers, the inevitable foreword about the area the book was set in, and for new readers the ritualistic explanation about the Lone Pine Club and its members.

And the obligatory endpaper map.

Endpaper maps deserve a few paragraphs of their own. They are both a signal and an invitation to a special kind of reading game. I believe the first major children's book to have a pictorial endpaper was *The Secret Garden*, illustrated by Charles Robinson. It was an *art nouveau* design brilliantly linking the growth of the girl in the picture with the growth of the garden – and, of course, linking the book-design with the central themes of the novel. In the early years of the twentieth century many children's books (and the more expensive annuals) had decorated endpapers, for example the works of Mrs Ewing in the uniform edition illustrated by M.V. Wheelhouse, and all the *Doctor Dolittle* stories with endpapers designed by the author.

The practice of the decorated endpaper was adapted by Arthur Ransome for the presentation of a map covering the area associated with each story in the *Swallows and Amazons* series. Some readers never look at these maps, but for others they are an essential aspect of the particular discourse associated with camping and tramping stories. They connect each story with a specific place, often a real one, and signal the author's allegiance to the unique character (and characters) of the landscape chosen for the story.

Ransome's endpaper maps were carefully designed to indicate the specific character of each of the novels. The first had been designed by Steven Spurrier in a rather stylised and fussy manner, but the other eleven were all presented as if drawn by the characters themselves – simpler, clearer and uncluttered picture-maps of a landscape or seascape. In most, the places are renamed in the imagined landscape of the children's make-believe, with Rio, Spitzbergen and the River Amazon. But in his East Anglian stories, exploration of a real area is supported by real maps. Not infrequently they associate the fiction with journeys, and they are particularly effective in quest stories, sailing adventures and tales of exploration, with routes indicated by dotted lines, often printed in salmon pink. The map of the North Sea for *We Didn't Mean to Go to Sea* provides an uncompromising sense of the enormity of the children's unintended sailing trip to Holland, whereas the map of the Atlantic for *Peter Duck* suggests its fantastic nature, with pictorial representations of a dolphin, a whale and a waterspout, all playfully out of proportion. Often

Ransome's maps provide a shorthand version of the story in a shape dictated by geography rather than narrative sequence: journeys, shown in pink or red, often distinguish between an inward and an outward route, together with references to key events: 'Here they rescued a kitten and met Dutch fishing boats',[21] or 'Here Nancy and Peggy got ashore'[22] – inviting the reader to take part in a sophisticated extension to the usual reading games and to read the text with some incomplete fore-knowledge provided by the map.

Game is the appropriate word, for Ransome's endpaper maps also express a kind of writerly *jouissance*. In the case of *Missee Lee*, one of the characters speaks directly to the reader in an insert:

> BASED ON THE MAP WE FOUND AND ON WHAT WE SAW. SOME OF IT WE HAD TO GUESS AT. WE NEVER HAD A CHANCE TO DO A PROPER SURVEY.

> NOTE – WE ARE NOT PUTTING IN THE LAT. AND LONG. BECAUSE IF THE GOVERNMENT KNEW IT MIGHT SEND GUNBOATS AND PEOPLE TO SHOOT MISS LEE OR EVEN PUT HER IN PRISON BECAUSE OF WHAT SHE IS DOING. THIS WOULD BE VERY UNFAIR AS SHE IS ONLY DOING IT BECAUSE OF HER DUTY TO HER ANCESTORS.

> NANCY BLACKETT (CAPT.)
> WE HAVE PUT IN JUNKS INSTEAD.[23]

Malcolm Saville's maps are altogether simpler and much more serious, with usually an unpretentious explanation in a cartouche:

> David Morton drew this map of Jenny's Neglected Mountain and the district around after the adventure.
> It was difficult to get everything in.[24]

They are businesslike black-and-white pictorial sketch-maps, emphasising mountains, roads, railway lines and key buildings in the narrative. Their role is explanatory. His narratives involve different groups of children going on separate journeys, their paths occasionally converging or failing to converge in ways that are crucial to the plot. Accuracy is therefore essential. As a young reader, I always felt I had to check the maps for accuracy: if the text refers to a public house just past the second turning on the left, I would expect to find the map was consistent. It always was. These maps help the reader to visualise a landscape of roads, tracks and footpaths, and grasp the ways in which their geographical layout holds the plot together. They are an aid to 'seeing', an extension to the author's descriptive power.

Endpaper maps are always richly suggestive of journeys, discoveries and places, and they remained part of the accessories of camping and tramping fiction for three decades, up to the point when Alan Garner used them in *The Weirdstone of Brisingamen* (1960) and *The Moon of Gomrath* (1963), and Tolkien used elaborate fold-out maps in the three volumes of *The Lord of the Rings*. It is no coincidence that Enid Blyton did not make use of endpaper maps, for her landscapes are general and unlocated. Saville, on the other hand, set his stories in real places in Shropshire, Romney Marsh, Dartmoor, London, the North Riding of Yorkshire and the East Anglian coast.

Saville's work has not been judged kindly by the critics. It has been said that he deals in outdated gender stereotypes and his prose is flabby. But such judgements are mostly based on the revised editions – the Blytonised versions – and it is hard not to agree with one of my students who believed that the best features of Saville's work were the most dispensable, and that the heavily edited versions were responsible for his poor critical reputation.

Yet it is not as simple as that. He was a far better writer than Enid Blyton, more serious about his work and more concerned to make an intelligent provision for children. But he was not a great writer, nor an original one, and his good authorial intentions were not able to conceal the fact that series fiction had been proceeding along a blind alley. He did avoid to a great extent the formulaic and repetitive plots which were the hallmark of Blyton's work, but he shared with her the same fundamental aesthetic. It was an aesthetic based on a number of assumptions: that children's fiction should be direct and open in structure and style; that readers' imaginations could be quickened by clarity of description; and that fictional richness could be made available in the explicitly literal.

This aesthetic is founded on a belief in the imaginative innocence of children and the social benevolence of the adult world. Its limitation is always that it is tempted to be content with surfaces, to show only what can be visually conjured by words, or by what the author deliberately points out. It presupposes young readers without much curiosity or scepticism, and a social and psychological order without doubts, without ambivalences, and – above all – *without secrets*. The world represented by Enid Blyton and Malcolm Saville is composed of surfaces which deny inner structures and unacknowledged hierarchies. Their writing is not equipped to deal with obliquities and moral ambiguity; it cannot represent the dark places in the individual psyche or in society. It speaks in its confident prose to readers assumed to be confident in their cultural entitlement. What you see is all there is, it seems to say to the reader; good characters are reliably and consistently good, and established institutions are entirely dependable; so there is no need for you to be concerned with anything else.

But in 1955, when the *Lone Pine* series had reached its eighth title and the *Famous Five* its fourteenth, a young author published a book which was moving in an entirely different direction and worked on a different aesthetic. William Mayne is not usually thought of as a series-writer – though he was in the 1960s and 70s frequently named in opposition to Enid Blyton in debates about literary excellence. Mayne did write one series, a quartet of novels, set in the choir school of an English cathedral. *A Swarm in May* established Mayne's reputation as an exciting and innovative writer for children. It was followed by *Choristers' Cake* (1956), *Cathedral Wednesday* (1960) and *Words and Music* (1963).

This sequence is distinguished from other fiction of the period by Mayne's extraordinary ability to capture the physicality of place intimately perceived from *within* a child's sensual understanding. This account of a choirboy waking up in winter is an example:

> Andrew found his breath on the windows when he got up. There was sunshine on the cathedral, splashed on the South side, so that there were columns of shadow up the tower. Andrew looked out of the window at it, then closed the window against the air, and put more breath on the pane, close and hot, to clear a peephole on to the city.[25]

'Description' does not quite do justice to this kind of writing, with its intimate shifts of perspective and distance. Mayne was not content to provide simply a faithful record of what can be observed; he demonstrated a unique ability to concentrate in a few apparently easy sentences the complex connections between a boy's mental life and his physical movements. In these opening sentences from *Cathedral Wednesday*, many different narrative things are happening simultaneously in the deceptively simple words:

> Andrew Young overtook a bus and raced down the London Road. The thing he had in mind was to get to the level-crossing before the gates were closed for the four-fifteen train from the North; but he was too late, and the gates began to swing as he

came near. He put his left foot down to the ground and let the bicycle droop whilst he felt in his pocket for the book with the engine-numbers in. The engine was almost certain to be one of the Ashford tankers; but – sometimes – Stanhope had said so – a Midland engine did the whole journey.[26]

Like his contemporary, Alan Garner, Mayne provided few narrative explanations. The choir school novels, despite their distinctive cathedral background, refer to a culture of grammar schools and boarding schools familiar to many young readers in the 1950s and 60s. They make full use of the shared idiom of a closed community, with numerous jokes requiring a knowledge of music, the Bible, or Latin ('knottus grannius fecit'). The provision for the determined reader is a dynamic sense of private and communal experience, often muddled, fleetingly grasped, and only partly understood by the young characters themselves. The shock of Mayne's writing to a reading-culture based on *explanatory* fiction can hardly be exaggerated.

This is an aesthetic which values the *inwardness* of personal experience and is absorbed by the *implicit* and perhaps dubious bonds which uphold the social and historical structures of the choir school. The way these four novels are preoccupied with the mysterious structure and practical maintenance of the great cathedral – in constant need of being patched up – resembles the way they are interested in the social and individual construction of a schoolboy's sense of himself. Mayne's aesthetic tries to do justice to fleeting, fragmentary and half-understood experience. Above all, it is an aesthetic which offers readers new challenges and leaves them gaps to fill and puzzles to work out. Any similarities between Saville – even at his best – and Mayne are superficial: each is in the most fundamental way opposite to the other, the one committed to an absolute and simplified surface clarity, the other to a permeable suggestion of infinite depths and provisional insights.

In 1950 another series had begun with the publication of *The Lion, the Witch and the Wardrobe*. This series became hugely popular all over the world, enjoying cult status in the USA at one period. However, for all its inventiveness, its brilliant story-telling and its engaging touches of fantasy and magic, its aesthetic was not as radically new as Mayne's.

Lewis is an extraordinary story-teller and these seven linked novels constitute a uniquely complex and rich experience for the young reader. To have created a fantasy universe – with not just a geography of its own but an entire cosmos, and with constantly evocative suggestions of a spiritual reality too – is an astonishing myth-making achievement.

But Lewis is still essentially a 'describer', often combining a Chaucerian freshness with a filmic sense of Technicolor and depth.

> ... the newly risen sun was at their backs and, of course, everything looks nicer when the light is behind you. It was a wonderful ride. The big snowy mountains rose above them in every direction. The valleys, far beneath them, were so green, and all the streams which tumbled down from the glaciers into the main river were so blue, that it was like flying over gigantic pieces of jewellery.[27]

For Lewis, writing is *showing*, and reading is *seeing*. It is the principle of the Narnia books that seeing precedes understanding. His artistic method was well served by his illustrator; Pauline Baynes' pictures have a lovely miniaturist and closely focused purity of design, like looking through the wrong end of a telescope and somehow seeing more clearly. Lewis provides for young inexperienced imaginations, tutoring them and leading them into metaphor and simile. You can see it happening in this passage.

> Have you ever had a gallop on a horse? Think of that; and then take away the heavy noise of the hoofs and the jingle of the bits and imagine instead the almost noiseless padding of the great paws. Then imagine instead of the black or grey or chestnut back of the horse the soft roughness of golden fur, and the mane flying back in the wind. And then imagine you are going about twice as fast as the fastest racehorse. But this is a mount that doesn't need to be guided and never grows tired. He rushes on and on, never missing his footing.[28]

We can sense Lewis' authorial concern for his reader in a passage like this:

> You may have been in a room in which there was a large window that looked out on a lovely bay of the sea or a green valley that wound away among mountains. And in the wall of that room opposite the window there may have been a looking glass. And as you turned away from the window you suddenly caught sight of that sea or that valley, all over again, in the looking glass. And the sea in the mirror, or the valley in the mirror, were

in one sense just the same as the real ones: yet at the same time they were somehow different – deeper, more wonderful, more like places in a story: in a story you have never heard but very much want to know. The difference between the old Narnia and the new Narnia was like that. The new one was a deeper country: every rock and flower and blade of grass looked as if it meant more. I can't describe it any better than that . . .[29]

Lewis' tactic here is not simply to tell how it is, but to make readers work by opening their imaginative eyes to the possibilities of language, then retiring modestly at the end of the paragraph, trusting that the mind and the senses of the young reader will have been enkindled.

Readers are thus welcomed into the story and encouraged – often with quite homely similes – to work their own cinematic magic. That repeated 'you' works like a talismanic invitation, tactfully handing over imaginative power so that even inexperienced readers can see the impossible and 'vision' the transcendental. It happens in the next example, the writing easily and comfortably leading the reader into the astonishing conceptual and poetic climax of 'climbing up light itself'.

But before Jill had time to notice these things fully, she was going up the Waterfall herself. It was the sort of thing that would have been quite impossible in our world. Even if you hadn't been drowned, you would have been smashed to pieces by the terrible weight of water against the countless jags of rock. But in that world you could do it. You went on, up and up, with all kinds of reflected lights flashing at you from the water and all manner of coloured stones flashing through it, till it seemed as if you were climbing up light itself . . .[30]

However, in spite of its vast imaginative generousness, the Narnian universe derives from the closed world of the prep-school and fear of what lies beyond its walls. And its aesthetic is the old conservative one – though practised by a far greater writer than Blyton and Saville.

In one respect, though, Lewis pointed the way forward. The next great fiction series were all fantasies.

Part III
Fantasy

7   *The Borrowers*
Brief encounters and a little air

Since *Gulliver's Travels*, the Lilliputian narrative idea has proved a seductive one. It is rich with ironies of perspective, remembered impulses that have to do with childhood make-believe, and the excitement and satisfaction of small clever creatures outwitting big ones. To any child who has played with toy cars, trucks, dolls'-houses, action men and model railways – or who has made bottle-tops, matchboxes and thimbles into tiny objects of furniture – the imaginative and beguiling world of *The Borrowers* must seem the very essence of pretending itself, transformed into an abiding narrative and toughened by an uncompromising naturalism.

But precisely because of the potency of these narratives of perspective and the concrete visual authenticity of Mary Norton's descriptions, most adults commenting on *The Borrowers* seem incapable of seeing beyond this immediate appeal. Marcus Crouch, for example, ends his perceptive account of the first in the series by referring to 'this marvellous story of Pod, Homily and Arrietty and of the lovely home they made under the floorboards'.[1] It seems to be the misfortune of this series that the surface story of a tiny race of people who make an enchanting miniature world for themselves under the floorboards of houses is so often seen to be the fictional total, an imaginative tally which few commentators get beyond. Since Mary Norton is such a seductive story-teller, this is hardly surprising.

This tendency towards minimalist readings afflicts the whole of children's fiction. And it is a genuine difficulty. The fact that children's writers are highly skilled story-tellers, and that children themselves seem to be possessed by a readerly lust to 'find out what happens', are powerful factors seducing adults into the belief that any other way of approaching children's fiction is inappropriate. But minimalist approaches to children's reading inevitably have a diminishing effect, for they ignore the personal emotional forces moving beneath the narrative surface and providing the energy of language which keeps the reader reading.

A minimalist approach to *The Borrowers* series is capable only of seeing a superficially cheerful and comic story about survival, tenacity and courage. It *is* undoubtedly such a story; but Mary Norton simultaneously gives her young readers a sober world-view of humanity doomed to loneliness and disappointment. Almost certainly, the readerly desire which impels a young reader from beginning to end of this series finds its gratification and delight in the detailed and painstaking resourcefulness of the Borrowers and in the way they survive such terrible dangers. Mary Norton has an extraordinary ability to keep this readerly lust simultaneously aroused and satisfied. And yet her characterisation in the series amounts to a melancholy representation of *loneliness and disappointment*. I believe that this aspect – this sad emotional colouring of the fiction – enhances the desires of the impassioned reader and provides its own deep gratification. What I want to show in this chapter is that *The Borrowers* is a narrative representation of a psychological world of melancholy and disappointed hopes, an elegiac story of loss of hope, a chronicle of failed intimacies and transitory fulfilments of deeply felt longing.

Arrietty gives the series its unity, and young readers might like to know that her name, like everything the Borrowers possess, is both borrowed and adapted. An arrietta is a small aria, or a little air, and that Arrietty should be named after a diminutive melody is particularly appropriate. She is a romantic, an archetypal adolescent girl with a deeply held belief that beyond the limiting constraints of her parents' understanding is a bigger and more generous imaginative world in which people lovingly and trustingly make contact with each other. Poor Arrietty! – it doesn't seem much to ask of life.

Arrietty's very first utterance is a question: what happened to Eggletina? – and immediately after that we are told that she gazes longingly out of a tiny brick grating to where she can see blooming crocuses and blossom drifting from an unseen tree.[2] In just a few lines readers are given two of the three essential facts about her: she wants to *know* and she wants to *escape* – 'to be out of doors . . . to lie in the sun . . . to run in the grass . . . to swing on twigs like the birds do . . . to suck honey . . .'[3] But desire runs directly into prohibition – and is there a child (or, indeed, an adult) anywhere in the world who does not understand the centrality of that conflict? The most serious of all the Borrowers' taboos is being 'seen' by 'human beans'. At one level, this is comical and has to do with the survival of a small parasitic race dependent on secrecy. But the language of solemnity associated with this powerful taboo invites into play the experience of all young readers who have unwittingly invoked the moral disapproval of grown-ups in which they sense a resonance they cannot quite understand.

Pod and Homily give her a long and serious talking-to, in which she learns to her dismay that the many barriers protecting their underground home are not there, as she thought, to keep out cats and rats, but to *keep her in*. 'Couldn't we emigrate?' she says to her scandalised parents.

> Arrietty raised her tear-streaked face. 'Late or early, what's the difference?' she cried. 'Oh, I know papa is a wonderful bor-rower. I know we've managed to stay when all the others have gone. But what has it done for us, in the end? I don't think it's so clever to live on alone, for ever and ever, in a great, big, half-empty house; under the floor, with no one to talk to, no one to play with, nothing to see but dust and passages, no light but candlelight and firelight and what comes through the cracks.'[4]

That reference to candlelight and firelight begins a pattern of images of darkness and radiance, enclosure and spaciousness, which is sustained through the entire series. By the end of Chapter 6 we know a good deal about Arrietty – her passion, her reckless outspokenness, her loving, forgiving and generous nature, and the 'dreamy, secret something about her lowered face'.[5] We also know that she can read, and can therefore imaginatively travel beyond the limited pragmatic world of her semi-literate parents. At the end of that chapter, Arrietty, half dozing, gazes up at the ceiling made for her by Pod out of an old cigar box.

> 'FLOR DE HAVANA,' proclaimed the banners proudly. 'Garantizados ... Superiores . . . Non Plus Ultra . . .' and the lovely gauzy ladies blew their trumpets, silently, triumphantly, on soundless notes of glee . . .[6]

This is brilliant writing, the melodic language of evocation masquerading as the language of statement, delicately suggesting the appeal of strange foreign words and a promise of some kind of heraldic celebration of a mysterious or secret happiness. Ending the chapter on that note, with the three dots, suggests promise, a desire waiting to be fulfilled. Not many private readers will have noticed those dots

– but, if asked, not many would be unable, however stumblingly, to explain why they are there.

That carefully composed chapter-ending cadence is a perfect illustration of the way in which good writing for children habitually masks the complexity of its effects.

Arrietty's yearning for an expansion of her limited world is reflected in the titles, which indicate a progressive movement outwards – afield, afloat, aloft. It also leads to moments of descriptive lyricism when Mary Norton uses words of radiance and colour to suggest Arrietty's delight as she escapes for the first time from the darkness under the floorboards.

> As she scrambled past the jagged edges of the hole she had a sudden blinding glimpse of molten gold: it was spring sunshine on the pale stones of the hall floor . . . She saw the gleaming golden stone floor of the hall stretching away into distance; she saw the edges of rugs, like richly coloured islands in a molten sea, and she saw, in a glory of sunlight – like a dreamed-of gateway to fairyland – the open front door. Beyond she saw grass and, against the clear, bright sky, a waving frond of green.[7]

At first I thought this kind of celebratory writing was Wordsworthian, but I have come to think that Arrietty's joy in the beauty of transfigured colour owes as much to Gertrude Jekyll and Clarice Cliff as it does to the poet's Romantic conception of childhood. Arrietty's emergence into the sunlight is the realisation of everything she had imagined, and almost always combines a closely focused myopic observation of natural detail with a rapturous response to radiance and colour.

> Oh, glory! Oh, joy! Oh, freedom! The sunlight, the grasses, the soft, moving air and half-way up the bank, where it curved around the corner, a flowering cherry-tree! Below it on the path lay a stain of pinkish petals and at the tree's foot, pale as butter, a nest of primroses.[8]

And in one explicit statement from *The Borrowers Afield* Mary Norton links desire, imagination and an almost sanctified achievement:

> It was a glorious day, sun-lit and rain-washed – the earth breathing out its scents. 'This,' Arrietty thought, 'is what I have longed for; what I have imagined; what I knew existed – what I knew we'd have!'

She pushed through the grasses and soft drops fell on her benignly, warmed by the sun.[9]

Arrietty is transfixed.

What a world – mile upon mile, thing after thing, layer upon layer of unimagined richness – and she might never have seen it! She might have lived and died as so many of her relations had done, in dusty twilight – hidden behind a wainscot.[10]

Behind this rhapsodic celebration of wonder there probably lies Mary Norton's memory of her own childhood, half-blind and with inappropriate spectacles – and the heady and exciting discovery of clearly viewed distances when her condition was at last addressed. At first the writing focuses on tiny details:

a glorious bank, it was, filled with roots; with grasses; with violet leaves and with pale scarlet pimpernel and, here and there, a globe of deeper crimson – wild strawberries!

Then the description moves outwards:

She saw in the distance the lonely group of trees: they still seemed to float on a grassy ocean. She thought of her mother's fear of open spaces. 'But I could cross this field,' she thought, 'I could go anywhere . . .'[11]

Yet almost at once she is asking herself: Does enterprise always meet with disaster? This whole chapter is a glowing account of delighted exploratory play in a world of expanding possibilities. She pauses to observe the tiny creatures of this outdoor world, refreshes herself with a wild strawberry, climbs delightedly to the top of a hedge where there is an abandoned birds'-nest, and is 'suddenly aware of her absolute safety'. Descending again to the ground is 'almost like surf-riding', and she allows the last bough to drop her lightly on the grass of the bank 'with a graceful elastic shiver'.[12]

But this chapter of Rousseauistic rapture, with its hints of a divinely protected world, ends on a sombre note, for where Arrietty sees endless possibilities, her father sees only danger.

'It's everywhere,' he said, after a moment. 'Before and Behind, Above and Below'[13]

– the capitals indicating that Pod's remark refers generally to the Nature of Existence, not specifically to the sparrow-hawk that happens at that moment to be above them in the sky.

Arrietty's longing for freedom and space is related to her other great wickedness, the longing to make contact with human beings. And a consideration of her friendships takes us directly to the source of the melancholy that underlies these five stories. Friendship is the clue to the *The Borrowers'* psychological world. Nothing – not her parents' anger, or the fact that she invariably leads the whole family into disaster and almost death – can stop Arrietty from finding out lonely human beings and becoming friends with them, sharing stories with them, talking philosophy with them. Arrietty's three desires – for freedom, light and friendship – are connected to one another, as she herself realises.

> 'I must see that boy,' Arrietty was thinking – staring blindly into the fire. 'I must hear what happened . . . I don't want us to die out. I don't want to be the last Borrower. I don't want' – and here Arrietty dropped her face on to her knees – 'to live for ever and ever like this . . . in the dark . . . under the floor . . .'[14]

This desire is, at several allegorical removes, sexual – an uncontrollable human urge to do what her appalled parents see as wicked.

> 'She was in the night-nursery,' said Pod quietly, 'talking to that boy.'
>
> Homily moved forwards, her hands clasped tremblingly against her apron, her startled eyes flicking swiftly to and fro. 'Oh, no –' she breathed.
>
> Pod sat down. He ran a tired hand over his eyes and forehead; his face looked heavy like a piece of dough. 'Now what?' he said.
>
> Homily stood quite still; bowed she stood over her clasped hands and stared at Arrietty. 'Oh, you never –' she whispered.[15]

Afterwards, Arrietty is always repentant and full of sincere apologies. Until the next temptation.

In the conversations between Arrietty and the Boy in the first of the series, there are many comic effects arising from her belief that human beings are dying out, that their role is to provide for the survival of Borrowers, and that borrowing is different from stealing. But the overriding impression is one not of comedy but of a serious developing friendship. Arrietty reads to the Boy, standing at his shoulder and telling him when to turn the pages.

She grew to know [his] ear quite well, with its curves and shadows and sunlit pinks and golds. Sometimes, as she grew bolder, she would lean against his shoulder. He was very still while she read to him and always grateful. What worlds they would explore together . . .[16]

But they explore no worlds. Her friendship with the Boy leads to disaster, and the Borrowers are threatened with poison gas, or being hunted out with a ferret. The horrors of extermination are vividly and dramatically represented by Mary Norton, and the reader is not even allowed to know for certain if the Borrowers have in fact escaped. Reviewers who belong to the 'delightful miniature world' school simply cannot have read this grim and equivocal ending. Even then, Arrietty does not learn her lesson. At the end of the next novel in the sequence, *The Borrowers Afield*, after another series of dangers, the Borrowers are rescued by another boy, young Tom Goodenough, and taken to his cottage to live in the lath-and-plaster wall with Lupy and Hendreary. Again, Arrietty's temptation comes upon her and, while the others are settling down – unable to control herself – she climbs down the inside of the wall and out into the candle-lit kitchen. The novel ends like this:

A face looked back at her, candle-lit and drowsed with sleep, below its thatch of hair. There was a long silence. At last the boy's lips curled softly into a smile – and very young he looked after sleeping, very harmless. The arm on which he had rested his head lay loosely on the table and Arrietty, from where she stood, had seen his fingers relax. A clock was ticking somewhere above her head; the candle flame rose, still and steady, lighting the peaceful room; the coals gave a gentle shudder as they settled in the grate.

'Hallo,' said Arrietty.
'Hallo,' said young Tom.[17]

It is a narratorially audacious ending, a closure which is at the same time an opening. At one level, it makes possible a sequel; but at another it has to do with temptation and desire, Arrietty's old desperate longing to find like-minded companions in a world full of unsympathetic people who do not share her needs or understand her feelings. And so Mary Norton ends the novel with a tiny girl and a huge boy – fated always to be divided – hopefully saying Hallo to each other.

In *The Borrowers Afield*, Mary Norton provides a surface adventure story of danger, risk, and temporary periods of rest and sanctuary, while at a deeper level the allegory of adolescence continues to explore the widening of Arrietty's cultural landscape. The tiny Borrowers are like pioneers discovering a huge new landscape – with frogs, snakes, wild strawberries, torrential rain. But there is one discovery she had not imagined – Spiller, an unknown Borrower, male, young, independent, slightly mysterious, resourceful and unruffled. Throughout the rest of the series Spiller repeatedly comes to their rescue and provides Arrietty with an ideal of the life she longs for – an outdoor life subject to no rules, free and mysterious, yet helpful and stalwart.

It is a matter of some significance – in fact, it seems to me to be the central determining factor in a reading of the series – that nowhere is there a friendship which endures. Brief periods of intimacy are repeatedly represented as seductive, precious and necessary, but always short-lived. Kate, the human girl who is the listener to the first of the stories is herself a lonely child, a dreamer, and companion to a lonely old lady, 'a wild, untidy, self-willed little girl who stared with angry eyes and was said to crunch her teeth'.[18] Kate is very like Arrietty, and in *The Borrowers Afield* she forms a brief and hurried friendship with old Tom Goodenough. It is a desperate and passionate relationship with a lonely old man who may just have time to tell her his account of the Borrowers before he is turned out of his cottage despite a promise that he would have it for life. Promises are not reliable in Mary Norton's imaginative world of stories; nor are the stories themselves. She tantalises her readers by constantly reminding them of the evocative unreliability of story-telling and by linking this with the unreliability of friendships. In this series, friendship *is* story-telling – and both are short-lived. Mary Norton wraps up in layers of mystery the origin of *The Borrowers*: the narrator is Kate (though that is not her proper name), who heard the tale from Mrs May, who heard it many years ago from her fanciful young brother, who might have made it up. In *The Borrowers Afield*, the first four chapters are devoted to establishing a dubious authenticity for the tale, and in *The Borrowers Afloat* the mystery of the telling is intensified as the source – Tom Goodenough – is described as 'the biggest liar in five counties'. So the 'story' of the entire series is an acting out of brief friendly contact, treasured but with uncertain status – and always ultimately lost.

All aspiration towards intimacy is doomed to collapse back on itself, or to lead to danger, destruction and disappointment. Perhaps

Mary Norton's most successful representation of this is the character of Miss Menzies, who first appears in *The Borrowers Aloft* as the lonely spinster helping Mr Potts with his model village – Miss Menzies, 'who believed in fairies'[19] and had seen the Borrowers in one of the miniature houses.

> And Miss Menzies spoke in such a high, strange, fanciful voice – using the oddest words and most fly-away expressions; sometimes, to [Mr Potts'] dismay, she would even recite poetry. He did not dislike her, far from it; he liked to have her about, because in her strange, leggy, loping way she always seemed girlishly happy, and her prattle, like canary song, kept him cheerful . . . Quick as a flash, she was; gay as a lark and steady as a rock . . .
>
> He knew she was not young, but when she sat beside him on the rough grass, clasping her thin wrists about her bent knees, swaying back and forth, her closed eyes raised to the sun and chattering nineteen to the dozen, she seemed to Mr Potts like some kind of overgrown schoolgirl. And sweet eyes she had too, when they were open – that he would say – for such a long, bony face: shy eyes which slid away when you looked too long at them – more like violets, he'd say her eyes were, than forget-me-nots. They were shining now and so were the knuckles of her long fingers clasped too tightly about her knees . . .[20]

We know nothing yet of Miss Menzies' personal background, but we know that her *imaginative* relatives are those other lonely longing girls, Arrietty and Kate – which is probably what Margery Fisher had in mind when she said: 'The Borrowers are not miniature humans; they are *reminders* of what humans are like.'[21] Poor Miss Menzies, who spends hours talking to Mr Potts without a word she says being heard or understood, could be said to exemplify one of Mary Norton's central preoccupations – loneliness, the desire for understanding and the failure to find it. But Miss Menzies is granted a brief period of happiness during which she watches and provides for the Borrowers. The writing is unequivocal here:

> With clasped knees, she sat smiling into space.
> 'I love them, you see,' she said softly.[22]

In the later books of the series, Mary Norton seems to have grown as interested in the human characters as in the Borrowers themselves and there is a great authorial compassion for the brave Miss Menzies.

'Not that I'm lonely, of course. My days' – Miss Menzies' eyes
became over-bright suddenly and the gay voice hurried a little –
'are *far* too full ever to be lonely. I've so many interests, you see.
I keep up with things. And I have my old dog and the two little
birds . . .'[23]

Miss Menzies' and Arrietty's needs are neatly brought together in the
narrative. As the human woman watches them, Pod reminds Arrietty
of the importance of being still. But Arrietty snaps back:

'Yes, of course I understand – you've told me often enough.
Stillness, stillness, quiet, quiet, creep, creep, crawl, crawl . . . What's
the good of being alive?'[24]

This is the old theme of restriction and limited vision. Of course, she
disobeys her father – again – and begins to talk to Miss Menzies.
And it comes as no surprise to the reader to learn that there had once
been a man in Miss Menzies' life.

'He married a girl called Mary Chumley-Gore,' said Miss
Menzies. 'She had very thick ankles.'
'Oh . . . !' exclaimed Arrietty.
'Why do you say "Oh" in that voice?'
'I thought he might have married you!'
Miss Menzies smiled and looked down at her hands. 'So did I,'
she said quietly.[25]

This new friendship is doomed too. The Borrowers are stolen and
imprisoned in an attic by a greedy pair of human beings who intend
to show them for money. And *The Borrowers Aloft* turns into an
adventure story.

We are given a date, 1911, and we know that Arrietty is now
almost seventeen. During the balloon flight, she announces her intention of marrying Spiller, an idea which scandalises Homily because
the mysterious Spiller is always on the move and none too clean. 'He
likes the out-of-doors, you see, and I like it too', Arrietty explains.
And then Arrietty's great longing is explicitly linked with Miss
Menzies' unhappiness.

'You see,' Arrietty went on quietly (she had been thinking of her
talks with Miss Menzies and of those blue eyes full of tears),
'[Spiller's] so shy and he goes about so much, he might never

think of asking me. And one day he might get tired of being lonely and marry some' – Arrietty hesitated – 'some *terribly nice* kind of borrower with very fat legs . . .'[26]

Mary Norton – in what for more than twenty years was regarded as the final story of a quartet – seems to have been preparing the reader for something like a routinely happy ending. But the melancholy conviction that all human intercourse ends in disappointment almost got the better of her. Arrietty has to confess that she has yet again made contact with a human being, she feels left out and hurt by her family, and – significantly – she has grown out of her clothes.

'I just don't know what any of you do want,' she exclaimed unhappily. 'I thought you might be pleased or proud of me or something. Mother's always longed for a house like this!' and fumbling at the latch, she opened the door, and ran out into the moonlight.[27]

There follows a strange and intense conversation in which Pod instructs Arrietty about the importance of family: 'say, one day, you had a little place of your own. A little family maybe – supposing, like, you'd picked a good borrower.'[28] Arrietty is thankful she is standing with her back to Spiller. If this *was* intended to round off the whole series, its mixture of a happiness promised and sorrow confirmed is characteristic – for in the closing pages Arrietty is made to promise that she will never again speak to a 'human bean'. She does, bursting into tears – and back into the imaginative arena comes the idea of Miss Menzies.

'Now I've promised,' gasped Arrietty, 'there'll be no one to tell her. She'll never know we escaped . . . She'll never know we came back. She'll never know anything. All her life she'll be wondering. And lying awake in the nights . . .'[29]

Then, astonishingly, Spiller promises to break the habits of a lifetime and tell Miss Menzies himself; Arrietty appreciates the significance of the promise; and Homily irritably mutters that she really has got to try and like him, presumably because she expects him to become her son-in-law.

So the original *Borrowers* quartet ends on a note of ambiguous hope: perhaps, it almost promises, Arrietty will get her heart's desire, a life of love and freedom, possibly with Spiller. But twenty years later *The Borrowers Avenged* was published – and added even more layers of melancholy ambiguity. The central authorial interest now seems to be the life of the village church. The daily activities associated with it – and the half-empty old rectory to which the Borrowers escape – are described with a gentle nostalgic affection and at more length than some young readers might like. The long-lost Lupy and Hendreary now live in a disused harmonium in the vestry, and several pages are devoted to Arrietty's wondering discovery of the church interior. The final climax of the story is set within the floral decoration of the church for Easter. Mary Norton seems to have become less interested in the Borrowers than she is in the village, the eccentricities of its people, and the modest loveliness of its church.

If we look at the end of the series, we see at once how it challenges conventional expectations about how a children's narrative should end. The Borrowers have at last, after several years of homelessness and wandering, found a secure home for themselves, and Pod and Homily are more than content with their new refuge in the old rectory. But what about Arrietty? Her new home is under a window-seat, with a grating that opens out to the sunshine – an important symbol for her. And yet the final chapter leaves her in some ways even worse off than she was at the beginning: she has had to make a solemn promise never again to speak to a human being. 'Would anyone, ever, begin to understand . . . ?'[30] says the tearful Arrietty, thinking of her beloved Miss Menzies whom she is forbidden ever to speak to again. Even her new friend – a Borrower-poet called Peregrine – is impatient with her interest in human beings and speaks 'sharply' to her about it. Arrietty has promised her father 'very gravely and sacredly' never to speak to any human being again, not in her whole life.

> Arrietty put her head down on her knees and burst into tears . . . They watched her helplessly: the little shoulders shaking with the sobs she tried to quench against her already damp pinafore.[31]

Arrietty's sustaining dreams of a radiant future are dimmed, if not entirely extinguished. She angrily rebukes Spiller for not keeping his promise, and he walks out of the narrative with his face set, throwing her a fierce glance which 'was almost one of loathing'.[32] Then Peregrine reprimands her, gives her a tiny egg – 'creamy pale with russet freckles' – and a small lecture about the significance of Easter.

> 'I only wanted [Miss Menzies] to know we were *safe* . . .'
> 'Are we?' he said gently. 'Are we? Ever?'[33]

– which reminds us of Pod's remark in an earlier novel that danger is 'Before and Behind, Above and Below'. Both comments suggest a wider and possibly a religious application.

We are not told what happens to Spiller; nor whether Arrietty will marry Peregrine, the crippled poet who is allowed to have the last word. The loose ends of the narrative are not tied up and there is no closure, just a distancing shift of perspective and a final elegiac sentence referring affectionately to 'the ladies who come on Wednesdays and Fridays to do the flowers in the church'.

What kind of ending is this? It seems to place human longing and failure within the reassuring practices of the Anglican Church. It is certainly *not* the neat and tidily cheerful closure of homecoming or triumph that many adults think is one of the defining characteristics of children's fiction.

It has been my aim in this chapter to demonstrate how much more there is to *The Borrowers* than a charming adventure story about a tiny race of people who make lovely little homes for themselves. In fact, though, all I have done is to mine one particular seam, the desires and disappointments of Arrietty, Kate and Miss Menzies.

However, it is possible to approach the novel from many different directions. A quite different approach might have examined the dynamics – and comedy – of the family comprising Pod, Homily and Arrietty, and the rivalry and snobbishness of their relationships with other Borrowers. For alongside the insecurities of desire exemplified by the frustrations of Arrietty, Kate and Miss Menzies, Mary Norton represents the family as the only safe unit, the only social group that can remain true to itself and collaboratively ensure its own continuity. However, its nature is restrictive and conservative, and its survival is always threatened by time and change, as the repeated reminders of Pod's increasing age and weariness demonstrate. And in any case the family's only commitment is to the practical pursuit of the needs for survival in a life devoid of hope of imaginative expansion.

But what kind of family is this? There is a good deal of social comedy and realism in the series, especially in the character of Homily. A working-class mother who pronounces parquet 'parkett', she is prickly, proud, ignorant and brave. Diana Stanley's illustrations indicate a bony graceless figure, with spiky hair. The spirit of Eve Garnett's *The Family from One End Street* (1937) is never very far away. Arrietty is represented as a recognisably rebellious and disruptive teenager chafing at restrictions and 'educated' beyond the understanding of her parents – a dilemma recognisable to thousands of young grammar-school readers in the forties, fifties and sixties, and a feature of this country's working-class domestic life since the beginning of compulsory state education. As Hardy had said of Tess in 1891, between her and her mother 'there was a gap of two hundred years as ordinarily understood. When they were together the Jacobean and the Victorian ages were juxtaposed.'[34]

Or one might equally well explore the view that *The Borrowers* is an allegory that leads the reader ultimately to the certainties of the Anglican Church; or a deliberation upon the dynamics of possessions, ownership and theft.

Power and powerlessness lie at the heart of the series, and it would be equally appropriate to examine the assumptions implicit in an extended narrative which represents its most ambitious and intelligent protagonist as a girl repeatedly rebuked and restrained by men. It is interesting to note that the series privileges masculine inventiveness, improvising and 'making-do' while frustrating Arrietty's longing for wider intellectual horizons. However, feminist readers might take comfort from the fact that the family's escape by balloon – a powerfully appropriate symbol of both flight and aspiration – is Arrietty's idea and is made possible only because she can read.

> One day Arrietty came beside [Pod] as he sat there, dully thinking, in the corner of the box. She took his hand. 'I have an idea,' she said.
>
> He made an effort to smile and gently squeezed her hand. 'There isn't anything,' he said; 'we've got to face it, lass.'
>
> 'But there is something, 'Arrietty persisted. 'Do listen, Papa. I've thought of the very thing!'
>
> 'Have you, my girl?' he said gently, and, smiling a little, he stroked back the hair from her cheek.
>
> 'Yes,' said Arrietty, 'we could make a balloon.'
>
> 'A what?' he exclaimed . . .
>
> 'We needn't even make it!' Arrietty hurried on. 'There are heaps of balloons in those boxes and we have all those strawberry baskets, and there are diagrams and everything . . .' She pulled his hand. 'Come and look at this copy of the *Illustrated London News*.'[35]

Not only is she clever; Arrietty has sufficient tact to deal affectionately with her father's sensitivities.

Mary Norton's series challenges the usual expectations: it does not, except in some very obvious ways, 'progress' at all. The characters grow a little older, and they are constantly displaced and driven into a nomadic existence; but this movement is not forward and there is no progression towards anything. There is no resolution of the paradoxes implicit in the themes, and no solution to the conflicting needs of the almost grown-up Arrietty.

I cannot help feeling that, if Mary Norton had gone on to write other sequels, they could have done no more than repeat in different narrative colours the same underlying pattern of loneliness and longing. Though the characters move from place to place, the narrative simply circles over the same imaginative area. That is not meant to be a disparaging judgement. Her series is an extended figurative representation of 'the way things are'; and, if that was her vision of life, then the homely feel-good endings expected of much children's fiction would have seemed to her a kind of cheating.

The five novels in *The Borrowers* series – while appearing to be a simple linear fiction going in one narrative direction – in fact constitute a complex *fictional map* of the author's imaginative and perhaps spiritual convictions. Any of the possible avenues of reflection represented on that map will lead the reader by different routes towards the loneliness and desire which lie at the centre of Mary Norton's fictional world. No attentive reader can avoid it: by whatever critical path we tread, that is where we will arrive. We may analyse the characters, or their relationships, or the dynamics of power and gender, or the social representation of the family – but our analyses will invariably in the end lead us to the sadly elegiac centre of Mary Norton's imaginative world of longing and loneliness.

When we move from the consideration of text to a reader's private experience of that text, we take a step into the unknown. We know very little about the mysterious dynamics of another person's private reading and it is impossible to say with any confidence how – or even if – a reader is likely to be affected by the kind of emotional narrative colouring I have tried to elucidate. My guess is that the implicit is more likely than the explicit to slip unnoticed into the reader's experience of the narrative; and if it slips in along the grain, as it were, of the reader's own personal or cultural inclinations, it is less likely to be noticed or resisted. And so, since reading *The Borrowers* is likely to be a solitary and private experience – by young readers who themselves are beginning to long for an imagined future release into the guessed-at freedoms of adulthood – it seems likely that the very act of reading the series involves an unconscious act of solidarity with the yearning narrative voice.

So, while it is possible to discuss with some measure of objectivity Mary Norton's ability to describe, say, how Pod climbs a staircase, it is impossible to discuss this deeper narrative level without bringing into play the reader's own subjectivity. We won't know how children experience this unless we make it possible for them to tell us. And we won't allow this to happen if we have not even noticed it ourselves.

In practice, teachers do not 'teach' an entire series in class. But a single novel of the series might be addressed, and the teacher who is concerned to develop the responses of a class of young readers might well be tempted to move *outwards* and away from *The Borrowers* by introducing the children to *Gulliver's Travels*, *Mistress Masham's Repose* and *The Indian in the Cupboard*. And this is perfectly appropriate, provided such an activity does not become a substitute for looking closely and in detail *inwards* at the texts of the series themselves.

The study of children's books is beset with literalism. If adults can discuss them only in terms of 'what happens' in the story, they are unlikely to engage children themselves in precisely those aspects of the fiction which the young readers are unconsciously affected by. For we should be quite clear about this: the adult critic or teacher who sees in *The Borrowers* only a cosy story about tiny people in a miniature world *knows less about it than the young reader*. And it is difficult to see how adult commentators can contribute much to any discussion, let alone develop the responses of young readers, if they know less about a children's book or series than young readers who have read it – perhaps more than once – from beginning to end.

8   Watching passionately

Lucy Boston and the *Green Knowe* series

Few novels begin as beguilingly as *The Children of Green Knowe*, the first of Lucy Boston's famous series. The account of the arrival of the seven-year-old Tolly at his unknown great-grandmother's house where he is to spend Christmas must be one of the best openings of a children's book ever to have been written. *Arrival* is the exact word, for this is more than an arrival by train at a railway station, or by boat at an old house entirely surrounded by water. It is – though the lonely, unhappy and rather bewildered little boy does not yet know it – an arrival at a deep and richly satisfying level, a restoration to family and home, the discovery that he has a place in a complex pattern of time and landscape.

The house is the central feature of the series, an imaginative version of the actual house which Lucy Boston lived in for many years, said to be the oldest inhabited house in England, located at Hemingford Grey, near St Ives in Cambridgeshire, by the Great Ouse.[1] The series is essentially about age, time and childhood, and the house is presented as a house not just in present time but in *all* time, not just a repository of past history but a living container of its past lives. Readers who cannot respond to the loving descriptions of place, the magical evocations of old family possessions, will get nowhere with this novel, let alone the whole series; which is presumably what this ungenerous critic was getting at:

> [Lucy Boston] has little pretension to be a creator of memorable human characters or even an exciting story-teller, and reaches her highest level when describing scenery . . .[2]

It is true that Lucy Boston is not an exciting story-teller in the manner of Enid Blyton; but it is equally true that in *The Children of Green Knowe* a deep story is told, one of welcome and home-coming.

The opening is a carefully paced account of a lonely and rather puzzled little boy arriving in a strange flooded landscape. We know at once that he is a dreamer, a reader and a pretender – for he thinks of Noah and the Ark, that great biblical refuge for threatened animals. The unsettling dynamics of 'home' and 'far away' become part of the conversation with two strange but kindly local women who ask Tolly where his parents live.

> '. . . [My parents] live in Burma.'
> 'Fancy that now! That's a long way away. Where are you going, then?'
> 'I don't know. That is, I'm going to my great-grandmother Oldknow at Green Noah . . .'[3]

The fact that Tolly's parents are on the other side of the world contrasts strongly with the warm and voluble welcome the two women receive when they get out of the train at their station 'kissing the people who had come to meet them'.[4]

There is a flashback to the empty school where Tolly has spent many a lonely holiday. Then the narrative returns to the present and Tolly's journey becomes a gradual healing discovery of the possibilities of kindness and welcome. After the well-intended advice of the women on the train there is the gentle teasing of the taxi-driver. And then Mr Boggis arrives in a rowing-boat, holds the lantern up to the boy's face and greets him with the words:

> 'Pleased to meet you. I knew your mother when she was your size. I bet you were wondering how you were going to get home.'[5]

The boy's heart is cheered by the magical word 'home' and the reference to Tolly's dead mother introduces the central theme of time and past generations. He reaches the house, whose 'thick stone walls were strong, warm and lively', and meets his great-grandmother, whose face 'had so many wrinkles it looked as if someone had been trying to draw her for a very long time and every line put in had made the face more like her'.

> 'So you've come back!' she said, smiling, as he came forward, and he found himself leaning against her shoulder as if he knew her quite well.

'Why do you say "come back"?' he asked, not at all shy.

'I wondered whose face it would be of all the faces I knew,' she said. 'They always come back. You are like another Toseland, your grandfather. What a good thing you have the right name, because I should always be calling you Tolly anyway. I used to call him Tolly. Have you got a pet name? I'm sure they don't call you Toseland at school.'

'No, I get called Towser.'

'And at home?'

'My stepmother calls me Toto, but I hate it. It's worse than Towser.'

'I think I agree with you. Here we are all used to Toseland, it's the family name and doesn't seem queer to us. So you shan't be Toto here. Do you mind Tolly?'

'I like it. It's what my mother used to call me. What shall I call you?'

'Granny,' she said. 'What does one generation more or less matter?'[6]

By this stage in the novel – barely seventeen pages – the attentive reader has been introduced to a complex time-picture. The past is all around Tolly, in a variety of forms. It is literally there in the solid and actual antiquity of the house and the objects in it; it is imaginatively there in the half-heard voices of the ghost-children; it is in old Mrs Oldknow, who was Tolly's mother's grandmother; later, it is seen to be there in the various stories of past times that the old lady tells him; and, most strangely, it is inside Tolly himself, in his own features, which, as the old lady implies, always reappear across the generations. Finally, it is in his name, which is no less his because it had also belonged to several of his forebears. Clearly the whole business of naming is important: the various people in his lives who called him Towser or Toto have failed to address the person he really is. Only his mother, and now his great-grandmother, understand that naming is recognition, and recognition has to do with belonging to a place.

In many respects this novel is unusual: it does not tell a straightforward story, relying instead on moments of magic, strangeness and beauty. It works more like a tone poem than a children's novel, its unity ensured through the author's judicious use of repeated images – the ghost-children from the time of the Great Plague, the real and the topiary animals, the sound of elusive music, the statue of St

Christopher, and the presence of snow, frost and flood. Lucy Boston resists the customary expectations of children's books and makes considerable demands on young readers. It is a 'mood-narrative', oscillating repeatedly from fear to comfort, from doubt to reassurance, from emptiness to love. It is more concerned with feeling and psychology than with an orderly series of events, and its apparently rather random episodic structure reflects the uncertainty and insecurity of an unloved and forgotten little boy who continues to have moments of fear and needs repeated reassurances.

'[Tolly] felt with all his heart that he was at home', we are told,[7] and this sense of belonging is repeatedly reinforced by the birds who fly into his bedroom, the time-travelling children who play with him, the magical flute-playing. But this joyous confidence proves to be little more than a passing mood; it is always vulnerable to moments of childish passionate despair. Often, it is sufficient to go indoors and be healed by the presence of his great-grandmother making tea by the fire. But Lucy Boston knows too that grandmothers are themselves subject to doubts and unhappiness, and that the assurance they are expected to dispense is to some extent a pretence. Once, when the two of them are discussing a sword that once belonged to seventeenth-century Toby, she introduces death into the narrative.

> 'Why doesn't he want it now?' . . .
> 'Because he's dead,' she said at last.
> Tolly sat dumbfounded, with his big black eyes fixed on her. He must have known of course that the children could not have lived so many centuries without growing old, but he had never thought about it. To him they were so real, so near, they were his own family that he needed more than anything on earth. He felt the world had come to an end.
> 'Are they all dead?' he said at last.
> 'They all died together in the Great Plague. The farm bailiff, Boggis, had been to London on business and he brought the infection back with him. Toby and Alexander and Linnet and their mother all died in one day, in a few hours. And little Boggis too. Only poor old grandmother was left, too unhappy to cry.'

This is uncompromising. The novel becomes a kind of meditation on how to tell children the truth about time and death while at the same time sustaining their faith in life and their own future. Lucy Boston represents dying as not so much an absence or disappearance but rather an insignificant shift into a more elusive state.

'After all,' she said, 'it sounds very sad to say they all died, but it didn't really make so much difference. I expect the old grand-mother soon found out they were still here.'[8]

There are repeated instances of such moments of cold fear, always followed by loving reassurance. Once, after playing and talking with the 'ghost chidden', Tolly looked up but 'found he was alone. They had all gone':

> Never was a little boy more desolate than Tolly. He wanted them so much, every minute of every day, and he no sooner found them than they vanished.'[9]

But he is cheered up almost at once by the discovery of a long-lost silver bracelet. Often in this way he is restored to optimism by some narrative incident; but mostly it is his great-grandmother who must provide the loving comfort, the healing of doubts. But here there is that poignant irony again, for Lucy Boston knows that old people are just as subject to doubts too. The climax of this sequence of oscilla-tions occurs when the old lady and the little boy are tired after decorating the Christmas tree. They hear coming from another room the sound of a woman's voice singing a cradle song, *Lully, Lulla, Thou little tiny child.*

> 'Who is it?' he whispered.
> 'It's the grandmother rocking the cradle,' said Mrs Oldknow, and her eyes were full of tears.
> 'Why are you crying, Granny? It's lovely.'
> 'It is lovely, only it is such a long time ago. I don't know why that should be sad, but it sometimes seems so.'
> . . . 'Granny,' whispered Tolly again with his arm through hers, 'whose cradle is it? Linnet is as big as I am.'
> 'My darling, this voice is much older than that. I hardly know whose it is. I heard it once before at Christmas.'
> It was queer to hear the baby's sleepy whimper only in the next room, now, and so long ago. 'Come, we'll sing it too,' said Mrs Oldknow, going to the spinet. She played, but it was Tolly who sang alone, while, four hundred years ago, a baby went to sleep.[10]

The play of time and time-travel is more than a device to suggest the past; it indicates the abiding continuity of time and the generations.

But it is more even than that, for this time it is the child who comforts the old lady, while the narrator comforts the reader. We are all,
it seems to say, subject to moments of unhappiness when time and
dying come into our thoughts – and only love can restore us, suggested by the archetypal picture of an old grandmother singing a
child to sleep, and consoling herself at the same time.

The Chimneys of Green Knowe works at a more steady rate. It is a
novel of *attentiveness*, not anxiety. There is less of the emotional
insecurity than there was in the first of the series, no swinging from
fear to consolation, or from the dangers of the outer garden to the
comfort of the fireside. Tolly is being taught to pay attention to the
world he is part of. And there is a more adventurous game being
played with time-travel, with a greater part of the novel concerned
with stories from the past, and characters from past and present
affecting each other's lives, not unlike the way they do in Philippa
Pearce's novel, *Tom's Midnight Garden*, published in the same year
(1958). Tolly spends a good deal of time being a detective, finding
old lost objects and learning the stories associated with their owners,
so that there are, in effect, two plots – the one from the past with
an exciting thriller-climax of danger and rescue, and the one in the
present, a low-key (but deeply satisfying) business in which Tolly
finds the long-lost jewels so that he and his great-grandmother will
be able to have the old house restored.

There are signs, however, of two related developing authorial interests which were to come to fruition later in *A Stranger at Green
Knowe*: one is the set-piece description, especially of any phenomenon evocative of vastness or strength; the other is the seeking-out of
stylistic challenges – a determination to use words to describe the
indescribable. Lucy Boston had in the first novel shown an astonishing
ability to word-paint (snow, flood, night frost); now she goes beyond
that, as if seeking a new linguistic challenge. In the character of the
blind Susan, and in Tolly exploring an underground passage, she finds
words to describe what it is to lack sight, to create word-pictures for
a pictureless existence, to image a consciousness devoid of imagery.
And there are hints of a kind of transcendentalism, too, with Tolly
becoming aware through *hearing* of a wider universe presented as
authoritative, uncompromising and fundamentally benevolent.

> Tolly sat listening to his great-grandmother's needle pricking in
> and out of the paper that her bits were sewn on, and the harsh
> sound of the thread pulled through it. His eyes wandered over

the patterns in the folds of the quilt, and he heard the fire and the clock, and the blackbird in the beech tree, and Orlando galloping in dreams as he lay flat on his side on the carpet, and aeroplanes going overhead droning in unlimited space. All these sounds seemed held in a very old and wonderful silence.[11]

This is a novel of *sounds*; things seen are also heard, and a description of dawn is composed as an orchestration of awakening sounds as well as a picture of stirring imagery.

He heard a startling rushing noise close behind him, and two swans passed low overhead, the sound of their flight, once they had gone by, continuing far up the river, and in the water underneath them their reflections flew upside down. After that the world began to tick, faint tuts and chucks and little flutters, and cracklings as the birds woke up, talked in their sleep, stretched their wings, scratched their ears, and shifted their position. And all the insects did the same. Even the leaves had a look of waking up, lifting themselves a little towards the sky as it got bluer.[12]

The *Green Knowe* series is held together by the house, and by related themes of homelessness, exile and sanctuary. In *The River at Green Knowe*, the third of the series, the concern with displacement becomes explicit as Lucy Boston introduces three new characters – Oskar, aged eleven, 'leggy and head in air with an obstinate thrust in his lips', whose father was shot by the Russians; a nine-year-old Burmese refugee whose name, HSU, comes out like an unpronounceable sigh and who is thereafter known as Ping; and Ida, eleven, undersized, and 'clearly the head of the group'.[13]

These three children do not resemble the fictional children that most young readers are familiar with; they speak like well-read and reflective adults, their friendship is an idealised one, and their understanding of their situation is both telepathic and poetic. They think in metaphors, speculate on metaphysics, and their play takes them to the dangerous heart of time, change and death. *The River at Green Knowe* is a novel *of* childhood, expressing Lucy Boston's understanding of the unfragmented and visionary knowledge of children. Mrs Oldknow is absent from the novel, the house having been let to two kindly but ridiculous elderly sisters who have little narrative significance; and, since Tolly is absent too, the entire novel exists as the concentrated experience lived and interpreted by these three imaginative outsiders.

Like its two predecesssors, the novel has no chapters; but, unlike them, its episodes could take place in almost any order. The effect, however, is not one of structural carelessness or episodic randomness. This novel operates like a huge and beautiful water-colour landscape, into which you might enter at any point and begin to understand the totality of its shifting and timeless vision. A linear narrative of events linked by cause and effect would have been counterproductive for a novel whose deep theme is Time, not as sequence and chronology but as the great immanent force of the universe, both benevolent and terrifying. Only the children understand this; the two adults are both hopeless, the one preoccupied with cooking and the other obsessed by an illusory academic 'history'. The novel's structure exemplifies its point.

Each of the *Green Knowe* novels is characterised by a feature which is not precisely a theme, but rather a poetic stance, or a pattern of related perspectives. In *The Chimneys of Green Knowe* there was a lot of carefully described tree-climbing, so that a good deal of the action took place at a great height, where more could be seen and more could be heard. The idea that dominates *The River at Green Knowe* is *thought*; while the imaginative eye is mostly at water-level looking upward and out; the narrative constantly juggles with a constellation of related ideas without ever quite allowing them to settle into fixed patterns, in particular, ideas and images of depths, surfaces and reflections. The three children speculate upon why the sky does not reflect water in the same way that water reflects the sky.

> 'Your eyes reflect,' said Ida. 'I can see a tiny pink sunset cloud and a tiny green pin-point earth. No colour photo was ever so *minute*.'
>
> 'I see them huge, though,' said Ping. 'The cloud is so big that if it was a mountain you never could possibly climb to the top, and the earth stretches all the way to where the sky begins. Miles and miles and miles with woods and rushes and waterfalls and water-wheels and nightingales and bells and singing fishes.'
>
> 'I shall like that,' said Ida. 'We'll have to go quietly by starlight to hear singing fishes. Do you *know* there are some, Ping, or are you just thinking it?'
>
> 'My father used to say,' said Oskar . . . 'that there isn't anything real except thoughts. Nothing is there at all unless somebody's thinking it. He said thoughts were more real than guns. He got shot by the Russians for saying that. But the thought

wasn't shot, because I'm thinking it now. So if Ping has singing fishes, let's try and hear some. Why not?'

'I'm in a hurry to begin,' said Ida. 'I *want* the river . . .'[14]

Reading *The Famous Five* will not have prepared a young reader for this kind of writing. Here are passion and hunger – but for experiential and intellectual richness. In just a few paragraphs, ideas and speculations crowd upon one another – ideas of great and small, political freedom, and the baffling question of whether we are in the universe or the universe is within us. The idea holding together this constellation is the notion of the power of thought, the ability of imaginative people to think themselves into new realities.

The three children think themselves into several strange situations. They encounter a herd of beautiful flying horses on a night-time island in the river, and an exiled giant terrified of being laughed at because he doesn't know what laughter is. And in one remarkable episode Oskar shrinks to the size of a harvest mouse. In none of these is there any mention of *play*, or *make-believe*, or *pretending*; the nearest the narrator comes to explaining such phenomena is when, after the shrinking adventure, Oskar says he grew tired of it and 'unthought' it.[15] These adventures are not like the 'time-slip' of the previous novels; the narrative does not slip backwards or forwards in linear time, but sideways into other modes of knowing, other kinds of vision.

Linking these mysterious episodes is the shifting imagery of the river, described with the stylistic faithfulness and clarity which is Lucy Boston's hallmark: the eel flung into the air and re-entering the water 'like a needle entering silk';[16] the 'inverted bowls of smooth water [which] travelled along with a suggestion of waltzing';[17] or Ida's view of a circus elephant bathing – 'a flat wrinkled drift of side-face, out of which a small humorous eye opened, saw her, winked and submerged again'.[18] But some of the longer watery descriptions go beyond an artistic faithfulness to a remembered scene, suggesting that the various manifestations of water offer the children clues to understanding the nature of being.

> The delighted children stopped paddling and every crease faded off the surface. The punt lay as if on a mirror which itself lay in empty space, for above and beyond the frame of bulrushes they could see nothing at all. There were white clouds above them and white clouds below, floating in a complete orb of hyacinth blue. When the swallows dipped, they disputed each fly with the

swallow that came up to meet them from below. The flies themselves in alighting on the surface met foot to foot with their
doubles. Even an ice-cream carton alone in the blue space had a
twin soul leaning towards it with the same enticing words in
pink written upside down. And all the doubles were mysterious,
both more shadowy and more brilliant than the originals because
of an azure varnish that alone distinguished them . . .
    . . . They never had a more delicious day. There was no sound
except the splash of their dives and the drip of their hair and
elbows as they sat in the punt, and their own happy nonsense.
The pool was a world as much their own as their most private
thoughts. Ida's nicest dreams for a long time afterwards were
ringed with a palisade of swinging bulrushes.[19]

In such moments, being becomes perception and neo-Platonism finds
an evocative place for itself in the imagery of water.

Nothing *is* explained because nothing *can* be explained. But there
is one precise moment of illumination for the three friends; it happens after the last of their imaginative adventures, when they have
a terrifying glimpse of the Wild Hunt, whose horned leader is described as 'a genius in horror'.[20]

They were standing at midnight, alone, under a sky that was
there before either earth or moon had been, and would be there
long after. In this agonizing second of revelation that ALL passes,
the bark of a disturbed heron caused them to clutch each other,
and jerked loose their tongues.[21]

Even Green Knowe, that solidly faithful centuries-old building of
stone, is subject to the processes of inevitable change. 'We are *really*
displaced now', Oskar says, glimpsing perhaps humanity's lonely
exile in an indifferent universe. But he is wrong. Time provides reassurance as well as fear:

Under [the moon's] lovely light Green Knowe was revealed again,
gentle, heavy and dreaming, with its carefully spaced bushes and
trees standing in their known positions enriched with moonlight
on their heads and shadows like the folds of Cinderella's ball
dress behind them.
    The children gasped with joy and relief, and slowly, taking in,
holding, and keeping what they saw, they moved towards home.

They all three slept in one bed that night. Because, as Oskar had said, it was too much.[22]

The River at Green Knowe is a remarkable novel, a holistic vision of time and the universe, and the children's place in it. But there was little in it to indicate what was coming next. *A Stranger at Green Knowe* is a masterpiece, a perfect union of style and structure, and in my opinion the greatest animal story in English children's literature. The previous three books in the series showed Lucy Boston's commitment to language – her desire to find exactly the right words, to groom her prose to glossy perfection. Here, this accomplished word-painting finds its perfect topic and its biggest challenge – to do what a wildlife camera might do, but also to capture the *inwardness* and integrity of a great primate, its animal strangeness and at the same time that which is recognisably human.

The structure of this novel is unusual. There are three long sections, unrelieved by chapters, with no natural breaks for inexperienced readers. Within the sections, there are massive paragraphs which many children might find daunting. Not infrequently, a single page-opening will contain only one paragraph break. These great bulks of concentrated prose almost mime the great bulk of the gorilla, or the gigantic thunderstorm, or the vastness of the jungle. This density of description invariably signals a moment of great seriousness, inviting approaching readers to draw breath and brace themselves for an imaginative effort. This may not be as difficult for children as we think, for many of them are so concerned with the treatment of animals that they are already halfway to sharing and understanding the passion on which this novel is founded. In *A Stranger at Green Knowe*, Lucy Boston is their natural ally. For most children today, the treatment of animals and concern for the environment constitute the first great ethical issues which they feel strongly about. What such readers might get, apart from narrative pleasure, is a refining of their own developing feelings about how humanity treats animals.

The first section begins with a lengthy and unhurried account of the baby gorilla in the 'immortal forest'[23] of the Congo, and ends with his capture and deportation to London Zoo. The set-piece word-pictures which Lucy Boston excelled in already are here developed into a kind of 'active description' which goes beyond scenic faithfulness, implying love and involvement, and serving to impassion the reader. The language repeatedly directs and commands; the novel begins with an instruction: 'Imagine a tropical forest . . .' and proceeds to give impassioned lessons in understanding and respect. 'Whoever lives here must surely have qualities to catch the imagination and a grandeur to inspire love',[24] the reader is told. This is where the gorillas live, and we are introduced to the young Hanno (though he has not yet been named). The description of the young gorilla combines the precision of an information book with the persuasive language of sentiment: 'Gorillas develop more quickly than humans, so this small furry person was like a child of five.'[25]

It is when the prose is concerned with the adult male that the reader first encounters what is to be the defining characteristic of this novel – a kind of passionate exactitude which commands in the reader an imaginative allegiance to both subject and style. 'All full-grown gorillas are natural kings',[26] we are told.

> A full-grown male may be six feet in height and weigh thirty stone or more. His face is coal black and majestic with a high crest like a Roman helmet. His eyes are deep set and far seeing, but neither sly nor cruel. He is superbly dressed in dense fur, different for the three parts of his body. Over his shoulders and arms he wears a kind of matador's jacket of long glossy black bearskin, open at the throat to show his bare chest. He has a cummerbund of silver grey. And his legs are covered in beautiful thick opossum. He has all the dignity and decency that chimpanzees so outrageously lack. To a little gorilla he was the one splendid figure in the world, the leader, the protector, the avenger, and of course as all fathers sometimes are in private, the big dangerous joke.[27]

Such combinations of metaphor, simile and contrast, shot through with understanding of the hierarchical animal family, amount to a generous anthropomorphic tribute (or, to be more precise, an acknowledgement of anthropomorphic identity), leading on to the wider context of the safe environment of the far-spreading jungle.

> And so the family went to sleep, heaped with leaves to keep them dry. No little boy tucked up in bed could feel more secure than a little gorilla tucked in by a seemingly endless forest, dreaming of happy games on its rich floor, where every day's direction is fresh and untrodden, all their own.[28]

Part 2 is an account, thirteen years later, of the visit to Hanno's cage by Ping, the little displaced refugee, 'trim, self-possessed and gay . . . so unlike his companions both in race and circumstance'.[29]

The narration immediately becomes Ping's thoughts, for he is intelligent, quiet and attentive. He has the kind of imagination that 'never dismisses anything as ordinary'.[30] The descriptions now are of an adult male gorilla in captivity, with the emphasis on confinement and the restriction of greatness. There is only the great animal's body in 'a space of nothingness. As if looking at *that* told you anything but the nature of sorrow.'[31] Ping is attentive and excited, enraptured by what he sees:

> a stupendous black figure standing like a horse; like a horse that was also a man, for it had a man's brow and compelling authoritative eyes, but its nostrils were large and soft like a horse's. Suddenly it sprang round facing him and stood upright. It *was* a man! It was a giant with a bare black chest ten times as wide as Ping's own.[32]

Steadily the carefully observed accounts of the gorilla's movements, and the judiciously phrased descriptions of his frustration – his 'age-long patient impatience' – lead the reader into an implied condemnation of displacement in all its forms. 'The very expression on his face was that of years of sitting. Ping had seen it in the refugee camps.'[33]

Lucy Boston had often, in the three previous books, brought her young protagonists in touch with the vastness of landscapes and skies, and with the enormity of time; but here vastness and power are precisely and dramatically focused in the concentrated figure of Hanno, tensely contained in the imprisoned gorilla. There is no possibility of its significance being missed; she has, in Ping, created the kind of boy who sees meaning in everything he perceives.

> 'Hanno,' he said in his gentlest voice. For Ping had, as it were, fallen in love. The world contained something so wonderful to him that everything was altered.[34]

Few child readers would be inclined to mock that, for most know what it is like to fall in love with an animal, real or longed-for. But I doubt if many of them realise what they are in for. This passionate and exact account builds up a powerful charge of *narrative desire* – a readerly lust for justice. This gorilla *must* escape. This is a children's story with the implied promise of a happy outcome; so the caged animal must, somehow, be freed. And when he does succeed in getting out, the reader's desire and need are rekindled into a longing for a permanent and happy resolution. But this narrative introduces its readers to the nature of classical tragedy, the desired in conflict with the inevitable, greatness and joy briefly grasped and understood, nobility allowed for a few moments to know itself before the darkness closes in.

In Part 3, Ping returns to Green Knowe and meets Mrs Oldknow. He is happy, dignified and discreet, 'twinkling and thinking things to himself'.[35] Like all the other refugees who come to stay, he finds something new there, and brings something new to it. And he finds himself caring for the escaped gorilla, Hanno, who takes up residence in the thicket, in a patch of bamboo.

> There he stood, at large, his untried power incalculable and arbitrary.
>
> Ping could not have moved if he had wished to. He was paralysed with the impossibility of either belief or disbelief. In any case he was watching so passionately nothing could have made him move. The very fact that Hanno was as great as he remembered him was a shock. He had, in his single-minded innocence, no feeling of danger. Who could mistake him, Ping, for an enemy?[36]

That phrase *watching so passionately* is characteristic of Lucy Boston's fictional children. Through Ping, the narrative passionately observes and describes the appearance and movements of the great animal, using similes and superlatives of size, shot through with words of passionate love.

> . . . his beloved giant.[37]

> . . . mixed with his huge splendour was a certain childishness and simplicity.[38]

> . . . something he had described as a kind of a man, but might just as well have called an outraged jungle god.[39]

> . . . sitting like a young chieftain.[40]

> . . . Hanno's eyes looking into his, piercing, haunting, commanding.[41]

> . . . an air of savage responsibility.[42]

. . . a natural force of the first order.[43]

. . . eyes which combined the directness of a lion's stare with the interchange of a man's.[44]

Peter Boston's illustrations for the whole series have mostly been delicately faithful pictorial representations of the descriptions in the text, a necessary help for young readers who have had no experience of living in an ancient stone house, or little idea what a statue of St Christopher might look like. His illustrations of the gorilla are his best, and at times he goes subtly a little further than his mother's authorial account. One of them shows Hanno in the thunderstorm, his huge face raised to the downpour with a smile of fierce pleasure.

No invitation to indulge in sentimentality is entertained. There can be no possibility of permanently freeing Hanno. He cannot be returned to the Congo, he cannot live wild in England, he cannot be cuddled or kept like a pet; and he *will not* return to captivity.

> His heart swelled with a fury that was like a great joy. He stood to avenge these wrongs. He was his own drummer, beating his passionate chest, his own herald with that roar so horrifying that it can never be described, presenting himself for single combat against all comers and this one in particular who was due to be torn limb from limb. He gave fair warning, but before he had launched his onslaught the unfair bullet tore at his heart. He put his hands to his breast and pitched face downwards on the ground. In less than a split second all that was Hanno had ceased to exist.[45]

Hanno is neither sentimentalised nor diminished. The language of jousting, the careful balancing of the 'fair warning' with the 'unfair bullet', the relentless pacing of the sentences, and the uncompromising final statement ensure that what young readers are given here is classical tragedy – not disaster, but *tragedy*, with choice and understanding at its heart. 'He's dead', Ping says a little later. 'It's all right. That is how much he didn't want to go back. I saw him choose.'[46]

In the last two novels of the series an authorial tidying-up is going on. *An Enemy at Green Knowe* differs from its predecessors in that the author formulates in a number of key explicit statements her belief in the specific and unique quality of the old house, as if trying to sum up and formulate the thinking implicit in the series.

... Green Knowe was full of mysteries. Certainly it was welcoming and comfortable and rejoicing and gay, but one had the feeling that behind the exciting colours and shapes of its ancient self there might be surprises from the unknown universe; that the house was on good terms with that too, and had no intention of shutting out the un-understandable. Of course, it was largely Time. Surely Now and Not-now is the most teasing of all mysteries, and if you let in a nine-hundred-year dose of time, you let in almost everything.[47]

A special house needs special people, and it is clear in this story that Tolly and Ping and Mrs Oldknow are an idealised and magical group of three. Again, this is made explicit: they do not quarrel, or sneer, or make fun of each other; 'Instead, they were three quite different people who loved being together and used their imagination for laughing and devising pleasures.'[48] Their secret is more than good-naturedness; they also have a magical understanding. The series began with a lonely little boy finding a *home* in the Fens; but the novels also increasingly work towards a mystical conviction that all of us may be in a much deeper sense *at home* in the universe. The boys have found a Stone of Power at a Welsh seaside resort and the narrator links this explicitly with the stones of which Green Knowe is constructed:

[The old house] lay in the garden as the Stone of Power once lay among sea ferns in a rock pool. *That* was part of the enclosed mystery and screening of the pool, which was part of the cove in which that stratum of rock lay, which itself was a reciprocal part of the great tides that flowed over it, which were one with the winds and moon and the sun, which is only a marginal detail of the Milky Way. Just as the Stone of Power held in its nature the truth of all of these, so the house of Green Knowe focused in itself and gave out again its own truth about being and knowing.[49]

Perhaps this interest in stone prompted the last novel in the series, *The Stones of Green Knowe*. The stones are both those the house is made of, and also a pair of ancient carved stone seats in the countryside which have the power to transmit characters through time. The boy at the centre of this novel is Roger, a Norman boy whose father is building the house which will become Green Knowe. The year is 1120. Roger goes forward in time, partly to discover the future history of his house and partly so that all the main characters of the series may be brought together at one magic meeting.

The Stones of Green Knowe is an outstanding historical novel in its own right, a perfect resource for any teacher concerned with the history of houses, or with early Norman England (the accounts of the wonder felt when walls were first built with windows to let in the sunlight, for example; or of the strangeness of having an open fire in a wall with a chimney instead of at the centre beneath a hole in the roof). Lucy Boston employs her extraordinary descriptive capacity to provide vivid and sensuous accounts of a wild and empty landscape which most of us would find it hard to imagine.

> The ground was soft from centuries of fallen leaves and the wind that had been so gay and rough outside did not stir the rich smell of mould, of endless growing and decaying that enclosed the boys, and while from the tops of the trees there came a sound like surf where the wind streamed through them, this was heard as a noise outside when one is indoors. Among the trunks there was a silence that could be recognised as spreading as far all round as could be imagined. Whichever way the boys looked the trunks rose up and shut out the horizon. Here and there was a little dell with a giant tree in the centre, where a shower of broken light came down . . .
>
> There was no birdsong, it being autumn, but occasionally the uncanny voice of a young owl and the rustling of unseen creatures. There was so strong a feeling of isolation, of silence, of secrecy and supernatural power (for trees are alive – they have a still, rooted, powerful life), such a sense of having been there since the beginning, that Roger was cut to the heart by his knowledge that in the future it would not be there.[50]

There are many such descriptions and, like this, they almost always direct the reader to the theme of Time.

> While he felt with all his senses the unconquerable presence of the forest and the awe of it that he had grown up with, he could not believe it could disappear. It was in its essence everlasting. And yet this would vanish . . .[51]

When Roger time-travels into the twentieth century he is stunned by the barren emptiness of what is left of the countryside, and wonders if some dreadful plague has destroyed what Lucy Boston calls 'the lovely worldful'.[52]

Some readers might derive from this novel a gloomily realistic representation of a world in decline, an environment continually being destroyed; undoubtedly there is in the writing an elegiac sense of loss. But it is not as simple as that, for there is also Lucy Boston's firm conviction that nothing is lost in Time, that all things remain in all things. Although her characters travel backwards and forwards in linear historical time, the novel's structure somehow suggests a circularity, or at least a coherence. Roger in 1120 is so exactly like Tolly in 1976 that he is mistaken for him, and he has a granny exactly the same as Mrs Oldknow, as if to suggest that the grandmother–schoolboy relationship transcends the changing generations.

I believe that Lucy Boston in her old age – she was 84 when this last novel of the series was published – felt the need for a thematic rounding-off, and that in *The Stones of Green Knowe* there is also something of the sacramental. If I am right in speculating that this book had a special private significance for a very old writer who believed that we are all trapped in time but at the same time capable of transcending it, it is also important to point out that she never loses sight of her young readers. This final novel is a narrative of *meetings and greetings* across nine hundred years of English history, and there is a perfect decorum in the way in which the issues of death and decline so important to the author are consolingly and cheerfully worked out in a fantasy for children.

9 The sun inside
the window, shining out

The Dark Is Rising quintet

Susan Cooper's subject is landscape – landscape not as setting but as plot.

Over Sea, Under Stone was published in 1965. It is an unremarkable children's novel – a competently told story, but instantly forgettable. Yet twelve years later it had become the first novel of the internationally acclaimed *The Dark Is Rising* quintet. How did Susan Cooper pull it off?

Its opening is composed of clichés characteristic of its genre:

three children arrive by train at a Cornish fishing-village for the summer holidays;
they are met by a benevolent but eccentric uncle with his dog;
in his battered estate car he drives them to their holiday home, the Grey House;
here, the exploring children discover a secret door behind an old wardrobe, and a staircase leading to an attic;
there, they eventually find a map with clues to the whereabouts of a hidden treasure.

Readers in 1965 were on familiar ground here; dozens of Johns, Susans, Colins, Alisons, Dicks, Julians, Sallys, Anns, Kays and Ians (with the occasional twins and an inevitable dog) had arrived on that same fictional train at fictional stations in Scotland, the Lake District or Cornwall, to be met by a benevolent adult and carried safely away to their summer holiday adventure.

I am not intending to scoff; such openings are no more ridiculous than 'once upon a time', and profoundly appealing. In fact, they are 'once upon a time' writ large. For thirty years between about 1930 and about 1960, hundreds of holiday adventure stories and camping-and-tramping stories offered young readers the pleasures of safety and predictability constructed on the premise that the British country-side was a safe playground for middle-class youngsters in the holidays. Alas, that generic fictional train no longer runs, and the branch-lines which had connections with several hundred children's stories for half a century have been closed down.[1]

As for Susan Cooper's three fictional children, apart from the young-est boy's interest in King Arthur, there is nothing distinctive in their characterisation to indicate that the author has much interest in them. They have no context but their adventure. They bring with them no past and, consequently, they have no psychology, only an empty readiness for adventure. Their only feelings are those inspired by what is immediately happening to them. Any individuality they pos-sess derives from Margery Gill's illustrations of them as cool and thoughtful children, high-cheekboned and rather remote.

But the story moves steadily forward in a businesslike way, mainly by means of dialogue; descriptions of place are brisk and impression-ist verbal sketches; and moments of excitement and tension are effi-ciently represented. However, readers are never permitted to be really frightened, and above all they are not allowed to be puzzled. For *Over Sea, Under Stone* belonged to a dying fictional ethos, before Alan Garner's *Elidor*, before the great commanding voice of Ted Hughes' *The Iron Man*, and before William Mayne turned his back on narrative security and moved into his great dark fictions – an ethos which assumed that a book for children must have a reassuring narratorial voice and that part of its role was to *explain*. Accord-ingly, in Chapter 6 Great Uncle Merry (alias Merlin) explains (at some length) that the missing treasure is in fact the Grail, and that it must not fall into the hands of the evil forces which are also seeking its whereabouts.

Susan Cooper provides hints that Great Uncle Merry is too big for his contemporary surroundings – that he belongs elsewhere and is preoccupied by mysterious business. And it could be argued that the Grail is too big for its place in this novel. A serious spiritual symbol at the heart of the Arthurian cycle of legends, and associated with Joseph of Arimathea and with the Crucifixion itself, perhaps should not be treated like a lost sports trophy and rescued by three undistin-guished children – without the aid of our greatest mythical magician because he had been duped by Cook into going off to Truro for the day![2]

All this may seem rather ungenerous. I do not mean to be severe on this novel, but rather to suggest that the differences between *Over*

Sea, Under Stone and its sequel were symptomatic of a wider cultural metamorphosis in the way people viewed children's books in the sixties, and what it was assumed young readers were capable of. I do not believe that the Grail, and the deep themes associated with it, should be barred from children's literature; but they were inevitably diminished by being forced into the comfortable narrative form in which Susan Cooper tried to fit them. The question is about form and structure: might there be a place in children's books for uncertainty, challenge, obliqueness, paradox and ambivalence? Could children's fiction do without the voice of the reassuring narrator?

It could, and it did. Alan Garner had shown in *Elidor* (1965) and *The Owl Service* (1967) that a writer needs to make few concessions for young readers. He provided no authorial explanations and frustrated at a stroke the traditional expectation that in children's fiction the authorial voice should provide constant reassurance. His fantasies are driven by anxiety or fear, and the only explanations the reader is given are those of the puzzled characters themselves. Similarly, in Susan Cooper's second novel in the series, *The Dark Is Rising*, the comfortable old cardigan of narrative reassurance is discarded. A new narrative voice is speaking here, obliquely and confidently.

In *The Dark Is Rising* traditional certainties are cancelled. In the realistic children's fiction of the previous three or four decades, readers could be sure of three things: place, time and character. In a novel by Arthur Ransome, for example, if the setting is a lake island, although any of the characters might pretend otherwise and its description might be written with all the writer's evocative authenticity, we are not meant to question its solidity or actuality; the time will be a particular sunny afternoon in August; and if a fisherman with a kindly face rows by, there will be no suggestion that he is anything but a kindly fisherman.[3] But in *The Dark Is Rising* these certainties collapse and become fluid. A housing estate can at any moment become a forest, the present-day can slip not just to another time in history but to *any* or *all* time in *both history and myth*, and the kindly fisherman might turn out to be Sir Lancelot. For *The Dark Is Rising* presupposes the parallel existence of four times, past, present, future and mythical, co-existing in a pattern of both Time and not-time.

The guarantee of this narrative fluidity is language and form. Susan Cooper writes with a new confidence and authority, with frequent touches of dramatic conciseness, often employing hyphenated coinages.

The snow lay thin and apologetic over the world.[4]

[rabbits] coming twitch-nosed forward to eat.[5]

The tall spinney of horse-chestnut trees, raucous with the calling of the rooks and rubbish-roofed with the clutter of their sprawling nests.[6]

The strange white world lay stroked by silence.[7]

Readers here are invited to enjoy language, to pause for a moment in their story-lust and acknowledge the pleasure of words. All children who love snow can appreciate the word-perfect appropriateness of that *stroked by silence*. Later, Susan Cooper puts this descriptive skill to use in vivid representations of blizzards, torrential rain and flood, not to mention all manner of 'special effects'. Her dramatic use of language is paralleled by a narrative grip on the reader's uncertainty. In a totally familiar setting of winter and Christmas, there are unfamiliar and menacing phenomena which remain unexplained. The reader can know only what eleven-year-old Will Stanton knows, and fear what he fears. It is not until page 47 that Merriman Lyon is introduced by name and only at that point can the reader see that this book is related to its predecessor. But *how* it is related remains a mystery. Readers might be half-expecting Simon, Jane and Barney Drew from the previous novel to appear, but they don't.

The mythological coherence which lies at the heart of this book is never totally explained; the reader learns it as Will learns it. And much of the writing is so heady that it is difficult for a reader's intellectual grasp to keep up with the pace of events – thus miming in the reading Will's own sense of frightened bewilderment, of things happening too fast for comprehension. Everything depends on the author's ability to present Will simultaneously as both an ordinary boy and a supernatural Old One. When Merriman tells him he has the power to extinguish a candle flame simply by wishing it, Will is simply distressed.

> '. . . Is that a possible thing for any normal boy to do?'
> 'No,' Will said unhappily.
> 'Do it,' Merriman said. 'Now.'

But Will rebels and turns his disbelieving powers to the fire instead.

> *Go out, fire,* he said to it in his mind, feeling suddenly safe and free from the dangers of power, because of course no fire as big as that could possibly go out without a real reason. *Stop burning, fire. Go out.*
>
> And the fire went out.[8]

There are many moments like this; John Rowe Townsend ascribes them to Susan Cooper's 'rare gift of being able to send a sudden electric shudder through the reader'.[9]

A reader cannot predict this narrative. Objects, places and characters change their form and meaning from one paragraph to the next. The landscape of this children's book is not single and static but multiple and fluid. Linear time-travel is not a difficult concept for young readers; but here they have to understand that all times and all places co-exist, and that, with them, is mythical time as well. And so there are none of the certainties of a single and orderly chronological narrative. Once you have accepted that the fictional 'reality' of Now is permeated by a hundred other realities from the historical or mythical past, the consequence is an unnerving narrative which can shift its ground alarmingly from one paragraph to the next, with no resting-places in the text, and no illustrations with their strange power to allay uncertainty.

There is one explanation, given – as it was in the previous novel – by Merriman. But it is not so much an explanation as a liturgy.

> '. . . For all times co-exist, and the future can sometimes affect the past, even though the past is a road that leads to the future . . . But men cannot understand this.'[10]

Now this is hard for young readers, who can hardly be expected to have studied Robert Graves' *The White Goddess*, the whole Arthurian cycle, not to mention Einstein on space-time. But in fact it does not matter, for what holds all this together is the fact that *The Dark Is Rising* is a profoundly *traditional* novel and has the conviction of its deep conservativism. Its central narrative is religious: an eleven-year-old boy's gradual discovery that the growing power within him is strong and potentially dangerous, that he must be responsible for it, and that he is surrounded by wise adults who forgive him when he makes mistakes and lovingly sustain him through this period of uncertainty. The Old Ones are priests and Will is a novice; his apprenticeship is an ethical rite of passage; he is a beginner, a learner, developing responsibility for his own actions and indeed for the whole of humanity and the whole of history. Once – in pre-1960s Britain – that scenario might have been thought of as an allegory for all boys.

It is difficult to have a religion without a doctrine; accordingly, on one occasion the narrative does stop to explain. To be precise, Susan Cooper lets the characters explain. It occurs at a point when the Dark has invaded and been driven out of the village church. The rector sees the crossed symbol on Will's belt and ascribes their success to that.

> 'That did the work, didn't it? The cross. Not of the church, but a Christian cross, nonetheless.'
>
> 'Very old them crosses are, rector,' said Old George unexpectedly, firm and clear. 'Made a long time before Christianity. Long before Christ.'
>
> The rector beamed at him. 'But not before God,' he said simply.

That is a good answer, and if the exchange had stopped there it would have shown orthodoxy gently correcting the playfulness of children's fantasy. But the rector's orthodoxy is diplomatically but firmly challenged.

> The Old Ones looked at him. There was no answer that would not have offended him, so no one tried to give one. Except, after a moment, Will.
>
> 'There's not really any before and after, is there?' he said. 'Everything that matters is outside Time. And comes from there and can go there.'
>
> Mr Beaumont turned to him in surprise. 'You mean infinity, of course, my boy.'
>
> 'Not altogether,' said the Old One that was Will. 'I mean the part of all of us, and of all the things we think and believe, that has nothing to do with yesterday or today or tomorrow because it belongs at a different kind of level. Yesterday is still there, on that level. Tomorrow is there too. You can visit either of them. And all Gods are there, and all the things they have ever stood for. And,' he added sadly, 'the opposite, too.'
>
> 'Will,' said the rector, staring at him, 'I am not sure whether you should be exorcised or ordained. You and I must have some long talks, very soon.'
>
> 'Yes, we must,' Will said equably . . .[11]

Now this is confident – and in some ways rather extraordinary – writing. The explanation is not this time given by an authorial all-knowing Merriman but by Will out of his developing understanding; and the effect is to suggest a naive inadequacy – a childishness – at the heart of the rector's Anglican faith. Perhaps the most confident touch of all is Will's quiet and untroubled sureness: most boys of his age would squirm with embarrassment and reluctance at the suggestion of long talks with the vicar; but Will just agrees equably.

This novel is about assuming power; and at the same time, and quite appropriately, it gives its readers the power to question religious faith. There have been hundreds of novels about faith, especially in the USA; and hundreds more that have entirely disregarded it. And a rather vague paganism located in the British countryside had been a feature in several popular works of fiction for children. But never before, I suspect, has children's fiction quite so explicitly offered benevolent Arthurian paganism as a superior alternative to Christianity.

Greenwitch, the third in the series, is about an image made by local Cornish women every spring out of branches and leaves, and thrown into the sea as an offering. In this novel Susan Cooper brings together the three Drew children from the first novel with Will Stanton from the second. They have two tasks: they must recover the stolen Grail, and they must find the missing key to its meaning which has fallen into the possession of the Greenwitch herself. If the next phase of the struggle between the Light and the Dark is to be resolved, the Witch must be persuaded to return it.

John Rowe Townsend has expressed some reservations about the validity of this conflict.

> The Light and the Dark are obviously good and evil forces, but it is difficult to work out just what the Dark is, what it intends to do and what it actually *does*, other than create scenic and atmospheric effects.[12]

He undoubtedly has a point, because at this stage in the series it is impossible to see a coherence in the four main factors that in Susan Cooper's mythology have influenced the story of humanity. There are the Light and the Dark, and there is an older system, the Wild Magic, which is indifferent to the purposes of the other two, operating according to its own rules and rituals. Few readers will have any difficulty with this, especially if they are familiar with Lewis and

Tolkien. The problem lies with the fourth, which is the evil and violence which men and women themselves are capable of. Susan Cooper devotes an entire – and compellingly vivid – section to the depiction of a Viking raid on a Cornish village, in which 'blood ran bright over the quayside, and streamed down into the sea, clouding out dark and murky in the waves'.[13] But no connection is made between the evil of the Dark and the evil that men do, and, although I doubt if many young readers are troubled by this, it does weaken the mythic authenticity which ought to be the foundation on which this fantasy rests.

As for the 'scenic and atmospheric effects' which John Rowe Townsend refers to, there is no diminution of Susan Cooper's skill. The special effects are, as ever, brilliant. At one point, for example, Will and Merriman set off at a great pace towards a headland:

> an urgent loping running that took away their age and all sense of familiarity in their appearance; faster, faster, faster. And at the rocks ending the headland they did not pause, but went on. Will leapt up light-footed to the crest of Kemare Head and cast himself outwards into the air, into empty sky, arms spread wide, lying on the wind like a bird; and after him went Merriman, his white hair flying like a heron's crest. For an instant the two dark spread-eagled figures seemed to hang in the sky, then with a slowness as if time held its breath they curved downwards, and were gone.[14]

This is vivid and convincing word-painting; but it is not just word-painting. Certain phrases – *cast himself outwards, lying on the wind like a bird, as if time held its breath* – have the power to mime the inwardness of physical movement or hint at the elasticity of critical time.

That chapter-climax reminds us again that Susan Cooper is in fact a very traditional writer, for it takes Merriman and Will to the dark depths of the deepest seas, and the underwater descriptions are very much in the manner of John Masefield and T.H. White. Nor is she averse to scenes of horror in which the visual is intensified by an incantatory quality in the language:

> *And from out of the night*, over the roofs of Trevissick from the dark inland moors, *came sailing again* the phantom ship of Cornwall, single-masted, square-rigged, with a dinghy behind, that had sailed up *out of the midnight sea* in the haunting. Silently it

skimmed over houses and roads and quayside, and this time it was not empty, but had a figure at the helm. The drowned man, dripping and intent, whom Jane had seen glide up out of the sea, stood high on the deck at the wheel, *steering his black dead vessel* . . . [my italics].[15]

Susan Cooper is a very filmic writer, always striving for visual authenticity. But the italicised phrases (though no two readers would choose exactly alike) could not be replicated precisely on film – only background music could supply the missing quality.

As with so many children's books, the innovativeness of *Greenwitch* is so effectively disguised as to pass almost unnoticed. For this is a *feminine* novel, consciously or unconsciously involving itself in a debate with other children's writers. When Susan Cooper decided to bring together the characters of the two previous books in the series, it was a clever authorial move, creating in readers a feeling of expectancy and a sense of an overall design. And the reader is encouraged to anticipate that a rivalry will develop between Will and one or both of the Drew brothers. But, after some coolness, Will is simply accepted.

The dominant writer of fantasy for children in the sixties and seventies was Alan Garner, and the single most influential of his books was *The Owl Service* (1967), a novel which shocked (and in some cases outraged) a generation of adults because of its representation of violent and passionate hatred between two schoolboys, and their problematical relationship with a girl. In many respects, it is inappropriate to compare *Greenwitch* with *The Owl Service*; they are different types of fantasy altogether. However, Susan Cooper might have developed a rivalry between her two male protagonists, and she could have made it a violent one, central to the plot. Instead, she takes an independent narrative line and completely eschews adolescent male angst. Equally, she could have made Jane the focus of rage and the inspirer of passions, but instead she carefully represents her as the main resolving intelligence within the narrative.

Most of the great fantasies of the twentieth century have been masculine conflicts between good and evil in one shape or another. And any fantasy influenced by Malory will inevitably be shaped by deeply held cultural assumptions about the defining of masculinity, and the power of different versions of the feminine to inspire or disrupt it. Almost twenty years later Ursula le Guin was to face this issue when she wrote *Tehanu* as the revisionist fourth part of her great *Earthsea* trilogy. But in 1974 Susan Cooper in her very different way tackled a similar issue: what is the role of the fictional heroine in traditionally masculine fantasy for children?

In *Over Sea, Under Stone* Jane had been a derivative fictional school-girl who could have stepped straight out of any of a thousand holiday adventure novels. But in *Greenwitch* she is different from the outset. She is shown in the opening pages as more acute and more respons-ible than her brothers. She is also a peacemaker, the only member of the Drew family to want to be friendly with Will. Because she is a girl, she is invited to be present at the overnight making of the Greenwitch, a strictly female ritual which Jane finds alarming. Yet there is nothing particularly female about the Greenwitch itself; in fact, Susan Cooper stresses its indeterminateness, studiously avoiding any hint that the strange creature represents some hidden aspect of femininity.

> It looked, Jane thought, like a single representative of a fearful unknown species, from another planet, or from some unthink-ably distant part of our own past.[16]

Jane is horrified by the Greenwitch as an 'image of an appalling, endless loneliness',[17] and when she is told she may make a wish, her simple response is both apologetic and generous: 'Oh dear. I wish you could be happy.'[18]

Jane is presented as a thoughtful girl, constantly working things out, often slightly worried. She is the only one to be interested in and puzzled by Will, the Old One. She dreams of the Greenwitch deep beneath the sea, aware of her, telling her it has a secret, malevolently threatening to overwhelm her if she tells anyone what she knows. While the boys and Merriman have their adventures, Jane is given vision and understanding in one terrible episode in which, in a kind of waking nightmare, she sees all the brutality, mostly male, that has been part of the history of this Cornish village.

The great quest requires that the Greenwitch be persuaded to give up the 'secret' it has found, and much of the plot is concerned with the efforts both of the Dark and the Light to accomplish this. But, in spite of all their sound and fury – or what John Rowe Townsend calls their 'scenic and atmospheric effects' – each of them fails com-pletely, and Jane is left talking sadly to the Greenwitch in a dream. What triumphs in the end is her simple and generous impulse of compassion, for the Greenwitch gives the secret to her, because she is the first person in thousands of years to have had a benevolent thought for the feelings of this strange woman-made monster.

In the closing pages of the novel, Jane goes down to the water's edge to throw her silver bracelet into the sea, only to be stopped by Will. She explains:

> 'I know it sounds stupid,' she said reluctantly, 'but I wanted to give the Greenwitch another secret to keep. Instead of the one we took. In my dream,' – she paused, embarrassed, but went gamely on – 'in my dream, I said, *I will give you another secret*, and the Greenwitch said in that big sad booming voice, "*Too late, too late*," and just disappeared . . .'

Another act of generosity. But Will explains that silver will simply be blackened by the sea. Instead, he offers her a small gold strip with an engraved message, which he had prepared before as if in foreknowledge of her impulse of compassion.

> 'Here's your secret, Greenwitch,' Jane said, and she flung it into the sea. The little case vanished into the waves, their foam curling round the weed-fringed rocks. In the sunlight the water glittered like shattered glass.
> 'Thank you, Will Stanton,' Jane said. She paused, looking at him. 'You aren't quite like the rest of us, are you?'
> 'Not quite,' said Will.[19]

An interesting way to conclude the third novel of the series, with hints of an immanent understanding between masculine wizardry and feminine compassion, mind and feeling, boy and girl.

What Jane seems to represent is very English and no doubt very middle-class: ordinary feminine 'niceness' combined with a desire for fair play. What the Greenwitch represents is more problematical: something denied and repressed, ritually cast out into exile.

Unlike Blyton, who was mostly concerned with landscape as *arena*, all through the first three novels in the series Susan Cooper has been concerned to suggest the English landscape as a source of ancient drama, a many-layered and deeply rooted matrix of significance and mystery, caught in ancient mythical moralities of its own which affect the lives of everybody. Merriman and Will are priests of this sacramental landscape. Indeed, 'landscape' is not the best word, for it implies *surface* and what Susan Cooper is striving for in these narratives is a sense of a many-layered and abundant *depth*, an accumulated dynamism of mythical meanings in, on and under the earth, perpetually struggling to become manifest. In the last two books of the series she approaches what is to be the final apotheosis of this transfigured landscape, a climax specifically Welsh and Arthurian.

What prevents *The Grey King* and *Silver on the Tree* from descending into melodrama is Susan Cooper's unfailing ability to employ unpretentious descriptive prose in the service of a powerful sense of place. Landscape – mostly Welsh – is the *raison d'être* of these two novels. They are novels of muted colours, of greys and browns, of pale fading light, of dark and towering crags and gloomy clouds, of rain and mist, and of the slow wheeling of mountain birds over still cold lakes. Susan Cooper gives us in a thousand innocent phrases an entirely convincing, loving and authentic account of Wales in autumn. But she goes much further than describing the Wales of guidebooks and travel literature; she orchestrates or choreographs the landscape, making its myriad features dance to a complex Arthurian score. So the ordinary dramas of country-life – a fire on the hillside, sheep mauled to death, a farmer embittered by past events – retain their ordinary human dramatic power and at the same time are revealed as moments in an ancient and deeper drama as old as both Malory and the *Mabinogion*. And her extraordinary achievement is that the narrative perspective shifts so effortlessly from the parochial and everyday to the transcendental and back again that neither is diminished in the juxtaposing.

> Music was flowing out of the farmhouse in a golden stream, as if the sun were inside the window, shining out.[20]

That brief statement, combining two of the author's favourite preoccupations, music and light, exemplifies in miniature the novel's fundamental trope: an inside-out reversal, the ordinary transfigured from within. The hillsides contain a magic harp, the ancient Sleepers of so many Celtic legends, and the son of the great King Arthur himself. This wealth lies *within*, waiting to burst out '*as if the sun were inside the window, shining out*'. Simile, here, is not simply an aid to clarity and vividness; it is the illuminating gleam of quicksilver which relates the banal to the mythical. The italicised words in this next quotation, for example, refer back to one of the saddest aspects of the narrative, like a repeated musical phrase, structural rather than simply rhetorical.

> Then the mist closed over Llyn Mwyngil, the lake in the pleasant retreat, and there was a cold silence through all the valley save

for the distant bleat, sometimes, of a mountain sheep, *like the echo of a man's voice calling a girl's name, far away.*[21]

And when Will and Bran, earlier, find the great cave in the mountainside, they find to their amazement that it contains an entire cosmos.

> They stood, looking up. The stars blazed round them. There was no sound anywhere, in all the immensity of space. Will felt a wave of giddiness; it was as though they stood on the last edge of the universe, and if they fell, they would fall out of Time . . . As he gazed about him, gradually he recognised the strange inversion of reality in which they were held. He and Bran were not standing in a timeless dark night observing the stars in the heavens. It was the other way around. They themselves were observed. Every blazing point in that great depthless hemisphere of stars and suns was focused upon them, contemplating, considering, judging.[22]

Reversal again – a 'strange inversion of reality', in which the two boys are gravely studied by the stars from the remotest edges of the universe – inside a mountain!

The Grey King is a Wordsworthian narrative. William and Dorothy Wordsworth were never in their few creative years together content merely to describe landscape; he in his poetry and she in her journals strove to make words convey their sense of a countryside active and interactive between all its parts, and inspired to a dynamic responsiveness only by the imaginative and transforming power of the observer. Susan Cooper's fantasy achieves something similar.

> Already now the sky was a heavier grey than it had been, as the afternoon darkened towards evening and the clouds thickened for rain. But as the lilting flow of notes from the little harp poured out into the air, in an aching sweetness, a strange glow seemed very subtly to begin shining out of lake and cloud and sky, mountain and valley, bracken and grass. Colours grew brighter, dark places more intense and secret; every sight and feeling was more vivid and more pronounced.[23]

Dorothy Wordsworth would probably have had little patience with the magical harp – but the rest she would have responded to in instant recognition, especially the dynamic perception and enjoyment of light and colour.

In the last of the series, *Silver on the Tree*, time-slips are abrupt and frequent. The central idea is that the battle with the Dark which is happening in Will's own time is simultaneously the same battle fought by King Arthur at Badon. And there are other slips – to Roman Britain, for example, or the time of Owain Glyndwr, or nineteenth-century Welsh-speaking Aberdyfi. The most significant of these shifts takes Will and Bran to the Lost Land of Welsh legend, guided by Taliesin. This extended episode gives free range to Susan Cooper's extraordinary sense of variety and colour. The action moves rapidly, with the two boys surrounded by a carnivalesque and volatile sequence of unexplained images and characters.

> Faces flashed round them like a kaleidoscope's shaken images. A child swung a handful of bright streamers before their eyes, laughing, and was gone; a hopeful flurry of green-necked pigeons swooped by. They passed a group of people dancing, where a tall man decked with red ribbons played the flute, a gay, catchy little tune; they stumbled, almost, at a place on the smooth grey paving, over a fragile crumpled-looking old man who was drawing with chalks on the ground. Will had a sudden startled glimpse of the picture, a great green tree on a rounded hill, with a bright light shining out of its branches, before the flute-player led the dancers past him in a flurry of music, and he was whirled away.[24]

As with image, so with incident. The two boys are taken through a bewildering sequence of baffling challenges, riddles, terrors, tests and prophecies, everything highly charged with a strange dreamlike vividness and significance the precise meaning of which would be apparent only to a reader versed in the details of Celtic mythology and the *Mabinogion*.

There is a revealing passage at the beginning of the last section of the novel, in a chapter called *Sunrise*, when Jane, alone, walks down to the beach at dawn. It is a long unhurried and measured celebration of the land- and sea-scape of the estuary of the Dovey, recorded in lyrical detail. One paragraph must suffice to give some sense of its character:

> Flocks of roosting gulls rose lazily as she reached the smooth wet sand nearer the sea. Dunlins swooped, piping. Round any tide-left heap of seaweed thousands of sand-hoppers busily leapt, a strange flurrying mist of movement in all the stillness. The record of other flurrying was written already on the hard sand: gouges

and claw-marks and empty broken shells, where hungry herring gulls at dawn had seized any mollusc a fraction too slow at burrowing out of reach.[25]

Verbs and participles are the telltale authorial signature here; everything is in movement, or has left behind the signs of its movements. This description is not just a scene to be set, for, although the beach at Aberdyfi is charged with its own beauty and its own natural and savage dynamism, it is further charged with suspense and expectation, because throughout these last two books the very ground beneath the characters is alive and dynamic, enkindled by its own mythical past. And, sure enough, after three pages, 'two figures took shape in the flying sand, against the brilliant sun, like apparitions in a golden mist'[26] – and when Bran draws the sword which he has brought back with him from the Lost Land, 'the world brightened and filled with sudden colour as the sun shone out for a moment through a gap in the cloud'.[27] Susan Cooper's achievement is to have united authentic naturalistic description with a genuinely persuasive sense that the old Arthurian myths of the past are not lost at all, but currently and persistently active for our good, their dramatic moments spotlit by sudden shafts of radiant sunlight.

It seems perfectly appropriate that *The Dark Is Rising* should have come out of the same decade in which films like *Star Wars* and *Star Trek* upstaged the novel's ability to use special effects to kindle the mythopoeic imagination of a generation of readers and viewers. And what an achievement it was to cast a magic spell over landscape, history and myth, uniting them in one simple theory of time:

'For Time does not die, Time has neither beginning nor end, and so nothing can end or die that has once had a place in Time.'[28]

Furthermore, the five novels enact an idealised make-believe, a boy's longed-for dream – 'enact' because the narrative represents with a free-wheeling allegorical exactitude a child's sense of a secret inner life of pretending enmeshed within ordinary day-to-day living. I suggested in my chapters on Arthur Ransome's great series that there was a connection between fiction and play, between story and make-believe. I believe something similar happens in Susan Cooper's quintet; only here the series does not supply ideas for pretending – it exemplifies its essential nature, of imagination and fantasy enmeshed with the mundane facts of everyday life. This extended narrative does what so much childhood pretending does: it casts the boy as his own great hero, possessed of a secret wisdom so potent that he has to keep it hidden from the ordinary people around him; it provides him with a powerful sense of a story being acted out, of quests to be undertaken in the imaginative interstices of actual life, with complex rules to be learned, risks and dangers to be endured, not as an isolate but embedded in an ancient fellowship formed by the great mythical heroes of the past.

I will conclude with two embarrassing memories of my own wartime childhood. The first is of myself, aged nine or ten, coming out of the cinema where I had just watched Roy Rogers or Hoppalong Cassidy win his way through to a simplistic but satisfying triumph over wickedness. I recall making my way through the dark village streets, dodging behind streetlamps and shooting imaginary enemies in the dark with an imagined two-finger pistol, reeling occasionally when shot in the arm, galloping and rump-smacking my way across the allotments to arrive triumphantly in the safety of the backyard of my parents' house, where the moment of opening the backdoor was the transition – accomplished with the speed and ease of an eye-blink – back into ordinary living.

The second memory is rather strange, I suspect. It concerns a bizarre idea I secretly entertained that King Arthur and his sleeping knights would one day awaken and lead the Allied forces to a triumphant defeat of the Nazis. I believe I also put Robin Hood in the front line, too, together with Hereward the Wake. Later, this idea became more subtle and I wondered if Winston Churchill (whom I worshipped uncritically) was in fact the reincarnation of Arthur, speculating that the great mythical king would always come disguised in the form of a modern hero to assist Britain in her hour of need. I did not exactly *believe* this – I was, after all, not an idiot. But it was a kind of 'imaginative hypothesis' which I enjoyed playing with.

Perhaps that is why I cannot help recognising with such pleasure the climax of Susan Cooper's quintet, where Will rides to battle alongside the great King Arthur himself.

> '. . . *How goes the day?*' The voice rose into a searching shout, a question asked of no one visible, thrown at random into the grey mist.
>
> And out of the mist as if in answer a long shape loomed: a boat longer and larger than their own, taking shape nearer the bank as they drifted towards it on the stream. It was decked with weapons, filled with armed men, with plain green flags flying at

stem and stern; it seemed the boat of a general, rather than a king. But there was the bearing of a king in the figure at its prow: a square-shouldered man with sunburned face and clear blue eyes; brown hair streaked with grey, and a short grey beard. He wore a short blue-green cloak the colour of the sea, and beneath it armour like that of a Roman. And round his neck, half-hidden but glittering with a light like fire, he wore Will's linked circle of Signs.[29]

There have been other fictional children who have been permitted to gaze at Arthur in admiration; but Susan Cooper's fictional boy is a hero of today alongside the great hero of the mythical past, his comrade and his equal. The writing – as it has been throughout the entire series – is a perfect combination of control and dizziness, uniting in landscape and time: weather, myth, history, and the kind of heroic make-believe that any ordinary boy might unthinkingly create for himself.

But, alas for poor Jane! The promise of the third book – in which her specifically feminine intuitive kindness was decisive – is not fulfilled. Here, she gets to convey an important message; and we are told that Bran thinks she is pretty. That is all. She amounts to nothing in this narrative. In the end, Susan Cooper did not outsmart the overwhelming maleness of traditional myth and modern fantasy.

The time was not yet ripe for cultural super-heroines. And not once in all my memories of childhood can I recall any of the girls I knew smacking their rumps and galloping triumphantly across the prairies of my fenland village.

Part IV

In and out of school

10 Jane Austen has gone missing

Suppose that the novels of Jane Austen had been out of print since a generation or so after she died; that most general readers had never heard of her; that the literary histories rarely mentioned her; that literary critics paid her no attention; and that a few devoted enthusiasts worldwide paid three-figure sums for old copies found in second-hand bookshops, made illicit photo-copies for their friends, and kept in touch with fellow enthusiasts on a Jane Austen website. Imagine the diminishing of our experience of fiction if that were so – and the bafflement and frustration felt by the few who knew her work at their inability to bring the pleasure of reading it to the notice of the general reading public.

It is a preposterous hypothesis. But, within children's literature, a closely parallel situation *does* exist in the fact that the novels of Antonia Forest have been entirely out of print for years. There can hardly be a single young reader currently familiar with her work, and a good number of specialists in children's books have never heard of her.

I must choose my words carefully here: I do not mean to suggest that the works of Antonia Forest are 'as good as' the works of Jane Austen. Such a comment would be meaningless. I am, though, prepared to argue with some confidence that within the entire range of children's books published in the last hundred years she ought to occupy a position roughly comparable to that of Jane Austen in the wider world of adult fiction. There are similarities between them. Like Jane Austen, her piece of ivory is small – a single family and its members' various friends; like her, her social range is limited to the modestly well-off upper middle class, though with an awareness of what went on in the social shadows; like her, she has a brilliant ear for witty, intelligent and revealing dialogue; like her, she has a quietly ironic view of the shifty and devious compromises and backslidings of weaker characters; and, like her, her chief interest is the establishment of firmness of character, integrity and personal autonomy in an imperfect world. For her, as for Jane Austen, the Navy was a background ideal of potential courage and honour. And, like Jane Austen, she appears to tell her stories with such apparently casual ease that their subtleties can pass unnoticed.

Most importantly, Antonia Forest's novels teach young readers the nature of literary pleasure, inviting them as intelligent readers to participate in and reflect upon an optimistically ironic view of the world.

Antonia Forest wrote ten *Marlow* novels (twelve, if we include two related historical novels). If her work were in print she would be acknowledged as at least one of the best writers for children in English, and – in my view – the only writer of a sustained series who can be measured seriously alongside Arthur Ransome. Those readers who can see little psychological depth in the *Swallows and Amazons* series would probably value the *Marlow* series more highly, for Antonia Forest is a writer who is particularly interested in the complex ways in which a sense of social right and wrong may or may not grow out of private and egocentric feeling, psychology and motivation. And she developed and extended the series in totally original and ambitious ways, taking its worst clichés and transcending them.

There are ten novels in the series. The first was *Autumn Term*, published in 1948, a school story describing the experiences of identical twin sisters during their first term at boarding school. It has many of the features of popular school stories that have come to be regarded as clichés: the small injustices inflicted by teachers and prefects, the making and breaking of friendships, treacheries and deceptions, defeats and triumphs at games. But from the start Antonia Forest reveals an engaging determination to revitalise the clichés with a sharp authorial intelligence.

An example is the motif of identical twins.[1] The teachers in *Autumn Term* inevitably confuse them, but this first novel is more interested in the differences than in the similarities between the girls, Nicola and Lawrie – and in any case the muddles are usually more irritating or distressing than funny. Nicola – who is to develop as the central sympathetic intelligence throughout the series – is thoughtful, passionate, moderately good at most school activities; Lawrie is self-indulgent, often rather silly and weepy, but with the talent and commitment to become a brilliant and dedicated actress. They have four elder sisters, also at the school, and the difficulties of living up to the reputation of the family provide much of the comedy as the two youngest keep getting into scrapes.

I have referred elsewhere to the 'invisible excellence'[2] of much writing for children, its tendency to underplay its most complex and literary achievements. Antonia Forest's novels are in many ways especially exposed to the unjust neglect this characteristic can lead to. For me to take the easy road and tell the reader what these novels are 'about' would be to fall into the trap of recounting all the stereotypical features generally associated with school stories – thereby diminishing them. Plot summary is almost always reductive; the only way of acknowledging the particular quality of her writing is to scrutinise it *in detail*.

Autumn Term is a very funny novel, a good deal of the comedy arising from the character of Tim, another new arrival at the school and a niece of the headmistress. But more interesting than the surface comedy is the way Antonia Forest provides lessons for new young readers on how to read a 'literary' novel. Early in the novel when the main characters are still 'new girls', Tim helps herself to some pears from the headmistress' – her aunt's – private garden. She is challenged by one of the mistresses [my italics]:

> 'Where did that pear come from, Tim?'
> *Nicola jumped and blushed.* Tim said:
> 'I brought it with me.'
> 'From home?'
> *Now it would come, thought Nicola miserably.* And Tim would probably feel frightfully silly saying she'd taken it from Aunt Edith's garden. *Nicola ducked her head, cutting her bread and marmalade into babyish squares.*
> 'Yes, Miss Cartwright,' said Tim's voice easily.
> *Nicola gasped, a small choked sound, unheard in the steady clamour of the dining hall.*
> 'Extras from home are supposed to be kept for tea-time,' said Miss Cartwright in the kind impersonal voice the staff were using just now to explain breaches of rules. 'Remember another time, won't you?'
> 'But I like pears for breakfast,' protested Tim gently.
> 'Perhaps you do. But that's the rule.'
> 'Perhaps I'd better ask Aunt Edith about it,' suggested Tim.
> 'Is that your guardian? Because if so, and she particularly wants you to have fruit for breakfast, I should ask her to write to Miss Keith.'

'It *is* Miss Keith,' said Tim carefully.

Miss Cartwright frowned. '*Who* is Miss Keith?'

'My Aunt Edith. But she's not my guardian. I have two quite normal parents.'

Miss Cartwright gave Tim a quick, wary look, *as though, thought Nicola, to decide whether she was being ragged and if so, how much.* But Tim stared candidly back *as though there had been no silly evasion* over where the pears came from.

'If Miss Keith is your aunt,' said Miss Cartwright, still friendly, 'I think – don't you? – that you need to be rather specially careful not to ask for any special favours, even very small ones. I'm sure you'd rather, really, that Miss Keith didn't treat you differently from anyone else. Wouldn't you?'

'No,' said Tim tranquilly. 'I want a lot of special privileges, actually. All I can get.'

The friendliness went out of Miss Cartwright . . .[3]

This is characteristic of Antonia Forest's writing: while the surface is concerned with a trivial incident of school discipline, there is a deeper interest in the small moral shocks experienced by Nicola. The words I have italicised prompt a young reader into understanding that this episode is described not as it happened but as it is observed and *felt* by Nicola – her embarrassment for her new friend as she expects the truth to come out, her unnoticed gasp as Tim coolly lies about it, the shock to her expectations as Tim refuses to play the part of the self-effacing headmistress' niece. The young reader is being given lessons here on how to move in the ambivalent gaps between authorial and characters' viewpoints – an important readerly lesson for children who will go on to read the great classical novels.

Nicola is keenly interested in people, both children and adults. When she and Lawrie are enrolled as Guides, Nicola feels that there was a lack of appropriate drama in her part of it and, a little disappointed, sits back to watch her twin – the actress – do her part.

In her new, crisp uniform, [Lawrie] looked light and triumphant, as though at any moment she might fly. Her small, distinct voice saying the Promise made it sound like something real, not just a mumble of words to be hurried through because it was a formula which had to be said. Very erect, she saluted Captain, saluted the Colours, and then swung round to salute the Company as though – Nicola stumbled on her simile – as though she had just been given the V.C. and were saluting her regiment: a *cheering* regiment, thought Nicola, tucking her chin down to hide a wholly admiring grin.[4]

This is typical of Nicola – observant of herself and others, but generous and appreciative in her judgements – except when it comes to deliberate untruths. Lying and evasion are at the heart of this story, and indeed the whole series. One of the main events is the twins' dishonourable (and unjust) discharge from the Guides because their leader lies to cover her own shortcomings. Untruthfulness in this novel is more than a pivotal dramatic moment; it is the beginning of a sustained authorial interest in how a young person develops a sense of integrity and also manages to live in the real world without too many compromises. Nicola, at twelve years old, knows she despises duplicity, but a bigger difficulty is learning how to develop a *modus vivendi* for dealing with contemptible people you cannot help meeting every day. Truth to others and to oneself was to become a centrally unifying theme throughout the series.

By 1953, series fiction had divided itself fairly firmly into two types, the school story and the holiday adventure, reflecting fairly precisely the two different kinds of life experienced by children attending boarding school. However, the *Marlow* series broke new ground by switching freely from one to the other. The second in the series, *The Marlows and the Traitor* (1953), could hardly be more different from its predecessor. It is a naval adventure story and introduces the twins' brother, Peter, who is on holiday from Dartmouth College where he is a sea cadet. It is a beautifully paced and relentlessly exciting story about treason, detailing with considerable and chilling exactitude the realities for children caught up in the violence of the Cold War.

Much of the interest lies in Peter's personal struggle with his own private fears, but Antonia Forest also sets up a contrast between the different habits of thought of the twins, Lawrie and Nicola. When the children are captured at gunpoint, Lawrie manages to escape and the reader is given a sympathetic account of her thinking.

Like the others, [Lawrie] thought of spies and gangsters as people you met with chiefly in books and plays and films; but then to Lawrie, films and plays were never quite pretence; they were something, so Lawrie thought privately, which went on with a particular life of their own, even when the last performance was ended at the cinema or the curtain came down on the last act. When people burgled and spied and murdered in real life, it was, so Lawrie thought secretly, because the special life of the cinema and the theatre had overlapped the ordinary, safe, school-and-home life that she and her family lived. So to meet a man with a gun in an empty house seemed to Lawrie a perfectly possible thing to happen . . . Lawrie, in an odd way, was rather enjoying herself. She kept thinking: 'This is how it feels – this is how my feet go – when I'm in films I must remember this.'[5]

Lawrie's thinking is egocentric and – perhaps because of her totally serious commitment to acting – based on illusion. Nicola, still a prisoner, learns different lessons, often about herself. For example, when she manages to put sugar into the boat's fuel-tank, her captor is violently angry.

Somehow, his fury and the glimmer of panic behind his eyes, made her feel very cool and confident. The *Talisman*, caught between the current and the tide, was still being flung about like a bottle in a fast stream, but Nicola didn't care. She answered his questions briefly and truthfully . . .[6]

And later:

He shot [a question] at her. Nicola's cheeks felt as if they must crack, they felt so hot. Even though she wasn't particularly afraid of him any more, it took a fair amount of courage to answer at once: 'Because we think you're a traitor.'
    He looked at her with a queer violent expression, as if he would have liked to hit her. But before she could flinch, his expression altered . . .[7]

Not many children's writers could shift with such confidence from the escapades and rivalries of school life to this kind of narrative. But the writing does not falter, even when describing the physical dangers and suffering the children endure. In the best tradition of R.L. Stevenson, the ways in which the dangers are inwardly registered by the characters is always made available to the reader, often as the main clause alongside the syntactically subordinated outward details:

Nicola, dazed, soaked, chilled to the bone, her teeth chattering uncontrollably, still had room to feel triumphant.[8]

The novel ends with a moment of clear-thinking heroism on the part of Nicola's brother and the arrival of a Royal Navy destroyer ('motionless as a lance in rest'[9]) just in time.

In 1957 the third work in the series appeared. As if Antonia Forest was consciously determined to challenge the notion of the repetitively formulaic series, *Falconer's Lure* was yet another change of direction. This novel is a family story, set in the summer holidays, and its main interest is – unexpectedly – falconry. The Marlow family are spending the summer at Trennels, a rambling country house that belongs to their cousin Jonathan.

Like the series as a whole, *Falconer's Lure* defies generic definition. It is held together by a web of linked themes – flight and disaster, heights and depths, fear and courage, competition and friendship. The ecstatic delight felt by Nicola when her new friend's goshawk takes flight is set sharply against the fact that their cousin is a test pilot. At one point, Nicola and Patrick are out on the Downs with one of their birds, their companionable chat interrupted occasionally by hardly registered distant observations.

> Miles away and very high indeed, the plane turned, catching brightness from the sun. Then all they could see was the vapour trail thrusting across the sky.

And a few moments later:

> Nicola nodded enthusiastically. And then, as she stood up, it felt as if she had walked into a wall. For a moment, the landscape seemed to quiver. And then it was still again and she could move.

Then, after some puzzled conversation about that:

> The sky was quite empty now; the high white tracings had begun to fluff out in the wind. Over towards Rushton someone had lighted a bonfire. She could see the smoke drifting up.

This comfortable chapter – with its deceptively Ransome-ish summer-holiday feel of safety – concludes:

> The sun came down in slanting lines through the trees, and made a fishnet of light on the bed of the stream. It was doing that

when Nicola and [her brother] first met. It was still doing so, five minutes later. But by then Peter had managed to tell her that Cousin Jon had been killed when the plane crashed, and that made everything look quite different.[10]

This kind of writing leads readers towards adult fiction, requiring them to reread the chapter (probably), to confront (if they choose to) the way sudden tragedy changes everything around it, and to register (perhaps) that the chapter was ironically entitled 'Grand Stoop'.

Falconer's Lure is also held together by style, a vitality and integrity of syntax and language which seeks absolute faithfulness to experience and thought. The following extract is an example; it purports simply to describe what happens when Nicola arrives late for a meal and in need of first aid because she has been bitten by a goshawk [my italics]:

> Then [Rowan] asked what had Nicola really done to her hand and why was she so late, and, having been told, *advised iodine and haste*, and offered to make her explanations to the breakfast table. Nicola *accepted the advice reluctantly and the offer with gratitude*, and went upstairs to rummage in the first-aid cupboard in the bathroom and make *some rather gingerly passes at her thumb with the iodine bottle*. Then she wrapped her thumb in a large chunk of band-aid, and galloped downstairs to the dining-room. She said good-morning all round, kissed her mother, said Hullo to Tessa, the Afghan hound, who lay neatly curled in her usual mealtime place under Cousin Jon's chair, sat down *unobtrusively* between Peter and Lawrie, made a neat sandwich of *tepid* bacon and plain bread and munched it *hungrily*.[11]

This can be read as a simple account of the rumbustious energy of the young, but in fact the prose is constantly signposting the attentive reader's attention in all sorts of other directions: to the entirely commendable assistance of Rowan; the nicely stylised acknowledgement by Nicola that Rowan will forestall any family fuss ('Nicola accepted the advice reluctantly and the offer with gratitude'); her rather half-hearted courage with the iodine; while *unobtrusively* reminds us that she does not wish to attract her family's attention, *tepid* that she is late for breakfast, and *hungrily* that she has been out since dawn.

This kind of writing, with its vigorous capacity to shift its descriptive perspective, requires a reader to develop a deft ability to map-read what is going on. The next passage occurs when the family begins to accept the fact that, after the death of Jon, the farm now belongs to them.

> Nicola had stopped listening. She was shooting little glances round the dining-room to try to surprise it into telling her what it was going to be like, eating meals in it for ever. Ann, noticing, asked what she was looking for and had she seen a wasp? Nicola said Nothing, and No, she hadn't, and concentrated on finding the cloves in her apple tart so that they couldn't surprise her in the middle of a bite. But she went on staring at the dark red wall-paper and the mahogany side-board with the hunting scenes carved on the panels, and trying to discover what it was going to be like, living with them always.[12]

The shift from action to thought, from the outer to the inner, from the social to the private, from seeing to reflecting, from the cerebral to the physical, is reminiscent of another great contemporary writer, William Mayne. In addition, a *Marlow*-reader will appreciate and savour the fact that Ann's well-meant but inappropriate fussing is entirely characteristic.

Antonia Forest's faithfulness to experience and feeling is both a matter of style and a central concern of the series. Nicola's sister Ginty (partly under the influence of a school-friend called Unity Logan) is susceptible to emotional artifice, to a cultivation of sentiment and phoney feeling. During one family gathering, when Nicola has been reading aloud 'Fear no more the heat o' the sun', Ginty purloins Shakespeare's song and connects it with the death of their cousin.

> 'It'll always mean him, though,' said Ginty suddenly, in a special voice. 'Every time I hear it now, I shall think –'
>
> 'Oh, don't talk such *nonsense*,' said gentle Karen, so furiously that they all jumped. 'You talk as if Shakespeare wrote it specially with you and Jon in mind! Well, he didn't. He wrote it to fit a scene in a play about a perfectly imaginary character, who wasn't dead at all. And it doesn't apply to Jon any more than to millions of people who've died younger than they should. I simply can't stand that sentimental wallow you do with Unity Logan –.'
>
> 'We *don't* wallow,' said Ginty, her face flaming, and knowing suddenly what Amy March meant when she described herself as mortified. For it was quite true she'd only said it because it was the sort of thing Unity would have applauded and while it was in

her head it had sounded so well and so sensitive, she'd thought even her family would be impressed. Scarlet, and on the edge of tears, she reached for her book, and hunching her back to the room, made as if she'd begun to read again.[13]

Adolescent readers cannot fail to recognise the situation described in the last sentence – though they might not consciously note how the description has moved from Ginty's state of feeling to an observer's view of her as she sits miserably 'hunching her back to the room'. Furthermore, the shift is not only from outer to inner, but also from one character to another, not to mention the quick glance outwards to the wider world of literature and thought.

Peter's Room, the fifth in the sequence, marks a significant change of gear. It is one of the most complex novels ever written for children, a many-layered exploration of the often ambivalent ways in which literature, biography and history can enter the psychology of the young. I have already commented upon Antonia Forest's ability to point a reader's interest in several different directions, directed by the flexibility of syntax; in *Peter's Room*, a similar variety of narrative highways is apparent in the construction of the plot. The novel is shaped around the children's interest in the lives of the Brontës, and in particular their Gondal and Angria 'plays'. The reader is invited to share this interest as the novel operates on two concurrent levels – the actual daily life of the Marlows and the fantasy life they lead as they make up their own 'play' and tell it, or act it. Several sustained fantasy episodes are printed in italics, requiring the reader to read each dialogue utterance in two ways, one for its narrative significance in the 'play', the other for its emotional significance for the child 'playing' it.

Each of the children takes into the play some aspect of his or her secret self, half-exposing it, half-shaping it, and the momentum of the fantasy proves to have its own power over their actual lives. For Lawrie, it is chiefly a delicious opportunity to act; for Peter, a way of vicariously dealing with his mostly controlled tendency to bullying and violence, and his interest in his own capacity for treachery and betrayal; only Nicola is mistrustful (though she feels slightly ashamed about that as she admits to herself that she frequently enjoys make-believe in private). Their friend Patrick has already noticed that, although all the Marlow girls were quite nice-looking 'in their fair-haired, blue-eyed way', it is Ginty 'who had the real looks',[14] and through the 'play', she and Patrick are drawn together in an attraction which is never fully acknowledged by them as a real attraction.

It is here that *Peter's Room* rejoins the earlier novels' interest in truthfulness, openness and integrity. Ginty is much given to self-deception, and this Brontë-like 'playing' provides many opportunities. When Ginty accidentally sees a passage in Frobisher describing a frozen ocean *after* the children had made up just such an ocean for their 'play', her excitement is heady, seductive and – ultimately – dishonest. She plays with the attractive notion that what we imagine amounts to a stumbling upon some other kind of 'truth'.

> But Ginty's thoughts pranced and strutted, deliberately fantastical: reading and re-reading Frobisher's words she told herself . . . that by some side-stepping chance they had uncovered one of the secrets of the world: had come, unaware, to another dimension in which, it might be, Crispian and Rupert and the rest were true – had been true – and they themselves were only acting out something which had once been real. It could happen. It did happen. If one wanted proof one only had to remember those two plays of Priestley's – *I Have Been Here Before* and *Time and the Conways* . . . and always provided one didn't say it aloud (especially to Nicola) it was gloriously convincing; it was like Flecker's poem about the oldest of the ships – about the mast breaking open with a rose and all the planks putting on leaves again: a thing which could be true – if only it was.[15]

It is difficult to imagine a young reader graduating straight from, say, *The Famous Five* to a dazzlingly multi-faceted narrative like this. The overwhelming dominance of Blyton throughout the fifties and sixties determined for many adults their notion of what children's literature was. But our literary histories ought to acknowledge – despite the fact that Antonia Forest's writing is largely forgotten and Enid Blyton's has endured – that *both* were making provision for young readers. Although Blyton is credited with helping millions of children to discover the pleasures of reading, nothing in her linear and literal narratives could prepare them for the supple and vibrant complexity of Antonia Forest's writing. The *Marlow* series is consistently interested in the life of the mind, the way it enmeshes itself with feeling and desire, and its sometimes dangerous need for literature and ideas. Forest's children move in a living culture in which music, history and literature are not 'delivered' to the children but *needed by them* and sought out from motives that often lie too deep for explicit understanding. Literature in a very real way enhances and validates their everyday lives, and tests their character.

But this Brontë-like 'playing' has its dangers, as is seen when Ginty and Patrick devise a separate 'play' with themselves as lovers (Rosina and Rupert). They immediately conclude that the others can't be told about this: 'had they been asked why they would probably have said the others were too young'.[16] Immediately they become involved in secrecy and furtiveness, and Ginty being so given to self-flattery and slightly dishonest feeling is already halfway to being in love with Patrick. The sceptical Nicola suspects what is going on.

> All the same, they were behaving – oddly. Every so often their eyes would meet and a glance pass between them – and not at all an ordinary *isn't this fun?* or *isn't this murder?* glance either. She caught them at it quite a number of times and continued mystified until the moment when Patrick, lifting his glass, made the slightest gesture in Ginty's direction as of drinking to her. And then she recognised his Rupert face.
>
> She couldn't have said precisely how Patrick's Rupert face differed from his own: only that it was recognisably different.[17]

This 'difference' in them all worries Nicola as the 'Gondalling' becomes more and more dangerous. At one point, several pages of italicised 'playing' are interrupted simply by – in plain font,

> 'Get up and let's act this properly,' said Ginty urgently[18]

– requiring of the reader some swift-footed imagining. Why is it so 'urgent', and why for Ginty in particular? And how were they doing it before? The violence of the 'play' bursts out in a furious row between Peter and Patrick in which the latter determines (as Rupert) to shoot himself. His Rupert face again frightens Nicola, who knocks aside the old pistol he is holding to his head.

> Whereupon a number of things happened all together.
>
> Patrick exclaimed and doubled over, clutching his wrist: the pistol struck the edge of the table: there was a flash: the window-pane behind Lawrie's head starred and splintered: the explosion roared: the dogs woke and burst into hysterical barking: the cold bright air rushed through the broken pane: and from the spinney a furious voice shouted, 'Hey! Stop that! What on earth d'you think you're playing at?'[19]

– which serves to show that Antonia Forest can write straightforward fast-moving accounts of action when she needs to (though, even here, the outside speaker's angry choice of words has a nice ironic precision).

This almost-disaster is too much for Nicola. She had always been a reluctant and rather worried participant in the 'Gondalling'; now she suddenly and happily finds that her mind is made up. Despite their protests, she announces that she has had enough.

> 'But it's four to one,' hectored Lawrie.
>
> 'I don't care if it's a billion to a quarter,' said Nicola, discarding family democracy at the same time she put on her mackintosh. 'I think the whole thing's quite mad. And I think those Brontës must have been absolutely *mental*, still doing it when they were thirty, nearly!'[20]

That is Nicola's last word upon the seductive falseness and real danger of what they have all been doing. But it is not her last word on the Brontës, nor on the power of the recorded past to influence the experienced present. When her merlin, Sprogg, is found dead, Nicola consoles herself with the thought that she will be able to stay in bed longer like other people.

> Instantly, at the unguarded thought, tears flooded her eyes, and furiously she blinked them dry. If she was going to behave like this every time she thought of him, it was going to be simply ghastly . . .
>
> A sentence wrote itself across her mind: *Our poor little cat is dead. Emily is sorry.* She thought it again as she went on towards the house, and the clenched, wrung feeling inside her began to slacken. She couldn't have said why Emily Brontë's long-ago sorrow should have been comforting, but it was.[21]

Peter's Room is a very 'literary' work; it has an interest in literature and biography, and in the workings of the developing literary mind of young readers. It is the most complex of the series. In the next, *The Thuggery Affair* (1965), Antonia Forest takes a step in yet another new direction; it is the only one of the ten novels in which Nicola does not appear, concentrating almost exclusively on Lawrie, Peter and their friend Patrick, who find themselves caught up in a drug-running adventure. That was followed by *The Ready-Made Family* (1967), a family story in which Karen, the eldest of the Marlows, gives up her place at Oxford to marry a widower much older than herself with three small children, thereby involving some complicated

family rearrangements as the Marlow children have to accommodate
a new older brother aged 41. The next two works, *The Cricket Term*
and *The Attic Term* (1974, 1976), return to the school story genre,
the second of them picking up the account of Ginty and her love for
Patrick – and the duplicity this involves her in. Finally, *Run Away
Home* (1982) is a sea-adventure story in which the Marlow children
– except the virtuous Ann – rescue a runaway Swiss boy in care and
sail him across the midwinter Channel to be reunited with his father.

The editors of *Outstanding Sequence Stories* have drawn attention to
one important feature: 'Although published over a period of 34 years
this closely knit series covers only 28 months in the adventurous lives
of the land-owning Marlow family in the 1940s.'[22] That is so, and
the development of all the children in the family is represented in all
its complex and chameleon complexity. It is Nicola, however, who
remains the central interest in the series as a whole. In *The Ready-
Made Family*, she has to accommodate herself to some worrying new
ideas and situations. Her clever sister's new and older husband, Edwin,
does not take well to the lifestyle of the Marlow children, and there
are some tense family scenes like this one, in which Peter – speaking
in his Mummerzet dialect – challenges Edwin's authority:

> 'But gaffer, there 'baint no call for alarm, like –'
> 'That's for me to judge.'
> 'Nay gaffer, but be ee sure as ee be a true judge? 'Tes –'
> 'Peter, if Edwin doesn't want Charles and the others [his own
> children] to –'
> 'Nay, but 'tes sich foolishness. 'Tes jes' a windy ol' –'
> His voice suddenly loud and harsh, the two veins as suddenly
> noticeable in the centre of his forehead, Edwin said 'Don't inter-
> rupt your mother when she's speaking. And don't use that damned
> silly manner when you're talking to me.'
> Apart from [Edwin's children], who found it exquisitely funny,
> there was no one present who hadn't felt equally maddened, one
> time or another, by Peter and his Mummerzet; but any sympathy
> with Edwin on this score was entirely dissipated by his officious-
> ness on Mrs. Marlow's behalf; he was instantly outside the pale
> with all the other visiting adults who had, at one time or an-
> other, uttered such fatal words as *Do as your mother tells you;*
> silent hostility towards Edwin began to smoulder about the table
> and Karen's hands clenched in her lap as Peter said deliberately
> 'Nay, gaffer, wot be the 'arm in a quiet stroll along the embank-
> ment, like?'

[Edwin's children] sat round-eyed, bating their breath. Edwin's mouth thinned and tightened. 'You can walk where you please. I'm only concerned with the children.'

'Eh, m' dear, but there be no call –'

'*Peter*,' said his mother.

'Nay, Ma, nivver ee side with ol' wet-blanket. Dü ee tell un –'

'Binks, do pack it in,' said Karen desperately.

'Eh, m' dear, there's one thing I can tell ee, an' that's for sure. Your ol' man doesn't scare me any, let un huff an' puff howsomever –'

Chas spluttered. Rose looked frightened. Edwin's hand came down flat on the table and his voice rose as he said 'Don't be so damned impudent! And unless you drop that nonsensical manner –'

'Yes, brother,' said Peter. 'What then?'[23]

Also in *The Ready-Made Family*, there is a nice moment when, rather to her own surprise, Nicola refuses to give way to her twin's tantrums and leaves her 'to stop crying and come home by herself. Or not, as she chose.'[24] It is a small step towards self-knowledge and autonomy – as is her astonishing discovery that local people think rather highly of her: 'Mind yourself, now,' the station-master says to her. 'Good ones are scarce.'[25]

Towards the end of *The Ready-Made Family* Nicola's new and very young step-sister, Rose, runs away to Oxford where she used to live before her mother died. In her distress and confusion, Rose is befriended by a child-molester – and, in a totally convincing and compelling account, we are told how Nicola finds her and gets her out of this new danger. There are no schoolgirl heroics, just a careful faithfulness to experience:

'Will we ever see him again?' [Rose asked.]

'Good *heavens* no,' said Nicola: and saw she was wrong. On the other side of the road, a camel-covered coat kept pace with them.

There had been other occasions in her life when she'd said or thought *Gosh, I was absolutely petrified* and thought she'd known what she was talking about. But now, as her mouth dried and her heart raced and her limbs seemed to freeze, she knew fear of a quite different order. The road in which they walked seemed darker than before, the lights of St. Giles very far away . . .[26]

This novel began with the oldest sister, Kay, giving up English at Oxford in order to marry a widower with three children. How appropriate, then, that her younger sister Nicola should at the end of the novel go to Oxford instead. True, Nicola is only thirteen and has gone there to search for a little girl who has gone missing. But, before beginning her hunt, she allows herself to be briefly bewitched by Oxford[27] – its architecture, its skyscape, its clocks, and the way so much of Oxford life is enmeshed with history and literature, from Edmund Campion to Lord Peter Wimsey. Antonia Forest makes nothing explicit: but the implication is that Oxford awaits Nicola, and that the appreciative Nicola is readying herself for everything that Oxford means.

This suggestion (if that is what it is) is supported by a clever narratorial use of Latin. Nicola is pleased to find she can translate *Fortis est Veritas* without having to think about it; and, later, her Latin has an urgent practical use when she needs to explain to her step-sister's father – a Latin scholar – what has happened without letting Rose herself know how serious it might have been.

> And she said carefully, in deference to Edwin and Oxford, 'Ille homo – dixit Rosam – nuntius est ex mater. Dare nos cibus et – et propellent nos tuus domus –'
>
> '*What* did you say,' said Rose.
>
> But Edwin had caught the drift of her puppy Latin. He said, 'You mean you were – accosted? You weren't – nothing happened, did it?'
>
> 'I think it might have,' said Nicola exactly. 'But we got away.'[28]

Exactly is a precise authorial tribute to Nicola's good sense and lack of histrionics. And *exactness* is the defining characteristic of Antonia Forest's writing – even here, where dog Latin rather appropriately becomes *puppy Latin*. And again, later, when Rose and her father both admit how much they miss Rose's dead mother, Nicola remembers the phrase *sunt lacrimae rerum* and knew 'exactly what it meant'.[29]

The extended account of Nicola in nine of the ten *Marlow* novels is the fullest and sharpest representation in English children's literature of a child's development, her growth in self-understanding and autonomy, the firming-up of her sense of integrity and ability to judge others. A chapter similar to this could also have been written about the elusive dynamics of Nicola's friendships. Many other writers have mined this seam, but I know of none who has so richly shown the complex intermeshing of family and culture, of private values and social assumptions, and of physical, emotional and aesthetic pleasures. Furthermore, the ten stories do not set their main characters against a more-or-less static backcloth: the other members of the family, and the other children at school, are represented as complex and changing; and circumstances constantly change, too, the grown-up world beset with illness, death and real-life problems. In that context, the series subtly and unobtrusively champions the mind, providing a fictional enactment of the growth of reflective thought – a growth which never leads towards isolation or élitism but always towards life, people, and the great cultural expressions of humanity – religion, art, music, drama and literature.

Why, then, is the entire series out of print? The original publishers were Faber, but in 1978 a deal was struck which allowed Penguin to reissue the four school stories separately as Puffins. These were packaged and marketed as a series on their own and numbered in some editions 1 to 4 on the spine, seriously misleading young readers into thinking that here was a routine set of school stories, coherent in themselves. However, the second, third and fourth make so many references back to the other stories in the series that a new young reader would find it very confusing, possibly baffling. The result might have been predicted: sales in both the four Puffins and the titles remaining with the Faber imprint fell to the point when further reissues could no longer be justified. Since I wrote this chapter, Faber and Faber have announced that *Autumn Term* – the first of the series – is being reissued in the Faber Children's Classics series.

Perhaps there were other factors. The move in schools away from the 'literary novel', the shift from boarding school stories towards a fiction more representative of the lives of most children, and ideological misgivings about novels recounting the lives of families with servants and big estates, have all contributed to what must amount to the worst publishing misjudgement in the history of children's books in Britain.

We still have Jane Austen. But Antonia Forest and Nicola Marlow have gone missing.

11 The various voices of Gene Kemp

When *The Turbulent Term of Tyke Tiler* was published in 1977 it was an instant success. Adults and children were struck by its originality, and in particular by the way in which Gene Kemp had deceived her readers into thinking that the narrative voice was male, only to reveal at the end that it was female. It was undoubtedly a clever stroke, raising issues of both gender and narrative, and no doubt it unobtrusively taught many children that crucial readerly lesson – that reading and rereading must always be different experiences.

I recall an afternoon when I was observing a student-teacher with a Year 6 class (top juniors, they were called then). She had been serialising *The Turbulent Term of Tyke Tiler* and was to end the afternoon by reading aloud the final chapter and the Postscript, fully expecting hilarity and delighted amazement at the narratorial deception that had been practised on the unwitting listeners. Alas, it did not happen like that; there were a few minutes of puzzlement and confusion – and then great indignation all round. When it had been established beyond all doubt that Tyke the boy was in fact Theodora the tomboy, anger erupted – and especially from the girls. There was no hint of feminist triumph in them, just a sense of disappointment. They felt cheated. I hope I gave the student some appropriate professional advice: she should have allowed time to engage the children in appropriate discussion, gone back in search of early clues, studied the illustrations, and generally directed the class to some understanding of narrative in general and first-person narrative in particular. But it was 3.30 on a Friday and she had not allowed for any of that.

However, I confess I have some sympathy with those indignant children. I find *The Turbulent Term of Tyke Tiler* a difficult book to reread, because, although it employs a girl narrator speaking as if she were a boy, it still feels like a male text in narrative drag. However, no such considerations influenced those angry children that afternoon; both the girls and the boys *needed* Tyke to be a boy. And in some ways I believe Gene Kemp's brilliant ending was unfortunate. It has subsequently distracted readers from the fact that this novel – and indeed the whole *Cricklepit Combined School* series which developed from it – is original and innovative in ways that go far beyond the éclat of the discovery that Tyke is Theodora. Some adult readers, I believe, felt that Gene Kemp would never be able to pull off anything so spectacular again – whereas, in fact, she manages to pull off something entirely different and altogether more interesting.

There had come a moment in the history of children's books at which – to the dismay of many – there was a conscious move to abandon the 'literary novel' in favour of accessible and popular fiction generally. Rightly or wrongly, the 'literary novel' came to be seen as a literature associated with, and written by, the upper middle classes, often embodying ideological assumptions remote from the lives of most of the children attending state schools, and employing language and narrative forms that put off more young readers than they attracted. It was a division between literature and teaching. Whatever the rights and wrongs of this debate, it undoubtedly set children's writers a new challenge (or an old challenge made more urgent) – to write narratives which were richly evocative and multi-layered in language and form but which were at the same time straightforwardly accessible to inexperienced young readers. Or, to put it more bluntly, to compose in relatively easy language without being banal, and to make fiction whose complexities and subtleties did not act as a deterrent. A few writers managed it, none more successfully than the incomparable Jan Mark;[1] others adapted, as can be seen by comparing the early novels of Philippa Pearce with her last, *The Way to Sattin Shore*.

One of the consequences of the cry for accessibility and relevance was a flood of first-person narratives, often a recipe for sloppy writing. At its best, a first-person child or adolescent narrator can delight young readers by shocking them with recognisable idioms, forbidden vulgarisms, and subject-matter which would normally be taboo. It can create a secret readerly joy by seeming to invite the child into collaborations which will shock outraged adults. At its very best, it can take a young reader into sharply satirical and disturbing perspectives on the personal and social issues that begin to seem especially urgent in adolescence – sex, death, injustice, poverty and, above all, adult hypocrisy.

192 Reading series fiction

But, with a good many first-person novels of the period, authority (author-ity?) was sacrificed in favour of a bogus authenticity. The gain of an authentic first-person narrator was not always worth the loss of the personal authorial voice. A kind of confidence trick was played on young readers, who were assumed not to understand that a first-person narrative was just as much an artifice as any other – and, indeed, often 'artificial' in that its avowed authenticity was in the worst cases little better than a fake.

But what Gene Kemp makes the first-person narrative achieve is extraordinary. In *The Turbulent Term of Tyke Tiler* the voice of the unruly Tyke provides a richly ironic child-centred view of day-to-day life which is neither narrow nor egocentric. This, together with the comedy, would be enough. But Gene Kemp manages also to suggest a richly complex world-picture of overlapping circles of care and responsibility. One centre is the home; another is the school and its ethos and culture; within that is the particular community of the classroom; and all of these exist in the wider community, together with its local history and local politics. Moving from one to the other, the children carry their own wavering and developing sense of concern for each other. All this is achieved in what is in fact a very short novel of about 120 pages, held together by this strong sense of social continuity and connectedness. This is a major achievement and a significant development of the school story genre, which had in its most traditional forms emphasised insularity. At a stroke, Gene Kemp turned the school story inside-out. Not since William Mayne's *Choir School* quartet had a school itself – its eccentricities, muddles, dilemmas and essential structure – been so lovingly and realistically represented.

The Turbulent Term of Tyke Tiler seems to lend itself to perform-ance, which is perhaps why it was so popular for many years as a text to read aloud in classrooms. But there are important signs for the private reader, too. Its alliterative title; its dedication to an actual school; the cast-list of teachers, schoolchildren, family members and 'Fatty, a large piebald mouse'; its jokes, riddles and puns at the head of each chapter ('What did the crude oil say when it was coming out of the ground?' / 'Knickers'.); and its Postscript supposedly written by the class-teacher – all these peritextual features indicate to a reader that this is a new kind of novel. The consequence in the late 1970s was that the book enkindled a sense of lively expectation in both listeners and readers, an agreeable and bracing frisson of anticipa-tion, and an expectation of comedy. This promise is richly fulfilled. Furthermore, the humour and likeability of Tyke do not obscure the fact that a serious central theme is compassion and responsibility for others. The representation of a boy with special needs – and an acknowledgement of the comedy occasionally to be found in incidents involving him – was boldly innovative, and Tyke's concern for him is realistically unsentimental: loyal, but often irritated and frustrated.

Gene Kemp's style is the prose equivalent of sketching: the movement of the narrative is rapid, energetic, always suggestive of more than it depicts. The story is about caring communities – especially the school and the home – and the nurturing of respect and concern for *every* individual member of the group. Such a democratic premise required a democratically accessible narrative language. To readers of all kinds and from all social backgrounds, *The Turbulent Term of Tyke Tiler* succeeds in speaking about serious and central moral issues – not through overt didacticism but by creating a narrative which enacts and demonstrates its essential concerns.

It was not surprising that in 1979 Gene Kemp published a sequel, *Gowie Corby Plays Chicken*, set in the same school but concerning different children. Gene Kemp seemed determined to make full use of one of the most convenient characteristics of schools that make school stories so amenable to series fiction – the constantly changing characters as pupils (and sometimes teachers) move on. *Gowie Corby Plays Chicken* is in many ways an even more innovative work than its predecessor, as if the author was deliberately setting herself a fresh challenge and seeking new ways of avoiding the formulaic predictability of much sequence fiction.

The narrative voice of Gowie Corby right from the start is clearly that of a bully and a failure, with hints of the background factors which contribute to his outcast status. He is loathed by everyone in his class, particularly the pathetic Heather whom he especially victimises, and a few boys (notably Jonathan Johns) with whom he has a particularly vicious rivalry. He steals, he wrecks, he sneers, he enjoys horror films, and he immediately sees through all the highly skilled blandishments of his well-intentioned teacher. This is assured writing, and shows Gene Kemp's ability to 'do the voices' of the classroom:

> 'I hope we shall have a pleasant year together and do some interesting things,' [Miss Plum] goes on, and yes, miss, they all chorus like sheep bleating, baa, baa, the creeps. I jab the underside of the table with my little knife. She hands out cardboard.
> 'First, I should like you all to make folders to keep your work in, and record cards to record what you have been doing. You

may decorate the folders if you wish, with a suitable picture or pattern, and remember to write your names clearly.'

Soon we are all scribbling like crazy. I borrow Heather's new felt tips and draw bombs, machine guns and swastikas over mine, together with my sign, the vampire. It looks very nice and cosy when finished, so I sit and admire it, adding a few finishing touches from time to time. The teeth, with blood oozing, are particularly good.[2]

It is not easy to write an entire novel in the present tense; it is more likely to suggest artifice than immediacy. But here it adds a nerviness, an almost Swiftian *jouissance*, the voice shifting with a quick mercurial deftness from authentic schoolboy sulkiness to a clever parody of art criticism ('The teeth, with blood oozing, are particularly good'). But *Gowie Corby Plays Chicken* is an especially dramatic narrative, not because it is told in the present tense but because the narrator consciously revels in his role as dramatic villain, with an intelligent and malicious appreciation of the comedy he provokes.

Miss Plum was reading this poem called 'The Listeners'. It's a bit wet, but spooky, and outside the room, a pneumatic drill buzzes away as she shouts out the words to us, when suddenly it stops and she is heard bellowing at the very top of her voice:

'And his horse in the silence champed the grasses . . .'

We fall about laughing while she does a cherry right up her neck and over her face.

Afterwards we are supposed to write out a poem for our folder; I don't, I do a fantastic picture of Heather being tortured in a deep dark dungeon instead.[3]

It is extremely difficult to keep young readers interested in an unlikeable main character. Gene Kemp probably knew this, which is why there is a shift of emphasis in Chapter 3: Gowie loses his grim and boorish destructiveness and betrays a positive *joie de vivre* at the anticipation of disorder. He becomes chief mischief-maker, planning and savouring the enjoyment of mayhem rather than just grimly being a wrecker. In one episode he trips up the unfortunate Heather during the Harvest Festival in church:

There's a song my mother sings when she's had a few, that goes 'Something in the way she moves', well, that 'She' isn't Heather, I never saw a worse mover as she arches her back, throws up her feet, lets out a screech and flings her eggs wildly in the air, finally collapsing in the aisle, while the eggs fly out of their cartons right over the boy now tripping over her and who just happens to be . . . and my voice rises up to the roof with joy . . . Jonathan Johns . . . proudly carrying the biggest offering, he always brings the biggest, the great show-off, and it's a huge basket of fruit with cellophane and ribbon on it.

And JJ is showered with falling eggs, and Heather is wailing from her seat on the floor. Miss Plum rushes forward and tries to clean up the egg juice off Jonathan with a very wee small hand-kerchief. Sir gets Heather to her feet and keeps the procession moving. The Vicar hasn't noticed, but then, he is deaf, and Darren hasn't noticed, but I don't care, I'll worry about that later. Right now, we are about to sing:

'We plough the fields and scatter . . .'
Singing loudly, I join in.
'The rotten eggs on the land . . .'
And I turn round a little, full of happiness . . .[4]

Such lively writing is deceptive; it looks simple, straightforwardly moving along in the syntax of chat. But its farcical speed of movement is not unlike a *Tom and Jerry* film, and its swiftly sketched visual precision is reminiscent of a comic strip in *Beano* or *Dandy*. Furthermore, it is full of voices, requiring of a young reader (or a teacher reading aloud) a considerable deftness in moving between the language of the speaker's home, the popular music of an earlier era, the Bible, hymn-singing, and traditional schoolchildren's parody of hymn words – all contained within Gowie's convincing appreciation of the farcical disaster he has set in motion.

Gowie is eventually beaten up by a gang, and his account of his fear is grimly persuasive. It is a turning-point, for he is rescued by Rosie Lee, a black American girl new to the district, with a brace on her teeth and an articulate and fearless capacity to meet violence with firmness. Most young readers probably respond to the moment with pleasurable readerly anticipation, immediately predicting that she will befriend the wretched Gowie and 'reform' him. They are right; his conversations with her gradually reveal (like many a real-life case-study) that Gowie's dad is in prison and – more importantly – his brother Joe was recently killed in a motor-cycle accident. The novel becomes a novel about friendship like *The Turbulent Term of Tyke Tiler*, and about how one child can be rescued by another, both outsiders.

Writing of this kind (bracing, double-edged, irreducible, like Quentin Blake in prose) is fully tested when it has to represent a serious personal crisis, or suggest a real and serious depth of feeling. Such a moment comes when Gowie is about to be caned by the headmaster, and his present-tense interior monologue merges seamlessly with outer dialogue to uncover not only the tension of the moment and Gowie's grief and confusion, but also the headmaster's understanding and frustration.

Don't let him cane me, Don't let him cane me, DON'T LET HIM CANE ME. Then as in a nightmare I hold out my hand, the cane whooshes, it hurts, it hurts. I don't cry. He looks at me. Is he waiting for the tears?

'Corby, did that hurt?'

'Yes, Sir. On the outside, Sir.'

He puts down the cane.

'Not an inside hurt. Not like . . .?' He watches me.

I look away. I don't want to know. I don't want to be conned again, like Merchant cons me into telling things I don't want to say. Yet I do say.

'Not like with [my brother]. When he was dead, and my mother wouldn't stop screaming. Or seeing my puppet broken. Sir.'

'Go away, boy. Try to keep out of trouble. Where's [Rosie], today?'

'She's away, Sir. With a sore throat.'

'Stay with her and away from [Jonathan Johns] and you might get through the year. Go now, Corby.'

'Sir. Aren't you gonna cane me, any more?'

We look at one another, then he says,

'There isn't much point.'

'Thank you, Sir.' I wait, then –

'I did break the cistern, Sir. And my mother won't pay the money.'

'You want to be caned.'

'No. But I don't want not to be.'

The blows are sharp and swift. I cry as I leave the headmaster's study. Only, I'm crying for a lot of things that have nothing to do with having hands that hurt.[5]

– which is a perfect illustration of the fact that a simple surface directness of language can involve great dramatic complexity. Few authors can do this. And it is not just a glitzy trick – an author who can represent suffering and unhappiness in the ordinary and homely language of a schoolchild is thereby committed to the assumption that children, too, can experience suffering and unhappiness. The language exemplifies an entitlement.

Gowie Corby Plays Chicken is about grief, loneliness and courage. As its title suggests, it explores the meanings of *playing* chicken and *being* chicken. Gowie tests the limits of courage, and finally courageously admits[6] what it is he is scared of. It ends with an Epilogue – and that probably reminds the slightly puzzled reader that there was also a mysterious Prologue, about a mother and father and their four children. In the Epilogue the reader learns (with some surprise, probably) that dad is the grown-up Gowie, admitting that he had been saved by Rosie from a life of serious crime. Again a rereading is invited, though this time the invitation is less ostentatious: readers are simply obliged to distance the story, to understand it anew, and realise that this entire present-tense narrative was the adult Gowie telling his story to his own four children, and that he had grown up and married the tearful Heather.[7]

The third novel in the *Cricklepit* series is *Charlie Lewis Plays for Time*, published in 1984 at a time when debates about teaching, especially in primary schools, were at their height. This novel, while never for a moment losing sight of its young readers, is simultaneously addressed to teachers. For any historian of the future interested in understanding the point of view of those teachers who were so frequently derided in the press as 'trendy lefties', *Charlie Lewis Plays for Time* should be essential reading. Much of this address is in the form of swift asides and jokes for teachers, many of them slyly funny ('Quiet there. This is a language lesson so there should be no talking AT ALL'). This novel is overtly educational – and therefore political. It was perhaps inevitable, given the way its two predecessors had represented a child's voice and a child's view, that at such a time the author should so openly nail her colours to a child-centred mast. It is skilfully done, through a story of the conflict between Class 4M and a hated supply teacher who believes in traditional discipline, silence in the classroom, segregation, notes copied from the blackboard, and gender roles. But Gene Kemp is a tricksy story-teller, and towards the end the narrative suddenly reverses direction as the head declares with that sudden sharp jab of serious dialogue so characteristic of Gene Kemp:

'No one in this school is going to be victimised because of being different. Not, even, Charlie Lewis, a teacher.'[8]

If *Charlie Lewis Plays for Time* had articulated its contribution to an adult controversy and in the process lost its child readership, it would have constituted a failure of Gene Kemp's narrative conviction, which rests on the centrality of the child to schools and to children's story. Fortunately, there is no such failure, possibly because she kept to the formula of the previous two *Cricklepit* stories, focusing on the way three children in the top class look after one another – a gifted musician with a rich but mostly absent mother, a passionate and abrasive girl from a large family with an out-of-work father and a just-coping mother, and her disorganised and hyper-active brother. But the next novel in the series was a move in an entirely different direction.

Juniper: A Mystery (1986), unlike its three predecessors, is a complex thriller, the action taking place mostly in and around the heroine's home. There is no compromising about the danger here: Juniper – a thalidomide victim suffering from her mother's use of harmful substances – is caught up in the violence of her father's criminal past, and is in real danger from his former brutal associates who are using her as a bait to draw him back for a reckoning. Childhood rivalries and the slights and triumphs of the primary classroom are not part of the substance of this novel. *Juniper* is urgently concerned with the ways in which the crimes of the father and the folly and illness of the mother become the burdens of the child. This is a novel about the child-as-victim – a victim not only in the way she might suffer abuse and violence but in the way she is left feeling responsible for everything that happens. Juniper carries all the weight of the fear, as well as having to deal with the rent-collector, do the shopping and household chores, beg for charity from a rich relative, and cope with her own disability – what she calls her 'one point five arms'.

The form of this novel indicates a fresh authorial urgency, and a commitment to find new structures to deal with this new and serious theme. The first-person voice has been abandoned – which means that a young reader cannot enjoy the comforting luxury of knowing in advance that Juniper has survived to tell the story. Another feature of the early novels was the nonsensical epigraph at the head of each chapter – humorous in two of the novels, rather unnerving in *Gowie Corby Plays Chicken*. Here, though, the habitual verbal nonsenses are incorporated within the narrative to work as charms privately used by Juniper to ward off danger or fear ('Abbledy, gabbledy flook . . . I'm a silly sausage, drowning in gravy. Neggy, naggy, noggy, noo, won't you come and save me?'[9]).

Oddly, the third-person narrative takes the reader more comprehensively into Juniper's thoughts, feelings and perceptions than the first-person would have done. The complex substance of Juniper's life – her dreams, her moods, her occasional anger and quick reconciliations, her longing for her father, and above all the strange Christmas bargain she has made to risk violence because she wants so badly to see him again – needs an all-knowing and all-seeing authorial voice. Juniper's story is told from within, and seen from without. The language of a child-narrator could not do this without straining credulity. At the same time *Juniper* is also an ironic fairy-tale, with a benevolent fairy godmother who lives next door and cooks wonderful meals, a best friend who cannot fall in love with her because he will one day enter an arranged marriage, and an animal companion. Fairy-tales are never told by a first-person narrator.

Juniper gives the reader simultaneously a child's-eye view and an adult's representation of the ways in which adult ignorance or indifference impinges upon children. A number of literary echoes remind us that childhood has its own history in literature: the account of the carol service in Exeter Cathedral, for example, suggests William Blake's 'Holy Thursday':

> Row upon row of heads, brown, red, yellow, fair, black, mousy, straight, curly, long, plaited, cropped, frizzed, frizzled, punk, rasta, coloured, but none so bright as the gold leaf on the pillars and the ceiling bosses, and the green and the red and the blue.[10]

– an entirely appropriate allusion for, although this children's carol service signifies none of the institutional social hypocrisy that Blake's great poem exposes, there are still many children whose plight challenges adult pieties. The lesson Juniper has to read in the great cathedral is the account of the Massacre of the Innocents. 'How afraid they must have been', Juniper thinks, 'and how the mothers must have tried to hide their babies.'[11] With Juniper it has been the other way round: she has had to protect her mother.

The Grimm story of 'The Juniper Tree' also underlies *Juniper*, its hideous brutality towards children having a painfully precise relevance to the central theme:

> My mother slew her little son,
> My father thought me lost and gone,
> But pretty Margery pitied me
> And laid me under the Juniper Tree.[12]

Poor Juniper's head is filled with nursery rhymes and popular songs in wild and almost hysterical ironies. At a school disco –

> The songs blurred and joined, Save the Children, We are the world, Don't they know it's Christmas? Run, run as fast as you can, sounded in Juniper's head, As fast as you can, For you can't catch me, I'm the Gingerbread Gal. It'll be all right, all right, oh, Save the World, all the World, and all the other worlds, for the only tune that he could play was over the hills and far away.
>   Over the hills and a great way off, the wind shall blow your topknot off. She looked at Ranjit's and giggled.[13]

Gene Kemp, one of the first writers to deal with child abuse in a novel for children, does not lose sight of her young readers. The old theme of friendship is still there. In fact, Juniper is saved by friendship – in particular by the patient and faithful Ranjit – and by the benevolent guardianship of the woman who lives next door. And the classroom at Cricklepit School remains a refuge presided over by 'Mr Merchant Sir', still teaching in the fourth novel of the series. It is a refuge for young readers too, a comforting return to the more familiar narrative mode of the early novels. It is an agreeable readerly pleasure that Gowie Corby makes a guest appearance, 'a smiling six-footer who looked as if he could eat crocodiles for breakfast',[14] revisiting along with several others their favourite primary teacher on the last day of term.

Juniper must have a happy ending of sorts. Its commitment to the efficacy of love and to the transforming power of social concern *insists on* some kind of good outcome. A tragic or defeated closure would be a violation of the humanitarian and socialist premise on which the entire series rests. And so it is not, I think, mere narratorial sentimentalism that ensures that Juniper's mother begins slowly to recover, surrounds Juniper with people who have been looking out for her in ways that neither she nor the reader realised, and reunites her (briefly) with her father. In any case, any such sentimentality is nicely undercut on the final page, when it is revealed that the one person who has given Juniper money is in fact the villainous fat-cat master criminal who is behind most of the misery that Juniper and her mother have had to endure.

Children's literature has few guardians. Despite the burgeoning numbers of academics teaching on children's literature courses, and despite the diligence of a small number of writers in the handful of periodicals devoted to criticism and reviewing, children's literature is careless of its treasures. The complex realities of publishing and bookselling economics repeatedly condemn outstanding fiction to the backlist, quickly to become completely forgotten. There is, I hope, no chance of this happening to Gene Kemp, but her work (and this novel in particular) has been, I believe, seriously underrated. Juniper should be seen as one of the latest in a line of child-heroines who have had to grapple with wickedness and cruelty and fear, while not losing sight of their own capacity to love and be loved; to know evil without becoming cynical; to contain within themselves both their innocence and at the same time a consciousness of bitter experience; to accept the folly and failures of adults while continuing to love them. In spite of her jumbled words and frenetic syntax, and the constant 'close-to-the-edge' quality of her story, Juniper's literary place is alongside more carefully articulate heroines such as Sarah Crewe, Mary Lennox, Bobbie, and Kate Tranter.

The *Cricklepit School* series can be seen as a sustained attempt to find narratorial ways of representing the shifting and mercurial dynamics of a primary school. And a writer whose subject is school must in the end confront bullying. In *Just Ferret* (1990), the fifth of the series, Gene Kemp returns to the first-person voice of a child-narrator, a dyslexic non-reader with a violent father and no mother. It is an uncompromising narrative, with accounts of children beaten up by a gang of Year 6 bullies who are themselves hooked on glue-sniffing and gambling in amusement arcades. Ferret arrives at the school, a lonely outsider, a failure, and a victim. But he is tough – and eventually wins over the support of his intimidated classmates and exposes the whole racket. The school is composed to a great extent of fallible individuals: Ferret's classteacher was totally hood-winked by the bullies; the much-loved 'Chief Sir' and 'Mr Merchant Sir' (who has now become Deputy Head) had their doubts but no real evidence. So the outcome depends entirely on the persistence of the children, and there is no attempt to minimise the difficulties and even danger of children who find themselves in such a predicament.

Zowey Corby and the Black Cat Tunnel (first published in 1995 as *Zowey Corby's Story*) is probably the least satisfying of the series. It is another first-person narrative, told by Gowey Corby's younger half-sister. The novel has many of the features of the earlier ones, including jokes at the heads of chapters.

HEAD FRED IN ASSEMBLY: 'How do you have to be to get to Heaven?'
CHILDREN: 'Dead, Sir.'[15]

There is a new headteacher now, and a student teacher irreverently called Percy; Mr Merchant, described in the cast-list as a 'teacher and writer', has clearly moved on. Gowey is still around, along with Rosie, 'a black and beautiful, very tall, very thin girl'.[16]

It is not easy to say precisely why this book is problematical. The entire *Cricklepit School* series is characterised by the author's strong sense of the social and cultural connectedness of the School and the community it is part of. Accordingly, the patterns of narrative are concentric, with the school and a particular child at the centre of shifting and widening circles of cohesion. This cohesion is in constant danger of fragmentation through neglect, violence or cruelty. What distinguishes the series is, I believe, this double vision of centrality and disparity. The movement of Gene Kemp's narratives is in perfect balance, focusing *in* on the centre, while simultaneously swinging *out* towards the periphery. However, in *Zowey Corby and the Black Cat Tunnel*, the centrifugal energy is de-centred. There are too many peripheral narrative interests: the school opting out; the connections between boys and danger; the selfishness of parents; the morality of zoos; the undervalued under-achiever; racism; the relationship of Gowey and Rosie; fortune-telling; literary echoes ('Oh, horrible old world that has such people in it'[17]); quotations and misquotations.[18]

The novel is worth reading, however, if only for one outstanding chapter in which Gene Kemp, writing at her best, describes a crowd of twelve-year-old girls having a wild Saturday night at the market – heady, crazy, silly, funny, and more than a little dangerous.

Friendship is a central concern in all the novels. I say *concern* because the word *theme* seems to me to imply something different – a sustained authorial visiting of a subject, a careful and articulate working-out of its significance within the narrative, often leading to some kind of formulated clarity related to the main protagonists' own development within the fiction. We know how to read a *theme* because of our experience with the great Victorian fictions. And, because children's novels are so closely tied in with tropes of character-growth and transformation, they too incline towards thematic clarity, with explicit authorial accounts of significance often given as a character's moment of insight or epiphany.

But Gene Kemp's fictions do not do that. She convincingly represents friends and friendship in action; she recounts what friends say to each other and do for each other; and she persuasively provides us with the sometimes difficult or dangerous contexts in which friendships must find a place. But she has nothing to say *about* friendship. Similarly, *Just Ferret*, though openly concerned with violence, does not make explicit the potential ironies and contradictions of the violent world it inhabits: Ferret is bullied by his father, infants are bullied by older children – but the novel's resolution occurs only when this very violent father at last champions his son and violently confronts the violence head-on. The reader has a sense that the children are fully aware of the ironies in this situation – but they say little about it, and there is no authorial voice to nudge the reader into appreciating an articulated ironic understanding.

This, I believe, is why the *Cricklepit School* series is not given the credit due to it. Adults – especially literary adults – do not quite know how to read it. The absence of a worked-out theme looks suspiciously like the absence of thought. We ought, in a post-modernist multi-media culture, to know better. But because Gene Kemp does not provide quotable and conclusive wisdom in an adult authorial voice, her work can be regarded as slight, with many features characteristic of the experimental literacies of actual children.[19] The sexual violence near the end of *Zowey Corby and the Black Cat Tunnel* is a case in point: it comes out of the blue and is not readily linked to the rest of the narrative. But children who experience this kind of violence know that that is precisely how it seems: it does come out of the blue, and is apparently motiveless and incomprehensible.

Gene Kemp's ability to 'do the voices' of her child characters is both her greatness and her undoing. If I am right, it is a serious matter: for it means that her writing is undervalued precisely because of its closeness to childhood. This closeness lies in the way her narratives exemplify and enact the physical, conceptual and affective lives of children, employing linguistic structures which closely resemble the literacies of actual children.

The series is not yet complete; Gene Kemp intends at least one more novel to bring it back finally to where it began. But the series already has a complicated publishing history: some titles are in paperback, some only in hardback, one is out of print and one has two different titles. I hope that does not indicate that its publishers are losing faith in its integrity *as a series* with its own coherence. In seeking to find new ways of representing the inner and outer lives of children, Gene Kemp is a great innovator, bringing children's fiction closer than it has ever been to the literacies of actual classrooms. At a period in which the dangerous place of children is so centrally and problematically urgent in British culture, these novels provide a complex account of childhood in contemporary society; the fact that they are given in the words of children amounts to a challenge, for the closer these novels come to resembling the developing literacies of children, the harder it is for adults to see them as literary.

Conclusion
An invisible excellence

There are three interesting questions about series fiction:

Why do authors write it?
Why do children read it?
And what do children find in it?

The first is a matter of biography and it has not been the purpose of this book to do more than venture a few tentative speculations; it would require a biographer of the calibre of Richard Holmes to explore, say, the private connections between the *Green Knowe* series and the life and thought of its author.

Why do children read series? Since around 1920, children in their millions have eagerly read series fiction – an eagerness that can be explained in terms of a paradoxical search for familiarity combined with strangeness. Readers of a series want more of the same – but with a difference. This is not a form of readerly self-indulgence or childish laziness. Students of English have occasionally said to me that they wish Jane Austen had completed a seventh novel; this is not primarily because of a scholarly desire to see how she would have developed as a writer, but because they would enjoy the confidence of knowing absolutely the kind of readerly pleasures that it would provide.[1] Similarly, when adults read sequels by different authors continuing the narratives of *Pride and Prejudice* or *Mansfield Park*, there is the same kind of readerly nostalgia in their motivation. When adults reread their own personal classics, what they desire is a repetition of past literary pleasure – probably the safest and most fulfilling kind of nostalgia there is, for the activity rarely fails to keep its promise. Being devoted to a series has something in common with that desire; there is a *promise* made by a series-writer, and a *recognition* of the readerly desires of young readers. J.K. Rowling's understanding of this desire and of her responsibility to keep the implied authorial promise partly explains the success of the *Harry Potter* series. And, like the best of the great series-authors, she knows how to keep that promise without being strait-jacketed by it – each sequel taking both her own writing and the reader's reading into deeper narratorial levels of interest and reflection.[2]

An author who wants a series to constitute an extended *Bildungsroman* must find a way round the fact that fictional characters who grow up risk losing the very essence of their appeal. Many readers, for example, find the mature Anne Shirley of L.M. Montgomery's later novels less interesting than the charismatic child of *Anne of Green Gables*. A different kind of promise is made by such series, a promise of extended psychological authenticity.

Post-romantic fiction has to confront the risk that the passage from childhood to adulthood will be represented as a loss, and that writing about this diminution will itself be diminished in interest. The fictional moment in which Anne Shirley recognises this loss was also probably the actual point at which L.M. Montgomery acknowledged the implications for her own writing. It occurs in *Anne of Avonlea*, at the end of the novel – at the end of a day, and at the end of a wedding:

> Perhaps, after all, romance did not come into one's life with pomp and blare, like a gay knight riding down; perhaps it crept to one's side like an old friend through quiet ways; perhaps it revealed itself in seeming prose, until some sudden shaft of illumination flung athwart its pages betrayed the rhythm and the music; perhaps . . . perhaps . . . love unfolded naturally out of a beautiful friendship, as a golden-hearted rose slipping from its green sheath.
>
> Then the veil dropped again; but the Anne who walked up the dark lane was not quite the same Anne who had driven gaily down it the evening before. The page of girlhood had been turned, as by an unseen finger, and the page of womanhood was before her with all its charm and mystery, its pain and gladness.[3]

In spite of the references to charm and mystery, there is an acknowledgement here of something lost, an acceptance of the prosaic inevitability of approaching adulthood. It is a bold series-writer who proceeds beyond this point, for to do so must challenge the great western cultural assumption that the *potential* adulthood of the young is more charismatic than *achieved* adulthood. This authorial recognition is similar in concept if not in language to William Wordsworth's anguished question: 'Whither is fled the visionary gleam?'[4] However, while cleverly suggesting that the narrative progression of a fictional character is as inevitable and irrevocable as the actual progression of real people through time, the reference to the 'page' of womanhood and its turning by an 'unseen finger' (the reader's? – the writer's? – God's?) defines the difficulty as an authorial one for a writer committed to take on her heroine into adult life.

But this is not a difficulty for writers of the other kind of series: the magical children of Ransome's and Blyton's series fiction have their adventures always in the brightness of the Wordsworthian 'gleam' – reminding us that a good deal of children's fiction is close cousin to romance. The *Swallows and Amazons* series is not progressing towards adulthood; its characters are not, in one sense, going anywhere – though that does not mean they are static. Perhaps it is not a coincidence that endpaper maps have been a particular though not exclusive feature of this kind of series fiction, a clue to their real character, perhaps. The greatest series seem to me to constitute not a linear sequence of fictions but a kind of extended narratorial map of the imaginative life of the author, charting a complex landscape of culture, literature, childhood and values – perhaps constituting that author's own particular view of what Peter Hollindale has called 'childness'.[5]

Perhaps these differences indicate that children's series fiction is in need of a taxonomy. Certainly, a rudimentary classification is possible, distinguishing between series which are committed to a predominantly magical view of childhood and those concerned with an authentic representation of maturation. And immediately a third category has to be admitted, for there are some series-writers (Arthur Ransome, Antonia Forest, and perhaps J.K. Rowling) who have somehow managed to make promises of both kinds by allowing their characters to mature – but only by a few years.

This has the advantage of solving the problem of readership – whether to write for readers who themselves are growing older or for a succession of new generations of readers. However, the age (or ageing) of fictional characters has probably had less effect on readership profiles than is generally believed: I doubt if eleven-year-olds will stop reading the *Harry Potter* stories if the hero ends up as a sixth-former at Hogwarts School. But the readership might change if he were to go on to university and have problems with his sexual identity as an adult male wizard – though Sue Townsend in the *Adrian Mole* novels has demonstrated that this is possible if the narrative stance is predominantly comic.

The remaining question – what do young readers find in series fiction? – has been answered, I hope, in the preceding chapters. I have tried to show the complex varieties of interest and pleasure which are to be found in the great series fiction of Arthur Ransome, Lucy Boston and the rest. However, anyone seeking to analyse and demonstrate interesting and rewarding writing for children comes up against two difficulties specific to children's literature: good writing for children generally goes unnoticed – and is in any case intrinsically invisible.

Neglect is not a new problem. Academics, teachers and librarians were for many years aware of the sometimes ignorant and patronising lack of interest of their bigger brothers and sisters in English Faculties. And, although a more sympathetic and scholarly understanding has developed in recent years, in the wider world at large children's books are still given only a cursory critical glance by, for example, the main broadsheet newspapers.

There is in Part 3 of *A Stranger at Green Knowe* a description of a thunderstorm; it is too long to quote here.[6] I mention it because I find it extraordinary that this account is not known and admired by all literate people interested in the arts. If it were a painting, it would be in a national gallery hung beside a Turner and celebrated by an entire culture. Of course, such speculation is ridiculous; it is *not* a painting and the analogy breaks down at a hundred points. But if we compared Lucy Boston's thunderstorm with similar passages by Joseph Conrad, or Thomas Hardy, or Patrick O'Brian, we would not be conscious of any lowering, or bathos, or condescension – just a sharp and demanding prose commanding the attentive respect of the reader.

I am not the only adult reader saddened by the fact that writing of that quality is disregarded; all my colleagues can think of similar examples of their own. Even in this post-modern age, it ought to be possible to acknowledge good description when we encounter it – and perhaps analyse how it is done. And while the neglect of children's books is a familiar problem, series fiction is often dismissed as of even less significance. *The Oxford Companion to Children's Literature*, for example, summarises the plot of *Anne of Green Gables*, simply adding that 'L.M. Montgomery wrote a number of sequels to the original book' and listing the titles. One is entitled to wonder if that writer had taken the trouble to read any of the others.[7] So, with children's series fiction, neglect is particularly acute: there is a double deficit of critical attention.

The consequence of that deficit is that the excellence of a good deal of children's fiction remains *unnoticed*. But another factor is that such excellences are often by their very nature also *invisible*. Acknowledgement and analysis are especially difficult with fiction for children because complexity so often manifests itself in an apparent surface simplicity of language and form. What we have come to think of as 'multi-layeredness' is often made articulate in language so unpretentious that it seems to deflect or defeat critical attention. And yet this invisible excellence, this transparency of significance, is precisely one of the most important ways in which a writer can make provision for young readers. Such a provision is not just a matter of style, but also one of ideology, for it defines and represents an entitlement and an acknowledgement that intensity of feeling and habits of reflection are not restricted to adults with advanced vocabularies, a grasp of complex syntax and sophisticated habits of cultural allusion.

This understanding should lie at the heart of English-teaching in schools, an informing dynamic acknowledging that in the best and most interesting children's literature the rich and complex full-cultured concerns of humanity are not *belittled* or *set aside*; they are transformed and contained. Margaret Meek has told us that children sharing stories are aware of 'something that lies behind the words, embedded in the sense'.[8] This is so; what lies behind the words is culture, that vast and volatile language which the story belongs to. The great children's writers enmesh their readers in a complex sense of a whole rich culture – *not just a children's culture*. To sustain such a level of provision, this filtering for children of an entire cultural and personal consciousness – especially through an extended series of novels – is in my view an impressive achievement which we should attempt to understand.

But this child-centred rhetoric (to be found, for example, in the work of many of the best children's writers such as Edith Nesbit, Philippa Pearce, Jan Mark and Jill Paton Walsh) often takes the form of an understated and careful literalness which effectively silences so many reviewers and literary critics. The task for writers of children's fiction is to achieve simplicity without being banal. To put it another way, the complexities of good writing for children must be presented with a surface simplicity, for if they manifested themselves as complexities of syntax or semantics, or as ironically disjointed plot-structures, they would cease to appeal to the hurried appetites of inexperienced readers. This is to some extent true of all popular fiction; it is especially true of fiction for young readers. Its excellences are usually invisible and unnoticed. But this does not mean that the best children's authors are writing on the edge of banality, or that they can never be innovative or experimental. The exception is Enid Blyton, who successfully disguised her banality with the sheer momentum of her output. She was banal with gusto.

What it does mean is that literature for children is close to allegory or fable, and that its poetics needs to be understood and championed. The pedagogical task for teachers and librarians is one of enabling inexperienced readers to develop their ability to focus not only on the sparkling surface of narrative texts, but also upon the strange vitalities which move stealthily in the depths. We cannot hang Lucy Boston's storm-description in an art gallery, but we *can* develop children's awareness of their own literature in such a way that they begin to accord it some of the recognition it deserves.

An example of what I mean by 'invisible excellence' is the ending of Jan Mark's *Trouble Half-Way*, a novel concerned with identity, doubt, trust, language and community. The ending – which is unfortunately too long to analyse here – consists mostly of easy dialogue and a few authorial comments describing how the heroine, Amy, completes a train journey in Lancashire and takes a photograph of a mill. Few Key Stage 2 readers would find any reading obstacles here. However, these *simple* ingredients provide a *complex* confirmation and celebration of Amy's understanding of her place in adult society. This is a novel about a child's entitlement to trust and understanding within the immediate context of family and the wider context of community; in those closing pages what she has learned is both enacted and recounted for the young reader *in simple narrative terms which do not oversimplify.*[9]

But simplicity is problematical. As I said in the Introduction, simplicity is not always banal; but it is always vulnerable to neglect or mockery. Everyone interested in children's reading must understand that many of the best books for children are characterised by a simplicity which – in Margaret Meek's memorable phrase – is 'full of possibilities'.[10]

I have tried throughout this book to demonstrate the invisible or transparent excellence which young series-readers are enabled to discover; I would like to end where I started – with Arthur Ransome. Many readers think of the *Swallows and Amazons* as a series of twelve well-told stories about children, with a high standard of realism in descriptions of boating and camping. But a great deal more is going on in Ransome's narratives than realistic or authentic storying. In *Swallowdale*, for example, Ransome uses homely details of landscape and wildlife as poetic images to illuminate theme: here the swans – those 'great white birds' – are powerfully suggestive of distance and voyaging.

High overhead there was a creaking noise, like someone very quickly swinging on a big door that needs oil in its hinges. They looked up.

'Swans,' said John at once.

There were five of them, great white birds with their long necks stretched before them, flying past with steady, powerful wing-flaps towards the setting sun.

'Where are they going?' said Roger.

'There's another lake somewhere over there,' said John.

Over there to the west there were far dim hills beyond the rim of heather that shut them in like the horizon at sea. Beyond the heather was the unknown.[11]

What could be more unpretentious than this brief episode? Yet implicit in it is an acknowledgement of the value of knowledge (in this case ornithological), a recognition of beauty, and an invocation of the vastness of the world and the mystery of migration, together with the romantic appeal of distance and exploration – connecting this passing moment with the central themes of the whole series. At its heart is a view of children learning to be their own experts in a world in which they have a safe and respected place. But the homely and unchallenging language ensures that its effects are achieved so unobtrusively that the reader hardly notices.

However, 'notices' is a bland word that masks some further complications. To distinguish between the 'surface' of a narrative and its 'depths' is to employ a helpful and illuminating figure of speech; but it is not so illuminating if it tempts us into assuming that there is a similar division between 'surface readings' and 'in-depth readings'. You cannot peel off the surface of a pond and hold it up apart from its depths; the surface is simply where the water meets the atmosphere. The surface of a narrative is where the reader meets it. But no reader is obliged to focus only on the surface and, I suspect, all surface readings are partly driven along by powerful emotional undercurrents. Even the most hurried and inattentive reading of the story of Arrietty will take its colour from the strong melancholy and urgent narratorial longing which drive these narratives.

If commentators and critics are content to remain on the narrative surface and concern themselves only with what young readers have already noticed for themselves, what use can they be? Reviewers of *Harry Potter* have celebrated the fact that the stories are about a boarding school, magic and the battle between good and evil. But such literal accounts do not explain why the nation's children are so preoccupied with these stories. Young readers could find other books set in boarding schools, other books involving magic, and other books about good and evil. The reviewing of children's books is beset with such casual and cursory literalism. If adults can discuss them only in terms of 'what happens' in the story, how can they hope to engage children themselves in precisely those aspects of the fiction which the young readers are affected by? For we should be quite clear about this: the adult critic or teacher who sees in *The Borrowers* only a comfortable story about tiny people in a miniature world *knows less about it than the young reader*. And it is difficult to see how adult commentators can contribute much to any discussion, let alone develop the responses of young readers, if they know less about a children's book or series than young readers who have read it – perhaps more than once – from beginning to end.

Perhaps we need to remind ourselves that there are children who learn to love and savour words, and who 'read through' the complex layers of challenging and unlikely narratives with a blithe and untroubled confidence, relishing the phrasing, cadences and melody often implicit in persuasive descriptions, and making a mental note to return some day for a rereading. And the fact that children may also read current popular fiction, or watch popular soaps on television, means only that they enjoy trying everything.

Near the end of *The Borrowers Aloft* Mary Norton speaks in her authorial voice:

> Stories never really end. They can go on and on – and on: it is just that at some point or another (as Mrs May once said to Kate) the teller ceases to tell them[12]

– a point that has a particular appositeness to series fiction. And perhaps it is appropriate for me to indicate to my reader that I may have more to tell in my next book.

Of course, such a promise is subject to many outside factors. But there undoubtedly *is* more to be said – about, for example, such great series as Richmal Crompton's *Just William* stories, the *Jennings* stories by Anthony Buckeridge, Tove Jansson's *Moomintroll* books, the *Dicey* series by Cynthia Voigt, Lloyd Alexander's *The Chronicles of Prydain*, Diane Duane's *Wizardry* series, Philip Pullman's *Sally Lockhart* stories, and the extraordinary *Chrestomanci* series of fantasies by Diana Wynne Jones – not to mention the *Harry Potter* series.[13] Furthermore, a study is needed of series for much younger readers, from Edward Ardizzone's *Little Tim* books to the *Katie Morag* stories by Mairi Hedderwick and the exciting recent sequels and trilogies for younger readers by Henrietta Branford.

As for Philip Pullman's trilogy, *His Dark Materials*, that can be left to look after itself; it is a different kind of work, appeals to older readers, and will undoubtedly and rightly be subject to serious critical scrutiny alongside Ursula le Guin's *Earthsea* quartet, J.R.R. Tolkien's *The Lord of the Rings*, and Patricia Wrightson's *The Song of Wirrun*.

Neglect is not an issue for these writers, but it has been for other writers of series fiction for younger readers. It has been the purpose of this book to show that series fiction has played an enormous and unregarded part in the reading of twentieth-century children and, indeed, should be seen as central to what we usually think of as children's literature.

Notes

Introduction: a room full of friends

1 Humphrey Carpenter and Mari Prichard, *The Oxford Companion to Children's Literature*, Oxford, Oxford University Press, 1984, p. 76.
2 Charles Sarland, 'Revenge of the Teenage Horrors', in Morag Styles, Eve Bearne and Victor Watson, *Voices Off: Texts, Contexts and Readers*, London, Cassell, 1996, p. 71.
3 Ibid. p. 71.
4 Jan Mark, 'The Way We Were', in Styles, Bearne and Watson, *Voices Off*, p. 151.
5 Gabrielle Cliff Hodges, 'Encountering the Different', in Styles, Bearne and Watson, *Voices Off*, p. 269.

1 A fellowship of innocence

1 Arthur Ransome, *Swallows and Amazons*, London, Jonathan Cape, 1930, p. 202.
2 Ibid. p. 358.
3 Ibid. p. 16.
4 Arthur Ransome, *Swallowdale*, London, Jonathan Cape, 1931, p. 336.
5 Ibid. p. 181.
6 Ibid. pp. 338–9.
7 Ibid. p. 339.
8 Ibid. p. 223.
9 Ibid. p. 376.
10 Ibid. p. 325.
11 Ibid. pp. 241–2.
12 Ibid. p. 91.
13 Ibid. pp. 91–2.
14 Ibid. p. 420.
15 Ibid. p. 453.
16 This account of *Peter Duck* was first published, in a slightly different form, in *Signal No. 66*, September 1991, pp. 154–9.
17 Arthur Ransome, *Peter Duck*, London, Jonathan Cape, 1932, p. 111.
18 Ibid. p. 158.
19 Ibid. p. 183.
20 Ibid. p. 183.

21 Ibid. p. 216.
22 Ibid. p. 61.
23 Ibid. p. 382.
24 Ibid. p. 383.
25 Ibid. p. 387.
26 Ibid. p. 233.
27 Ibid. p. 234.
28 Ibid. p. 260.
29 Ibid. pp. 394–5.
30 Ibid. p. 381.
31 Arthur Ransome, *Winter Holiday*, Jonathan Cape, 1933, p. 235.
32 Ibid. pp. 33–4.
33 Ibid. pp. 172–3.
34 Ibid. p. 248.
35 Ibid. p. 99.
36 Ibid. p. 145.
37 Arthur Ransome, 'Introduction' to Katharine Hull and Pamela Whitlock, *The Far-Distant Oxus*, London, Jonathan Cape, 1937, p. 17.
38 Arthur Ransome, *Coot Club*, London, Jonathan Cape, 1934, p. 75.
39 Ibid. pp. 165–6.
40 Books on ornithology written between about 1900 and 1940 employed a similar style to Ransome's, an affectionate mixture of careful accuracy and vivid figures of speech. A book owned by my father, *British Birds and Their Eggs*, by J. Maclair Boraston (published in 1908 and bought by my father in 1920, I am embarrassed to confess, to aid him in his egg-collecting), is typical of many. It says of the heron, for example, he 'may be seen standing in the shallows, a gaunt, long-necked, long-legged, long-billed bird, the straightened neck held usually stiffly forward at a moderate declination from the perpendicular, and the bill projecting like the arm from a signal-post'. There is a loving attentiveness to style here. Apart from that 'declination from the perpendicular', Ransome himself might have written it.
41 Ransome, *Coot Club*, p. 184.
42 Ibid. p. 184.
43 Ibid. p. 330.
44 Ibid. p. 267.
45 Ibid. pp. 155–6.
46 As a young reader brought up in the Fens near Ely – in a landscape much of which is below the levels of the main rivers – I felt I had a special appreciation of Ransome's excitement. In such circumstances, reading becomes recognition.
47 See Chapter 6.
48 Ransome, *Coot Club*, p. 90.
49 Ibid. pp. 248–50.
50 Ibid. pp. 264–5.

2 The storm before the calm

1 Arthur Ransome, *Pigeon Post*, London, Jonathan Cape, 1936, pp. 209–10.
2 Ibid. pp. 265–6.

3 Ibid. p. 278.
4 Ibid. p. 140.
5 Ibid. p. 140.
6 Ibid. p. 152.
7 Ibid. p. 153.
8 Ibid. p. 154.
9 Ibid. p. 156.
10 Ibid. p. 156.
11 Arthur Ransome, *We Didn't Mean to Go to Sea*, London, Jonathan Cape, 1937, p. 157.
12 Ibid. p. 217.
13 Ransome, *Swallowdale*, pp. 19–20.
14 Ransome, *We Didn't Mean to Go to Sea*, p. 126.
15 Ibid. p. 145.
16 Ibid. p. 146.
17 Ibid. pp. 157–8.
18 Ibid. p. 166.
19 Ibid. p. 163.
20 Ibid. p. 172.
21 Ibid. p. 200.
22 Arthur Ransome, *Secret Water*, London, Jonathan Cape, 1939, p. 64.
23 Ibid. p. 65.
24 Ibid. p. 312.
25 Ibid. p. 278.
26 Hugh Brogan, *The Life of Arthur Ransome*, London, Jonathan Cape, 1984, p. 378.
27 Peter Hollindale, *Signs of Childness in Children's Books*, Stroud, The Thimble Press, 1997, p. 56.
28 Arthur Ransome, *The Big Six*, London, Jonathan Cape, 1940, p. 187.
29 Ibid. p. 187.
30 Ibid. p. 276.
31 Ibid. p. 294.
32 Ibid. p. 310.
33 Ibid. p. 399.

3 Nancy Blackett – champion of goodness

1 This account of *Missee Lee* was first published, in a slightly different form, in *Signal No. 66*, September 1991, pp. 159–68.
2 Arthur Ransome, *Missee Lee*, London, Jonathan Cape, 1941, p. 19.
3 Ibid. p. 29.
4 Ibid. p. 30.
5 Ibid. p. 30.
6 Ibid. p. 29.
7 Ibid. p. 32.
8 Ibid. p. 36.
9 Ibid. p. 40.
10 Ibid. p. 34.
11 Ibid. pp. 93–4.
12 Ibid. p. 47.

13 Fred Inglis, *The Promise of Happiness*, Cambridge, Cambridge University Press, 1981, pp. 133–5.
14 Ransome, *Missee Lee*, p. 48.
15 Ibid. p. 117.
16 Ibid. p. 129.
17 Ibid. p. 131.
18 Ibid. pp. 135–6.
19 Ibid. p. 161.
20 Ibid. p. 162.
21 Ibid. p. 170.
22 Ibid. p. 188.
23 Ibid. p. 317.
24 Ibid. p. 318.
25 Ibid. p. 321.
26 Ibid. p. 321.
27 Ibid. p. 336.
28 A friend once confided that her only anxiety when reading a series was that the author would die before the sequence was complete.
29 Arthur Ransome, *The Picts and the Martyrs*, London, Jonathan Cape, 1943, p. 97.
30 Ibid. p. 300.
31 Ibid. p. 42.
32 Ibid. p. 83.
33 Ibid. p. 59.
34 Ibid. p. 59.
35 Ibid. pp. 62–3.
36 Ibid. p. 173.
37 Ibid. p. 55.
38 Ibid. p. 146.
39 Arthur Ransome, *Great Northern?*, London, Jonathan Cape, 1947, p. 221.
40 Ibid. p. 11.
41 Ibid. pp. 69–70.
42 Ibid. p. 62.
43 Ibid. p. 99.
44 Ibid. p. 236.
45 Ibid. p. 301.
46 Inglis, *The Promise of Happiness*, p. 126.
47 John Rowe Townsend, *Written for Children*, London, Penguin, 1987, p. 165.
48 Thomas Hardy, 'Candour in English Fiction', *New Review*, June 1890.
49 See also Chapter 6.

4 Camping and tramping fiction, 1920–1960

1 Most titles were published a year or two earlier in the US.
2 *The Girls of the Hamlet Club*, while not strictly speaking one of the series, was a fore-runner and was published in 1914.
3 Dating and listing is problematical, since some stories were reissued with different titles, and many were issued with no publication date. A further

complication is created by omnibus volumes. Readers particularly interested in school stories should consult Rosemary Auchmuty's excellent work, *The World of Girls*, London, Women's Press, 1992.

4 Ibid.

5 M.E. Atkinson, *August Adventure*, London, Jonathan Cape, 1936, p. 25.

6 I am indebted to Margaret Courtney and Paul Moynihan for their help in drawing my attention to the range of fiction associated with Guiding and Scouting.

7 Marjorie Lloyd, *Fell Farm Campers*, London, Puffin, 1960, pp. 100–2.

8 Under the influence of the Society of Wood Engravers, engraving went through a considerable revival in the 1920s and 1930s.

9 David Severn, *The Cruise of the Maiden Castle*, London, Bodley Head, 1948, p. 92.

10 Ibid. pp. 15–16.

11 Ibid. pp. 29–30.

12 Margaret and Alexander Potter, *A History of the Countryside*, London, Penguin Books, undated, [no. 37], series editor Noel Carrington.

5 The great Nanny-Narrator and the children of the War

1 Enid Blyton, *The Sea of Adventure*, London, Macmillan, 1948, pp. 290–1.

2 Enid Blyton, *The Mountain of Adventure*, London, Macmillan, 1949, p. 1.

3 Enid Blyton, *The Castle of Adventure*, London, Macmillan, 1946, p. 220.

4 Blyton, *The Mountain of Adventure*, p. 6.

5 Ibid. p. 5.

6 Ibid. p. 8.

7 Ibid. p. 14.

8 Ibid. p. 17.

9 Ibid. p. 22.

10 Ibid. p. 24.

11 A comparison with Ransome is not to Blyton's advantage; it is inconceivable that Ransome should ever tell us that Titty's or Susan's knees ever 'went queer'!

12 Blyton, *The Sea of Adventure*, pp. 264–5.

13 Arthur Ransome, *Swallows and Amazons*, London, Jonathan Cape, 1930, pp. 221–2.

14 In fact, there was a third in the series, *Up the Faraway Tree* (1951), a comic-strip story illustrated by Dorothy M. Wheeler.

15 Enid Blyton, *Five on a Treasure Island*, London, Hodder and Stoughton, 1942, pp. 7–8.

16 Ibid. p. 15.

17 Ibid. p. 16.

18 Ibid. p. 19.

19 Ibid. p. 20.

20 Ibid. p. 24.

21 Ibid. p. 31.

22 Ibid. p. 34.

23 Ibid. p. 108.

24 Ibid. p. 183.
25 For an example of this, set at a key dramatic moment, see Enid Blyton, *Five Go Adventuring Again*, London, Hodder and Stoughton, 1943, p. 134.
26 Enid Blyton, *Five Run Away Together*, London, Hodder and Stoughton, 1944, p. 35.
27 Ibid. pp. 37–8.
28 Enid Blyton, *Five on Kirrin Island Again*, London, Hodder and Stoughton, 1947, p. 14.
29 Ibid. p. 98.
30 Ibid. p. 192.

6 Malcolm Saville: the price paid

1 Margery Fisher, *Intent upon Reading*, Leicester, Brockhampton Press, 1961, p. 28.
2 Humphrey Carpenter and Mari Prichard, *The Oxford Companion to Children's Literature*, Oxford, Oxford University Press, 1984, p. 45.
3 I am grateful to Catriona Nicholson for introducing me to this excellent writer.
4 Malcolm Saville, *Mystery at Witchend*, London, Newnes, 1943, p. 9.
5 Malcolm Saville, *The Secret of Grey Walls*, London, Newnes, 1947, pp. 11–12.
6 Malcolm Saville, *Lone Pine Five*, London, Newnes, 1949, pp. 245–6.
7 Saville, *The Secret of Grey Walls*, p. 13.
8 Actually the text reads 'nuder' for 'under', a rare case of a Freudian misprint?
9 Saville, *Mystery at Witchend*, pp. 128–9.
10 Malcolm Saville, *Mystery at Witchend*, revised edition, London, Collins, 1969, p. 96.
11 Ibid. p. 198.
12 Malcolm Saville, *The Neglected Mountain*, London, Newnes, 1953, p. 23.
13 Ibid. p. 59.
14 Ibid. p. 75.
15 Malcolm Saville, *Man with Three Fingers*, revised edition, London, Collins, 1969, pp. 54–5.
16 John Rowe Townsend, *Written for Children*, London, Penguin, 1987, p. 165.
17 Catherine Storr, *Marianne and Mark*, London, Faber and Faber, 1960.
18 Saville, *The Neglected Mountain*, p. 145.
19 Ibid. p. 154.
20 Ibid. p. 212.
21 Arthur Ransome, *We Didn't Mean to Go to Sea*, London, Jonathan Cape, 1937, endpaper.
22 Arthur Ransome, *Missee Lee*, London, Jonathan Cape, 1941, endpaper.
23 Ibid. endpaper.
24 Saville, *The Neglected Mountain*, endpaper.
25 William Mayne, *Cathedral Wednesday*, London, Oxford University Press, 1960, pp. 123–4.

26 Ibid. p. 1.
27 C.S. Lewis, *The Magician's Nephew*, London, Bodley Head, 1955, p. 153.
28 C.S. Lewis, *The Lion, the Witch and the Wardrobe*, London, Geoffrey Bles, 1950, pp. 151–2.
29 C.S. Lewis, *The Last Battle*, London, Geoffrey Bles, 1956, pp. 171–2.
30 Ibid. pp. 174–5.

7 *The Borrowers*: brief encounters and a little air

1 Marcus Crouch, *Treasure Seekers and Borrowers*, London, Library Association, 1962, p. 116.
2 Mary Norton, *The Borrowers*, London, Dent, 1952, pp. 16–17.
3 Ibid. p. 35.
4 Ibid. p. 48.
5 Ibid. p. 47.
6 Ibid. p. 51.
7 Ibid. pp. 55–6.
8 Ibid. p. 63.
9 Mary Norton, *The Borrowers Afield*, London, Dent, 1955, pp. 51–2.
10 Ibid. pp. 55–6.
11 Ibid. pp. 52–3.
12 Ibid. p. 56.
13 Ibid. p. 58.
14 Norton, *The Borrowers*, p. 94.
15 Ibid. p. 102.
16 Ibid. p. 119.
17 Norton, *The Borrowers Afield*, p. 194.
18 Norton, *The Borrowers*, p. 7.
19 Mary Norton, *The Borrowers Aloft*, London, Dent, 1961, p. 21.
20 Ibid. pp. 21–3.
21 Margery Fisher, *Intent upon Reading*, Leicester, Brockhampton Press, 1961, p. 104.
22 Norton, *The Borrowers Aloft*, p. 28.
23 Ibid. p. 30.
24 Ibid. p. 35.
25 Ibid. p. 41.
26 Ibid. pp. 121–2.
27 Ibid. p. 141.
28 Ibid. p. 151.
29 Ibid. p. 152.
30 Mary Norton, *The Borrowers Avenged*, London, Kestrel Books, 1982, p. 282.
31 Ibid. p. 282.
32 Ibid. p. 283.
33 Ibid. p. 285.
34 Thomas Hardy, *Tess of the D'Urbervilles*, London, Macmillan, 1957, p. 25.
35 Norton, *The Borrowers Aloft*, p. 95.

8 Watching passionately: Lucy Boston and the *Green Knowe* series

1 It is possible to visit the house of Green Knowe by appointment (tel. 01480 463134).
2 Humphrey Carpenter and Mari Prichard, *The Oxford Companion to Children's Literature*, Oxford, Oxford University Press, 1984, p. 77.
3 Lucy M. Boston, *The Children of Green Knowe*, London, Faber and Faber, 1954, Puffin edition, p. 8.
4 Ibid. p. 9.
5 Ibid. p. 12.
6 Ibid. p. 16.
7 Ibid. p. 21.
8 Ibid. pp. 73–4.
9 Ibid. p. 102.
10 Ibid. pp. 132–3.
11 Lucy M. Boston, *The Chimneys of Green Knowe*, London, Faber and Faber, 1958, Puffin edition, p. 85.
12 Ibid. p. 88.
13 Lucy M. Boston, *The River at Green Knowe*, London, Faber and Faber, 1959, Puffin edition, pp. 8–9.
14 Ibid. p. 11.
15 Ibid. p. 69.
16 Ibid. p. 21.
17 Ibid. p. 70.
18 Ibid. p. 113.
19 Ibid. pp. 93–5.
20 Ibid. p. 106.
21 Ibid. p. 107.
22 Ibid. pp. 107–8.
23 Lucy M. Boston, *A Stranger at Green Knowe*, London, Faber and Faber, 1961, Puffin edition, p. 7.
24 Ibid. p. 9.
25 Ibid. p. 10.
26 Ibid. p. 15.
27 Ibid. p. 17.
28 Ibid. p. 21.
29 Ibid. p. 37.
30 Ibid. p. 39.
31 Ibid. p. 38.
32 Ibid. p. 39.
33 Ibid. p. 41.
34 Ibid. p. 44.
35 Ibid. p. 93.
36 Ibid. p. 98.
37 Ibid. p. 101.
38 Ibid. p. 110.
39 Ibid. p. 121.
40 Ibid. pp. 123–4.
41 Ibid. p. 127.
42 Ibid. p. 132.

43 Ibid. p. 160.
44 Ibid. p. 160.
45 Ibid. pp. 164–6.
46 Ibid. p. 166.
47 Lucy M. Boston, *An Enemy at Green Knowe*, London, Faber and Faber, 1964, Puffin edition, p. 15.
48 Ibid. p. 38.
49 Ibid. pp. 115–16.
50 Lucy M. Boston, *The Stones of Green Knowe*, London, Faber and Faber, 1976, Puffin edition, pp. 93–4.
51 Ibid. p. 94.
52 Ibid. p. 103.

9 The sun inside the window, shining out: *The Dark Is Rising* quintet

1 These trains must have returned empty: I cannot think of a single novel in which three or four country children, full of anticipation, arrive at Paddington.
2 Susan Cooper, perhaps as a kind of acknowledgement, writes only of 'the grail', not the Holy Grail.
3 He might, of course, be a crook *disguised* as a kindly fisherman, but that simply reverses the expectation without annihilating it.
4 Susan Cooper, *The Dark Is Rising*, London, Chatto and Windus, 1973, Puffin edition, p. 11.
5 Ibid. p. 12.
6 Ibid. p. 13.
7 Ibid. p. 31.
8 Ibid. p. 51.
9 John Rowe Townsend, *Written for Children*, London, Penguin Books, 1987, p. 235.
10 Cooper, *The Dark Is Rising*, p. 64.
11 Ibid. pp. 164–5.
12 Townsend, *Written for Children*, p. 235.
13 Susan Cooper, *Greenwitch*, London, Chatto and Windus, 1974, Puffin edition, p. 117.
14 Ibid. p. 83.
15 Ibid. pp. 127–8.
16 Ibid. p. 43.
17 Ibid. p. 40.
18 Ibid. p. 41.
19 Ibid. pp. 151–2.
20 Susan Cooper, *The Grey King*, London, Chatto and Windus, 1975, Puffin edition, p. 57.
21 Ibid. p. 189.
22 Ibid. pp. 83–4.
23 Ibid. p. 180.
24 Susan Cooper, *Silver on the Tree*, Chatto and Windus, 1977, Puffin edition, p. 151.
25 Ibid. p. 224.
26 Ibid. p. 225.
27 Ibid. p. 226.

28 Ibid. p. 203.
29 Ibid. p. 253.

10 Jane Austen has gone missing

1 The first of Enid Blyton's stories about the twins at St Clare's School had appeared in 1941, and five further sequels had followed by 1948.
2 For a fuller account of what I mean by 'invisible excellence', see the Conclusion.
3 Antonia Forest, *Autumn Term*, London, Faber and Faber, 1948, Puffin edition, pp. 49–50.
4 Ibid. pp. 89–90.
5 Antonia Forest, *The Marlows and the Traitor*, London, Faber and Faber, 1953, pp. 88–9.
6 Ibid. p. 129.
7 Ibid. p. 148.
8 Ibid. p. 192.
9 Ibid. p. 244.
10 Antonia Forest, *Falconer's Lure*, London, Faber and Faber, 1957, pp. 48–53.
11 Ibid. p. 31.
12 Ibid. p. 64.
13 Ibid. p. 135.
14 Antonia Forest, *Peter's Room*, London, Faber and Faber, 1961, p. 49.
15 Ibid. p. 106.
16 Ibid. p. 169.
17 Ibid. p. 172.
18 Ibid. p. 215.
19 Ibid. p. 221.
20 Ibid. p. 223.
21 Ibid. p. 128.
22 Alasdair Campbell, *Outstanding Sequence Stories: A Guide to Children's Books that Carry the Reader Forward*, Swansea, Librarians of Institutions and Schools of Education, 1998, p. 48.
23 Antonia Forest, *The Ready-Made Family*, London, Faber and Faber, 1967, p. 116.
24 Ibid. p. 127.
25 Ibid. p. 158.
26 Ibid. p. 185.
27 Ibid. pp. 164–6.
28 Ibid. p. 187.
29 Ibid. p. 189.

11 The various voices of Gene Kemp

1 *Trouble Half-Way*, for example, is at the same time an extremely simple novel and an extremely complex one – tailor-made for the term *multi-layered*, which began at about this time to be widely used.
2 Gene Kemp, *Gowie Corby Plays Chicken*, London, Faber and Faber, 1979, Puffin edition, p. 17.
3 Ibid. pp. 34–5.

4 Ibid. pp. 37–8.
5 Ibid. pp. 94–5.
6 Ibid. p. 118.
7 The Prologue and Epilogue create a chronological puzzle. We are told that the events of the story took place shortly after Tyke Tiler was at the school. But, if the story is now being told by the adult Gowie to his four children, that either pushes *The Turbulent Term of Tyke Tiler* back by about twenty years or sets the Prologue and the Epilogue twenty years in the future.
8 Gene Kemp, *Charlie Lewis Plays for Time*, London, Faber and Faber, 1984, p. 110.
9 Gene Kemp, *Juniper: A Mystery*, London, Faber and Faber, 1986, p. 43.
10 Ibid. p. 71.
11 Ibid. p. 76.
12 Ibid. epigraph.
13 Ibid. pp. 85–6.
14 Ibid. p. 93.
15 Gene Kemp, *Zowey Corby's Story*, London, Faber and Faber, 1995, p. 5.
16 Ibid. p. 26.
17 Ibid. p. 119.
18 For example, ibid. p. 122.
19 The poetry of Michael Rosen has been similarly misunderstood.

Conclusion: an invisible excellence

1 I am indebted to Mary Nathan, a colleague and former student, for this suggestion.
2 The *Harry Potter* series has been planned as a series of seven stories; at the time of writing this chapter, only the first three have been published.
3 L.M. Montgomery, *Anne of Avonlea*, 1909, British edition, Harrap, 1983, p. 252.
4 William Wordsworth, 'Ode on Intimations of Immortality from Recollections of Early Childhood', first published in *Poems in Two Volumes*, 1807.
5 See Peter Hollindale, *Signs of Childness in Children's Books*, Stroud, The Thimble Press, 1997.
6 Lucy Boston, *A Stranger at Green Knowe*, London, Faber and Faber, 1961, Puffin edition, pp. 142–9.
7 Humphrey Carpenter and Mari Prichard, *The Oxford Companion to Children's Literature*, Oxford, Oxford University Press, 1984, p. 25.
8 Margaret Meek, *How Texts Teach What Readers Learn*, Stroud, The Thimble Press, 1988, p. 20.
9 Jan Mark, *Trouble Half-Way*, London, Viking Kestrel, 1985.
10 Meek, *How Texts Teach What Readers Learn*, p. 12.
11 Arthur Ransome, *Swallowdale*, London, Jonathan Cape, 1931, p. 268.
12 Mary Norton, *The Borrowers Aloft*, London, Dent, 1961, p. 153.
13 For an account of current series in print for young readers, see Alasdair Campbell, *Outstanding Sequence Stories: A Guide to Children's Books that Carry the Reader Forward*, Swansea, Librarians of Institutions and Schools of Education, 1998.

Index

Graves, Robert 157
Great Northern? 65–8
Green Knowe series 6, 135–52,
 205; death in 138–9, 152; exile
 and displacement in 141; Hanno
 145–9; Hemingford Grey 135,
 221 (note); Ping 141, 142–3,
 146–50; time in 136–8, 142,
 151–2; time travel in 139–40,
 143, 151–2; Tolly 135, 150
Greenwitch 159–63
Gregory's series 74
Grey King, The 164–5
Grimm, Jacob and Wilhelm 199
Guiding and Scouting fiction 77–8
Gulliver's Travels 119

Hale, Kathleen 76
Half Magic 75–6
Hann, Dorothy Osborn 78
Hansel and Gretel 63
Hardy, Thomas 69, 132, 208
Harry Potter series 205–6, 207,
 211–12, 224 (note)
Haymond, Alison 83
Hedderwick, Mairi 213
Heward, Constance 76
Hildick, E.W. 68
Hill, Lorna 75
His Dark Materials 213
History of the Countryside, A 84
Hodges, Gabrielle Cliff 8
Hogg, Garry 75, 80
holiday adventure stories 177; *see
 also* camping and tramping
 fiction
Hollindale, Peter 207
Hughes, Ted 154
Hull, Katharine 75, 102

Ian and Sovra series 75
Inglis, Fred 56, 68
Intent upon Reading 101
Iron Man, The 154
Island of Adventure, The 88
Island series 75

James, Grace 74
Jane Eyre 1
Jansson, Tove 212

Jennings Goes to School 75
Jennings series 212
Jill series 82
Jilly Family series 75, 102
John and Mary series 74
Johns, Captain W.E. 73–4
Jones, Diana Wynne 5, 212
Josephine stories 76
Junior Captain, The 74
Juniper Tree, The 199
Juniper: A Mystery 198–200
Just Ferret 203
Just Jane series 74
Just William series 212

Katie Morag series 213
Kemp, Gene 9, 190–204
Kiddell-Monroe, Joan 78, 79
 (illustration), 102
King-Smith, Dick 100
Kipling, Rudyard 22, 70, 78

La Rochelle series 74
Lady Chatterley trial 109
Ladybird Books 8
Le Guin, Ursula 161, 213
Lewis, C.S. 114–16
Leyland, Eric 75
*Lion, the Witch and the Wardrobe,
 The* 114
'literary' novels 191
Little Brown Mouse stories 76
Little Grey Rabbit stories 76
Little Princess, A 201
Little Tim series 213
Little Women 181
Lloyd, Marjorie 6, 78
Lockett Family series 76–7
Lofting, Hugh 73, 110
Lone Pine series 6, 75, 85, 104–14;
 endpaper maps in 110–12;
 paperback editions bowdlerised
 106–10; Petronella Sterling
 104–10; sexuality in 108–9
Lord of the Rings, The 112, 213
Lucy and Humf series 102
Lyon, Elinor 75, 102

Mabinogion, The 164, 166
Magic Faraway Tree, The 94

Mahy, Margaret 5
Malory Towers 75
Malory, Sir Thomas 161, 164
Mansfield Park 205
Marianne and Mark 109
Mark, Jan 4, 191, 209, 210
Marlow series 6, 173–89;
'literariness' of 176; Ann 181;
Ginty 181–3; Karen 181, 185–7;
Lawrie 174, 177–8, 182; Nicola
174–88; Patrick 179, 182, 184;
Peter 177, 179, 180, 182, 184,
186–7; Rose 187–8; Rowan 180;
Tim 175–6; twins in 174–5
Marlows and the Traitor, The
177–9
Marston Baines series 102
Mary Plain stories 76
Masefield, John 160
Mayne, William 4, 5, 68, 102,
113–14, 154, 181, 192
Meek, Margaret 3, 209, 210
Mike and Mary series 102
Milly-Molly-Mandy stories 76
Missee Lee 45, 50, 52–61, 111
Montgomery, L.M. 206–7, 208
Moomintroll series 212
Moon of Gomrath, The 112
Mountain of Adventure, The 88–91
Mr Gumpy's Outing 99
Mumfie stories 76
Mystery at Witchend 85, 102–3,
106–7, 108
Mystery Manor 77
Mystery series 75

Narnia series 6, 114–16
Nash, Frances 78
Nat and Jonty series 75
Nathan, Mary 224 (note)
Naughtiest Girl in the School, The
75
Neglected Mountain, The 107
Nesbit, Edith 6, 27, 209
Nettleford series 102
Nicholson, Catriona 219 (note)
Norton, Mary 1, 9, 119–34, 12

Orlando 76
Out with Romany 78

Outstanding Sequence Stories 186,
224 (note)
Over Sea, Under Stone 153–5, 162
Owl Service, The 155, 161
Oxenham, Elsie J. 73, 74
*Oxford Companion to Children's
Literature, The* 1, 102, 208

Pardoe, Margaret 75
Pearce, Philippa 68, 140, 191, 209
Peg series 78
Perkins, Lucy Fitch 73, 74
Peter Duck 19–23, 110
Peter's Room 182–5
Picts and Martyrs, The 61–4
picturebooks 5
Pigeon Post 33–8, 41
Point Horror 2, 4
Point Romance 3
pony stories 82–3
Potter, Beatrix 37, 76
Prance, Bertram 105, 109
Prelude, The 13
Price, Evadne 74
Pride and Prejudice 3, 205
Priestley, J.B. 183
Promise of Happiness, The 68
Psammead, The 6
Puck of Pook's Hill 78
Puffin Books 101
Puffin Picture Books 82
Pullein-Thompson, Christine,
Josephine and Diana 82–3
Pullman, Philip 212
Punchbowl Farm series 83

Rae, Gwynedd 76
Railway Children, The 201
Ransome, Arthur 6, 73, 76, 82, 92,
93, 108, 110–12, 155, 167, 174,
207, 210–11
Ready-Made Family, The 185,
186–8
Red Riding Hood 52
River at Green Knowe, The 141–5
Robin Hood 70
Robinson Crusoe 14, 22, 66, 70
Robinson, Charles 110
Rocklands series 74
Romney Marsh series 83